A Sheffield Boy

Best Wishes
Keith Farnsworth
June 2011

A Sheffield Boy

KEITH FARNSWORTH

First published in Great Britain by The Breedon Books Publishing Company Limited
Breedon House, 44 Friar Gate, Derby, DE1 1DA. 1998

Paperback reprint published in Great Britain in 2011 by The Derby Books Publishing
Company Limited, 3 The Parker Centre, Mansfield Road, Derby DE21 5SZ

ISBN 978-1-85983-948-5

Printed and bound by CPI Antony Rowe, Chippenham.

Contents

Introduction

*A*SHEFFIELD BOY which began as an attempt to recapture some memories of growing up in the East End and Pitsmoor districts in the 1940s and 1950s, has ended up spanning the first twenty-five years of my life up to the early 1960s when I finally became a newspaperman and joined the reporting staff of the old *Sheffield Telegraph* – a step into daily journalism marking a major turning point with the realisation of a boyhood dream which had once seemed far beyond my reach.

There is a sense in which the story is representative of my generation, for it contains much that will strike a chord with many who grew up in the same era. But, of course, autobiography is essentially a personal exercise, and, though I doubt whether my own tale is particularly significant compared with what many contemporaries have experienced and achieved, it cannot really be described as typical.

When my good friend Anton Rippon at Breedon Books looked at some autobiographical notes and urged me to convert them into a finished manuscript, I was delighted to accept an opportunity to do something we all dream of doing. Like many others, I have often looked back and felt an urge to place some memories on record in the hope they might have some lasting merit.

Now the job is done, I admit to feeling humble and inadequate, plagued with a kind of stage-fright and questioning the wisdom of seeking to interest anyone in the reminiscences of an ordinary Sheffielder who, if he has gone rather further than some might have predicted when he was a boy, has nevertheless achieved little that can be called exceptional. However, it is often said that we all have a book in us, everybody has a story to tell, and, if mine is not especially remarkable, I think it will amuse, intrigue and perhaps surprise those who know me only as a football writer, journalist and author, and, hopefully, these episodes from my early life will entertain and even enlighten.

Like most of us, I suffered a few trials and traumas along the way, and my early background was less than ideal, but, while I might have wished for a better start and particularly regret my limited formal education, I think I was always a happy boy well able to take the positive view and make the best of circumstances. I was lucky enough to discover early what I wanted to do, and to have got there in the end when perhaps it was easier to have failed.

Of course, I was also a bit of a rebel, often tended to be impulsive, and sometimes did daft things which did not help my progress – a habit that has plagued me all my life! However, I was fortunate in not suffering as much for my mistakes as might easily have been the case, and if I look back and blush at some of the more foolish episodes, I don't pretend they didn't happen.

One of the problems about recalling the distant past is the world has changed so much since that it is difficult now to recreate events in the context of their time and place in a way later generations can grasp. So many things we now take for granted didn't exist, and attitudes, habits and a wide range of conditions were so different that what once seemed natural may now appear old-fashioned, unremarkable and unsophisticated.

INTRODUCTION

We were what we were because of the circumstances existing at that moment in time. Our horizons, opportunities and expectations were very much more limited, and we could not then have imagined a world which, thanks to a remarkable social revolution and the dramatic effects of technology, has seen so much that was once familiar disappear to be replaced by developments which have changed many aspects of life beyond recognition.

When we were young, the year 2000 seemed so distant we could not really believe it would ever come, but now, in the era of computers, fax machines, the Internet and E-Mail and similar wonders, the world we knew as youngsters seems just as remote in retrospect. Who can imagine the days when communication meant writing letters in pen and ink (if we were lucky, we laboriously knocked them out on a manual typewriter) and walking a couple of miles to catch the last post? Or when making a telephone call meant an expedition to the nearest public box? When we were learning to master the mysteries of Buttons 'A' and 'B', mobile phones would have seemed like something out of science fiction!

Outside toilets, homes without central heating or hot water on tap, washdays without washing machines, the wonder of the first black-and-white television sets, and the days when it was mostly only the 'posh' who owned motor cars – how long ago and far away it all seems. Remember when the big night out of the week was a trip to a suburban cinema, where getting tickets for the second house on Saturday night and rounding off the evening with fish and chips was the height of sophistication? Words like videos, microwave ovens, digital TV and a thousand others didn't exist.

Of course, what we didn't have or didn't know didn't prevent us from enjoying life, and, if the quality of that life was not as good in the sense that we didn't have many of the benefits and facilities we now take for granted, we were not without compensations and I doubt if many of us really felt we were living in the wrong period in history. We had plenty that we might sometimes feel made the world a better place than it is today!

I might look back on my childhood and youth and wish our family circumstances had been better, but I don't think I would want to have grown up in a different age, and I wouldn't wish to have missed knowing the people and places that have shaped my life. If the pattern had been different and more pleasant in certain parts, it might have changed the rest – and denied me much that I remember with gratitude.

My old grandmother often said it was better to be born lucky than rich, and there is not much doubt that the greatest good fortune any man can have is the love of a good woman. On that count, I have been twice blessed, and count myself the luckiest man in the world.

My first wife, Kathleen, who died when she was thirty-seven, transformed my life and gave me the stability, emotional security, self-discipline and sense of purpose I had lacked. It was remarkable how everything suddenly began to happen for me after I met Kathleen, and I owed all I achieved to her influence and inspiration. When she died in late 1976, I could not believe I would ever enjoy the same happiness again. However, miracles do happen, and Linda, whom I met in 1982, came along to restore the kind of joy to my world that makes life worthwhile and renew my enthusiasm for a career that had reached a crossroads.

Meeting Kathleen coincided with a turn for the better in my career with a step in the right direction when I moved into the Press Office at Newton Chambers, and, within seven months of our marriage in 1963, I joined the old *Sheffield Telegraph*. Of course, I was very much a beginner in 'real' journalism, but, after fearing I might struggle to make the grade, I did reasonably well, and, since finally finding my niche, I have managed to make a living by writing ever since. If I haven't written too well at times, it's still the only thing I'm any good at!

I have always been grateful to have had the chance to do a job that has suited my natural if limited talents, but I have never pretended that what I have achieved is notable other than in the context of my beginnings. Few who knew me as a boy expected me to do what I have done, and many marked me out for failure, but I got lucky and my modest abilities have enabled me to make something of my life. Ironically, with the benefit of hindsight, at the age of sixty I can look back and admit I could have gone much further with more effort and ambition – and but for a chronic reluctance to leave Sheffield.

We live now in an age when technology has transformed the media and it sometimes seems that anybody can set themselves up as a journalist. More young people are better equipped to recognise their potential, and there is not only a greater awareness of opportunity but a more widespread determination to seize it. There were fewer open doors forty years ago, especially for unqualified late starters, and those who, like me, managed to squeeze into newspapers by the back entrance were a fortunate minority.

Naturally, once I had fulfilled my romantic dream and gained a place on the editorial staff of the *Sheffield Telegraph*, it took a while to identify what direction I wanted my career to take, but, once again, the fates were kind because, within a couple of years, I found myself, almost accidentally, on the sports desk – and that proved the making of me.

It might seem curious, but, at the outset, I didn't aspire to switch to sport. It was enough just to be a reporter, and, once I had found my feet, I was thrilled to be producing stories and getting regular by-lines (such fame!) that served to show I was making progress. I loved it so much, I was churning out articles in my spare time for fun, and, after taking time off to interview such favourite authors as Howard Spring and J. B. Priestley and winning some acclaim for my efforts, I began to fancy a career as a feature writer – preferably one with a literary bent!

However, the move on to the sports desk, which came at the instigation of Benny Hill, then acting sports editor, was a crucial step. I doubt if I could have developed as well and as rapidly as I did in any other area of the paper, and I look back on my ten years in that department as the most satisfying of my career. It may sound rather juvenile, but covering football and travelling with Sheffield United and Wednesday seemed the peak of fulfilment, and, when, in 1971, I suddenly found myself made sports editor, I cannot explain the sense of achievement I felt.

I don't think I have ever worked harder or given more of myself to a job than I did in my time in the sports department, especially after I was put in charge. Looking back, I can hardly believe the hours I worked, or the sheer effort and commitment. I smile now when I recall my regular 12-14 hour shifts divided into administration, writing and page-planning. I got so absorbed in what I was doing, I often forgot to eat the sandwiches Kathleen had packed and put in my brief case. In photographs from this period, I'm thin as a rail – and no wonder considering how often I worked a full shift without eating!

We were seldom without problems and always seemed short staffed, but I loved the job. My main weakness was in managing people, and I must admit my enthusiasm for my own role, and my reluctance to give up writing to concentrate totally on running the department, sometimes blinded me to the needs of the team. I always thought I did my best, but I was a long way from being the ideal captain. If I had my time to come again, I would do it differently.

Because I loved it, and it meant so much to me, people have often asked why I suddenly gave it up, and I have been reluctant to explain because the circumstances which prompted the decision were complicated, and a pattern of events conspired to persuade me that it was time to move in a new direction – though, frankly, I didn't know then what it might be.

During the spring of 1976, Kathleen began to complain of having trouble with her mouth, and, after several weeks during which the local doctor seemed to think she was imagining things, she visited a specialist, who sent her into hospital for an exploratory operation.

I shall never forget the May day when, just after I had arrived at work, Kathleen telephoned to say she could go home. I walked to the Royal Hospital in high spirits which evaporated the moment I reached the ward and was whisked in to see the specialist. He revealed Kathleen had cancer of the tongue, and at the most had a 50-50 chance of surviving.

She lived for only six more months, and, of course, it was a traumatic spell, what with a period of treatment followed by a phase when she fell into a sharp decline. In the last months, when she was unable to talk and communicated with written notes, the gradual deterioration in her handwriting reflected her weakening hold on life, and I could only marvel at her courage.

I remember it now as a time when I have never felt more tired, wearied by a sense of disbelief and exhausted by a need to block out all thought of the future. Everything seemed so unreal. Of course, I continued to work, but, as my normal duties involved working from lunchtime until after midnight every day, I elected to temporarily relinquish my role as sports editor in order to spend more time at home with Kathleen, and to have the freedom to come and go as might be necessary without affecting the running of the department.

Sadly, the arrangement did not work, and the situation induced misunderstandings which, to say the least, were unfortunate. The fault was probably mine in that, perhaps unexpectedly, I took little time off, and, when I was at work, I was deliberately cheerful and reluctant to dwell on what was happening at home. Moreover, my self-imposed demotion seemed to cause embarrassment and my presence led to confusion over who was exactly supposed to be in charge.

We are all only human, and sometimes see the world only through our own eyes, and, regrettably, myself and Benny Hill, my deputy and the man to whom I had handed my duties, each took a different view of a switch of responsibilities which had been approved by the editor, Michael Hides. Benny couldn't understand why, if I was still working, I couldn't continue to run the department, while I stressed that in my current circumstances I needed to be free of the burden. He seemed to believe I was exploiting a personal situation that was not as bad as I made out, while I felt he was being unreasonable and unsympathetic.

In the time we worked together, Benny and I always had an uneasy relationship. It didn't help that he had once been my boss, and I had been promoted over him – 'You've got my job,' was his greeting when he learned I'd been made sports editor. We respected each other as journalists, but, as individuals, we were very different. He was a good operator, knew his job, and, when he wanted, there was nobody more capable. However, while I was the romantic enthusiast, he was the cynical professional. Whenever we had a production problem, such as getting a paper out with a reduced staff, my attitude was 'let's show 'em what we can do', while he tended to resent being asked to shoulder the burden.

I don't think any colleague had more time off with illness than Benny during my time in charge, but, frustrating as it was to run a department without him on many occasions when the pressure was at a peak, I had always tried to sympathise with his problems. It was disappointing to find that, in my own time of personal crisis, he could not appreciate my circumstances.

The situation got very complicated, and everything came to a head one evening when I finally discovered what was really bugging Benny. 'I'm doing your job, and the sooner you resume your responsibilities the better, because, frankly, the situation is getting me down – and, what's more, I'm not getting paid for doing the job,' he said.

'Well,' I replied, 'it's up to you to sort that out. Anyway, you can have the job permanently because I'm going.' I then walked out of the building, and, the next day, told Michael Hides I wanted a transfer to another department. Alas, Hides asked me to stick it for another week because Benny insisted the sports desk didn't have enough staff to cope until a couple of the lads came back from holiday. Ironically, Benny promptly took a couple of days off!

I knew I had given up the only job I had ever really wanted, but, at that moment, I didn't care. Later, of course, I sometimes wished things had not happened quite as they did, but, with hindsight, it probably happened for the best. The *Telegraph* closed within ten years anyway, and, in the meantime, I had rebuilt my career.

When Kathleen died, I was working as a feature writer, and, as the job was a temporary compromise, I soon decided the time was right to move on. As I didn't want to leave Sheffield, this was difficult, but, in the event, an opportunity arose to become editor of *Quality*, the Sheffield Chamber of Commerce journal.

I wasn't really cut out to be an industrial journalist, but I spent nearly eight years on *Quality* and coped reasonably well. Unfortunately, as a consequence of a recession which severely affected local industry and dramatically reduced the number of advertisers, the magazine ceased publication in 1985. However, in 1982, I had written my first book, a history of Sheffield Wednesday, and the dramatic success of this volume served to suggest I might be able to maintain a writing career by becoming a freelance. I have since produced fifteen books on a range of subjects, and, one way or another, managed to survive. Ironically, having begun to believe that my links with sports journalism were severed for good, in 1988 I suddenly found myself covering football again when the *Daily Telegraph* recruited my services.

Overall, it's been a funny old career, really, but, if I might have achieved more, what success I have enjoyed has been satisfying and fulfilling. Privately and professionally, I've been luckier than most, and I'm grateful for that.

Introduction to 2011 edition

I was about 60 years old when I wrote A Sheffield Boy, and I am glad I did it then, for now, a dozen or so years later, I am tempted to question whether I could do half as good a job, or complete it as quickly as happened around 1998–99. Time, plus asthma, arthritis and a heart attack (from which, happily, I have made an excellent recovery), have rather slowed me down, the levels of energy and stamina aren't what they were, and the memory, too, is not as sharp as it was!

In preparing for this paperback re-issue, it was an intriguing experience re-reading the book from start to finish for the first time since I wrote it. I was particularly surprised at how much I had forgotten about certain episodes, especially some of the minor details. However, overall I do think the book reads fairly well, though I will admit that there are a number of passages that the journalist in me would have loved to have had another go at; but the trouble with doing that is once you get started it can be difficult knowing when to stop!

Over the past 12 years there have been a few criticisms of some passages in A Sheffield Boy, and, in meeting up again with people from the distant past, my descriptions of a handful of incidents and individuals have been the subject of discussion. Happily, it has been accepted that I was sincere in what I wrote, and I think more people have praised my accuracy in those same instances than have questioned it. I can only say that told it as I saw it at the time, and I stand by what I said. All the same, the opportunity of to share a few memories with some of those involved has enabled me to see certain things in a slightly different context, and thus perhaps if I were writing about them now, I might say something very similar but add a few balancing words!

One of the pleasures of recent years has been the opportunities to renew friendships with old school mates from Newhall such as Derek Brown (who inspired a couple of reunions, in 2005 and 2007), Jack Shirley, Joan Renshaw (we sat together on our first day in Newhall nursery in 1941) and Arlene Turner (my sweetheart at junior school!); former works colleagues Harry Truelove, Christine Kilner and Donald Bird; and old Harrogate AAS pals Peter Gray, Laurie Dixon and George Ient. There was also an unexpected but very welcome message from the daughter of the late Police Constable 'Bobbie' Brookes, once of Swallownest, after she had read A Sheffield Boy and seen my praise of her father. (I also unexpectedly rediscovered a favourite boyhood book, A Chattertooth Eleven by Eduard Bass – see the chapter 'Football Daft' – 60 years after borrowing it from Burngreave Library).

On the negative side, it is sad that I was never able to re-establish contact with two of my best friends of years gone by, David Depledge and Ken Swindells, before it was too late and I learned that they had died – both following long spells of illness.

In the chapter 'Canny Street Kid', my memory of how the school team lined up was wrong, and the formation was: Sam Ashworth; Derek Brown, Peter Morton; Graham Watson, Jack Shirley, Maurice Salvin; Brian Hancock, Barrie Day, Eric Hancock, Barry Haythorne, Terry Carr.

It is good to see A Sheffield Boy available again after so long out of print, and I hope it will now reach those people who have been inquiring about its availability in recent years. I hope, too, that those who are discovering it for the first time will enjoy this record of the trials and tribulations of one ordinary boy's early years in Sheffield in the 1940s and 1950s.

Grenoside, February 2011

East End Roots

GROWING up in the Newhall area of Sheffield's East end in the 1940s, it was impossible to avoid being aware of the impact of the steel industry on the district. From the Wicker Arches to Tinsley and beyond, the Lower Don Valley was dominated by the furnaces, forges, rolling mills and engineering workshops of such famous firms as Firth Brown, the English Steel Corporation, Brown Bayleys, Sanderson & Newbould, Jessop's and Hadfields.

The region was invariably shrouded in smoke and grime heavy with the taste and smell of metal, while the valley vibrated day and night to the thud of mighty hammers and the sounds of drilling, grinding and cutting as ingots of metal, not long since tapped white hot from the open-hearth furnaces, were forged, rolled and sliced into a range of shapes, sizes and lengths for hundreds of different uses.

It was a long way from Paradise, but few complained because most people had grown so used to the gloom and noise they barely noticed it. Indeed, to those of us who were very young, the place seemed much brighter than it really was – as the poet said, Heaven lies about us in our childhood! Because the district no longer exists as it was in my schooldays, the houses and so many other familiar buildings having been demolished in the 1960s, I can't, so to speak, go home again and view it once more with the eyes of an adult. So, if in reality it was rather grim, distant memory only lends enchantment to the scene.

* * * *

No doubt there are people who have memories of the hardships and the mass unemployment caused by the slump in the early 1930s, and, indeed, despite the subsequent upturn when Sheffield's workshops played such a vital role during the war years and enjoyed some boom years afterwards, there was still plenty of poverty around.

I cannot honestly recall any personal experience of children without shoes in my time, though quite a few wore hand-me-downs which were either too big or too small; and, like me and my sisters, many of my Newhall colleagues qualified for free dinners when funds were low at home – and all the kids were grateful for the free school milk. The early post-war period, of course, was not only a time when few East Enders had much money, but when their difficulties were compounded by a shortage of so many things essential to everyday life. Who now can imagine that era of the Ration Book and clothing coupons, when everything from petrol to sweets were severely rationed?

I remember a time when bread was in short supply because, in my grandmother's house, there was a family joke: 'There's no bread left, so we'll have some toast.' The bread was kept in a bin (an old biscuit tin) which stood on the corner of the table, and grandmother used to cut the end crusts off a new loaf (no sliced bread then) and put them in the bottom of the bin. By the time they were the only items left in the bin, those crusts had invariably gone bone-hard – and the only way you could enjoy eating them was by toasting them before the open fire...always assuming Grandma hadn't used up her ration of coal! A shortage of fuel was a constant problem, and news that some coke was available at the local gas works prompted a mass dash to join long queues of people who were grateful to come away with a 28lb bag. In that bad winter of 1947, I carried many a bag of coke along Upwell Street and Brightside Lane in the snow – and, as I wasn't the strongest of kids, I was grateful when my pal Tony Clayton hurried ahead with his load and then came back to help me!

Today, in the late 1990s, smoking has come to be regarded as a social evil, and those who still enjoy a cigarette are considered to be not only damaging their own health but that of others. Attitudes were very different in the 1940s, and there was sympathy for the man who was 'dying for a fag' but couldn't always get his packet of Woodbines or Park Drive when he wanted because of rationing. Even if cash was short, the family breadwinner was seldom denied the luxury of his cigarettes when available, and I recall an instance when one man was so desperate for a smoke that he sent his kids out to search for 'dog ends' which had been dropped in the streets – and then converted them into fags on his hand roller!

Yet, whatever the problems and conditions, most people adjusted surprisingly well when financial circumstances were so stretched that they couldn't even afford the bare essentials, and at school it was never difficult to tell which of my mates had mothers who were masters at making ends meet. It has to be stressed that, while there was plenty of poverty, and many people lived so close to the brink of it that a sudden illness or spell of unemployment could plunge a family into despair, the majority succeeded in maintaining remarkably high standards. Being poor did not prevent them from living properly. The streets outside might be dusty and bleak, but the insides of most houses were like palaces – comfortable, spotlessly clean and reflecting the pride of the woman of the house. There was a place for everything, and everything had to be in its place. The goal was to be respectable and show a brave face to the world whatever the circumstances. Many might never aspire to a regular annual summer holiday at the seaside, and be content with a couple of day trips courtesy of the local working men's club. I recall a day trip to Cleethorpes with the school, but I also remember how some kids felt they had been to somewhere as good as the seaside when they visited Elsecar Dam in the heart of the South Yorkshire coalfield! Nobody had a chip on their shoulder about these things because most kids then didn't feel they were missing out on something better: they gladly accepted what pleasures and treats they were given. However, there were plenty of parents who scrimped and scraped all year round to save up enough for a week in Skegness or Blackpool even in the toughest of times. The Sheffield holiday weeks, the last week in July and the first in August, would see the big works closed down and a substantial exodus of East End residents – and those kids left behind because their parents couldn't afford a holiday might feel envy but found contentment playing with pitch in the sweltering streets.

* * * *

The majority of East End residents depended on steelmaking and related trades for employment, and, while there were many who seldom gave a thought to these things, no doubt there were plenty who took pride in being able to claim they played some part in maintaining a tradition which numbered Sheffield's special steels as the best in the world – a product sold in pounds rather than tons.

Indeed, among the most ordinary-looking men walking the streets of the district were some of the finest craftsmen of their day – to see them in their working clothes, or in their domestic surroundings, was not always to appreciate the knowledge and skills they possessed.

Curiously, although at school we learned about how Alfred burned the cakes and William conquered Harold at the Battle of Hastings, we weren't taught much about the history on our doorstep and the heritage shaping the lives of our families. As I recall, nobody at Newhall instructed or amused us with tales of such industrial 'kings' as John Brown, Thomas and Mark Firth, Robert Hadfield and Edward Vickers. Nor did anyone explain how their creation and expansion of such famous sites as the Atlas, Norfolk, East Hecla and River Don works had coincided with the dramatic growth of steelmaking in Sheffield and changed the face of the valley. True enough, when we were very young, the technical details of steelmaking might have been beyond our capacity to grasp, but the sheer romance in the stories of those early steelmasters and their rise would surely have captured our imagination – and been more relevant than tales of old monarchs.

Benjamin Huntsman, whose invention of the crucible steelmaking process in the 18th century transformed the local industrial scene and set Sheffield on course to lead the world, was a classic example. He had spent most of his life in Attercliffe (his cottage in Worksop Road subsequently formed part of the Britannia Inn, which still stands), but nobody made us aware of him or the fact he once trod the streets we now walked. Of course, up the road at Huntsman's Gardens School, the pupils may have been told about the man behind the name of the establishment.

I often wonder how many of our teachers knew that the legendary John Brown and Mark Firth had, in fact, been members of the original Sheffield School Board which, in 1873, inspired the building of Newhall. Indeed, those famous steelmasters were both present when the original property on Sanderson Street – by my time it had become the infants department – was formally opened as one of the earliest board schools in the country.

The teachers at Newhall were, on the whole, a pretty decent lot whom I'm sure many of my contemporaries remember with much affection, but they were probably unaware that the homes in which many of their pupils lived had been built by such local firms as ESC in the context of the drive to recruit and house a labour force to sustain the industry's remarkable expansion.

Incidentally, few of those houses boasted a bathroom, and many of the kids at Newhall were grateful for an arrangement the headmaster made with the nearby Maltby Street School which enabled us to use their showers once a week. It was a luxury we probably appreciated more for helping us to escape from the classroom than for the pleasure of being clean, but, anyway, on the way back across the bridge over the Don, we would break into the school song:

> We are the Newhall Boys,
> We never make any noise – not much!
> We win all our matches,
> We get all the scratches,
> Aye, Aye. Aye,
> We are the Newhall Boys!

Family Matters

O F COURSE I discovered quite early in life that my parents were genuine East End products with roots in the area, but it was many years before I understood how steel had contributed to the circumstances which shaped their destiny and brought them together – and it proved fascinating to learn something of the events which led to the meeting of Tom Farnsworth, my father, and Eliza (Betty) Jackson, my mother, in the early 1930s.

Grandfather Farnsworth, also called Tom, was born close to the Derbyshire-Nottinghamshire border at Upper Langwith in mid-November 1887, but, as the ninth of James and Elizabeth Farnsworth's ten surviving children at Pear Tree Farm, he saw no future in following in his father's footsteps.

The farm, on the Duke of Devonshire's estate, had been in his mother's family, the Turners, since the 18th century, and his father, having moved to the district from Kimberley in Nottingham when a small boy, had seen the family's farming links extended into nearby Palterton and Scarcliffe. However, as James and Elizabeth had six boys, and he was next to bottom of the list, Tom does not seem to have aspired to maintain the family tradition. When he was about fourteen years old, around the turn of the century, he insisted on moving to Sheffield to begin an apprenticeship as a turner at Thos. Firth's steelworks. In truth, Tom probably just wanted anything that offered an escape from Upper Langwith and the domination of a fiercely possessive mother who, though barely 5ft tall, had the capacity to strike fear in the hearts of her sons. In the event, his choice was influenced by a connection with Sheffield established by his oldest sister, Annie. Annie, fourteen years his senior, had moved to the city eight or nine years earlier to become housekeeper to Lewis James, a widower with three small children. Lewis, having started in steel in his native South Wales and built a big reputation in the industry, had recently been recruited as melting shop manager at John Brown's following a spell in a similar capacity on Teesside.

It was no surprise when Lewis married his young housekeeper in 1896, and one imagines that, over the next few years, Tom was a regular visitor to their 'Woodhill', Grimesthorpe Road home overlooking the Lower Don Valley. Tom liked the freedom he enjoyed in Sheffield, and, defying the wishes of his mother, was so determined to start his working life there that he ran away from home several times. Annie appears to have acted as peacemaker in what developed into a family crisis by promising to accommodate and keep an eye on Tom, while Lewis James was instrumental in arranging for him to be given a place in Firth's Norfolk Works. It was there that a significant development occurred when Tom was placed under the wing of Charles Johnson, one of the senior turners.

That was the accident of fate which set in motion events which, some seven years later, in February 1908, led to the marriage of Tom, not then quite 21, to Johnson's third daughter, the auburn-haired Annie, who was five days past her 18th birthday on her wedding day. Back at Langwith, old Elizabeth raged at the prospect of her son marrying into a Methodist family; while the Johnsons were just as disapproving. A mystery I was never able to solve was a suggestion that Annie was, in fact, pregnant at the time of the wedding at Pye Bank Chapel. During my researches, someone mentioned a son called Harry, who allegedly died soon after birth, but no documentary evidence appears to have survived – though such a development might explain why, according to family folklore, Charlie Johnson described Annie as 'another black sheep in the house'. The other black sheep was her sister Amelia – of whom more later.

Whatever old Charlie's feelings, Tom and Annie probably started their married life with the Johnsons at Wade Street, in the Page Hall district, but they were established in a house of their own at Irving Street, Darnall, by the time Tom Jnr, their only son, was born in February 1910.

Annie Johnson's parents were both at least second generation Sheffielders, and, on her mother's side, there were strong links with the cutlery industry. Her grandfather, Thomas Rowbotham, was a cutler who originated from Aston or Aughton, but he was based at Wadsley when, as a widower, he married his second wife, Ann Kay. Mary Rowbotham, their eldest daughter, met and married Charlie Johnson while her family was living at Grammar Street and Charlie's was based at nearby Gilpin Street, both in the Infirmary Road area. Charlie Johnson, whose father William had also been an engineer, spent all his working life at Firth's, having followed William into the Norfolk Works. His married life was passed in and around the East End – at Harleston Street, Bagley Street, Jansen Street and Wade Street. He and Mary had four children, all girls – Edith, Amelia, Annie and Mary.

* * * *

It was Charlie Johnson's second daughter, Amelia (his other black sheep!), who forged the initial link with my mother's family, the Jacksons, when, as the widow of Richard Holden, a steelworks labourer who had died aged 48 in March 1931, she became the second wife of my maternal grandfather, Charles Jackson, and they set up house at her home, 43 Paget Street, in April 1932.

Grandfather Jackson was an iron moulder by trade and spent most of his life in the East End. His father, also called Charles, was a tobacconist who had moved to

Sheffield from Gainsborough and married Mary Flowers. Although they were based at Eyre Lane in central Sheffield at the time of my grandfather's birth in August 1881, Charlie and Mary soon afterwards moved to Attercliffe. They lived for a while in Alfred Road, and, although the area was heavily industrialised, it is of interest to note that for some years the senior Charles Jackson combined shopkeeping with running a smallholding – which, apparently, was not uncommon in the East End at that time. It is intriguing to speculate on how the younger Charles Jackson met my grandmother, Mary Ellen Bamforth, for she was a native of Lound Side, Chapeltown, being the daughter of William Bamforth, a coal miner, and Eliza (Emma) Hague. It may have happened when she followed the custom of the day and went into domestic service. However, there was again a probable steel or industrial link, for two of Mary Ellen's brothers, Jack and Frank, moved to Attercliffe after finding employment at a local firm; and it seems likely they and my grandfather were workmates – possibly at Edgar Allen's Vulcan Road works. There was one drawback to grandfather's hopes of furthering his relationship with Mary Ellen – he was a Catholic. He solved the problem by changing his religion.

My Jackson grandparents, who were married at Attercliffe Parish Church in July 1905, had one son (Teddy) and three daughters (Elsie, Eliza and Charlotte Elizabeth) – my mother, Eliza (named after her maternal grandmother), being the third child and second daughter when she was born in May 1915, at which time the family lived at 48 Zion Lane.

A Mystery and Other Twists of Fate

THE lives and character of both my parents were considerably influenced by the early loss of one of their parents, and it is fair to suggest these developments had a significant effect not only in the short term but over a much longer period. One wonders how different the pattern of events might have been for both but for the dramatic change in circumstances induced by those deaths. Almost certainly they would not have met, and it is also probable that, influenced by the 'lost' parent and spared some of the instability they endured, they would have enjoyed benefits which better equipped them for when they became parents themselves.

My father was only four years old when his father died in mysterious circumstances at sea while returning from America aboard the *SS Oceanic* in March 1914. The mystery was compounded in that no explanation survives to explain the reason why Tom Snr had taken the dramatic and sudden decision to leave his wife and small son behind and cross the Atlantic in the first place. Of course, there may have been a simple and unremarkable explanation, but, somehow, that seems unlikely. Family legend has it that his brother-in-law, Lewis James, smuggled Tom out of Sheffield in a hurry. One of my father's cousins lent credence to the suggestion that something of a sensational nature was behind the development when, during my inquiries, he talked of remembering tales of a midnight dash from Sheffield and a family conference at Pear Tree Farm at which it was decided to get Tom out of the country without delay. Around the same time, incidentally, it seems that one of Lewis James' daughters was dispatched to Australia. Whether the two incidents were connected, we shall never know. What is known is that Tom's mother, Elizabeth, chose to arrange for her son to sail to Canada.

For Elizabeth it was the latest in a succession of family traumas – in the space of a few years she had lost both her husband and her oldest son (Frederick had died in tragic circumstances while on his morning milk round), seen one of her daughters widowed, and been helpless to prevent Tom from marrying against her will. Now she faced more trouble.

Elizabeth was related through marriage to Mary, the wife of the Rector of Langwith Bassett, the Revd Edwin Mullins, and, some years earlier, their son, Auburn, had emigrated to Saskatchewan. It promised a safe haven for Tom, who remembered

Auburn as a contemporary and close friend of his older brothers – and one of the great characters of Upper Langwith before he had gone off to Cambridge University.

Indeed, Auburn himself had been given the money and encouraged to go to America to spare his family embarrassment after failing his exams and being sent down. The parson's son, once one of the key figures in a boxing club the Farnsworth boys had formed, was very much an extrovert with a mind of his own – so much so that, on one occasion, after his father had been defeated in the local parish council elections, he went round and threw a brick through the window of the house of the man who had defeated the Rector!

How long Tom remained with Auburn Mullins in Canada is not known, but it was probably as little as a few months. Mullins had a farm, but the work did not appeal to Tom, and he migrated first to Philadelphia, then joined hundreds of others seeking to make their fortune by working on the building of the Panama Canal. Unfortunately, by all accounts the Panama episode proved a personal disaster, for conditions were horrific and the place rife with yellow fever, typhoid and malaria. Tom's misery was compounded when, within a few months, he fell seriously ill.

The irony was that, in the meantime, it almost certainly emerged that whatever had caused him to flee the country proved not to have been as serious as first imagined. Anyway, Elizabeth, who at the time did not know Tom had gone to Panama, dispatched her youngest son, Frank, across the Atlantic to bring his brother home.

At the age of 21 it proved a traumatic experience for Frank, sailing steerage class to Canada, finding his way to Saskatchewan and then travelling on to Philadelphia and missing his brother in both places. He hadn't either the funds or the heart to continue his quest with a trip to Panama, and sailed home.

It was about a year later that Tom, now recovered from his illness, quit Panama and sailed for New York, from where he wired his mother for money to enable him to get back to England. Soon afterwards, he booked a passage aboard the *SS Oceanic*.

He never reached home. According to the ship's log, on the evening of 21 March 1914, Tom Farnsworth Snr 'jumped overboard', the only witness being a deckhand. The Master, told the facts, decided there should be no further inquiry – which suggests, for some reason, he wanted the subject closed as soon as possible. Among Tom's belongings were found letters from his sisters Annie and Kate, and it was they who were notified of the incident after the ship reached Southampton. Annie was charged with the task of passing the news to Tom's mother and his wife.

Nobody who knew Tom ever believed the official verdict. He was 26 years old and had everything to live for. The theory within the family was that he suffered another attack of yellow fever and was in such a delirious state that he didn't know what he was doing – so stumbled across the deck and fell overboard. A more sinister alternative, that he may have been thrown overboard when it was found he was suffering from yellow fever or something worse, is not an unrealistic suggestion – Frank Farnsworth's experiences when he sailed to North America led him to believe anything was possible if you were an obscure steerage passenger.

It has been said that, when my grandmother learned of Tom's death, she travelled to Pear Tree Farm and insisted it was the Farnsworth's responsibility to bring up her son. She wanted to leave the boy with Elizabeth. In the event, she took him back to Sheffield, where, so I'm told, he was more or less brought up by his Johnson grandparents. During his schooldays, he did, in fact, spend some time at Upper Langwith, where, apparently, his rough city ways did not impress his country cousins. My father appears to have resumed living with his mother around the time she met and married John William 'Billy' Johnstone. This was probably just after the Great War. 'Billy' was a steelworks labourer who also dabbled in buying and selling second-hand clothes. They lived in the Woodside Lane area for a few years before settling at 58 Danville Street – a back-to-back house on the steep hillside off Grimesthorpe Road.

* * * *

Although my mother's misfortune was more prosaic in that she was sixteen when she lost her mother (who died in September 1931 after a long illness), it was more traumatic than my father's experience because she was sixteen and old enough to understand both what was happening and the implications. She recognised it as an event which transformed her environment, and never forgot that her world turned upside down at just the moment when she needed the stability and influence of a secure home base – and the support and guidance of a mother.

At the time of Grandmother Jackson's death at the age of 49, the family was living at 60 Clay Street, off Attercliffe Road. According to my mother's younger sister, Charlotte, Grandfather Jackson had begun an association with Amelia Holden even while his wife was ill – Charlotte recalled that in order to break the news of Mary Ellen's death to her father, she had to seek him out at Amelia's house.

Anyway, Charles married Amelia within eight months of being widowed, and the event united (some would say that was the wrong word!) the families of both my maternal and paternal grandparents.

My father was then 22 and had long been a regular visitor to his Aunt Amelia's Paget Street home. Now he met her new step-daughter and his new cousin, Eliza. My mother, it should be noted, was by now the only Jackson child remaining with her father – her brother Teddy and sister Elsie had long since moved out, while Charlotte, then thirteen, had gone to live with Teddy and his wife, Mary, at Grenoside, where she enjoyed a much more comfortable adolescence than my mother.

Tom and Eliza

THE 1930s proved an eventful, often traumatic and crucial period for both my parents. What happened then shaped the rest of their lives. My father, bright and especially clever with figures, held various clerical jobs and was a smart young man with the potential and opportunity to progress much further than proved to be the case. Somehow, he lacked ambition and, especially, guidance. You couldn't say he was without drive, for, when he wanted, he had the patience and determination to succeed at anything. Mother often said if he had spent as much time working at things that really mattered as he did studying the horses, he would have gone a long way.

He was probably handicapped as much by environment as any flaws in his character. He was a victim of his background, and perhaps it was not his fault that he was content to remain trapped within limited horizons. His mother doted on him, and, as he could do no wrong in her eyes, no doubt he was spoiled. However, he did not enjoy a comfortable relationship with his step-father, and, while 'Billy' Johnstone was not without his good points, he was hardly an ideal role model.

It may have been because of this conflict that, around 1933, father joined the Royal Air Force. Had he been able to break with home ties, escape his mother's apron strings and settle into his new career, it might have been the making of him. In the event, though he did, in fact, make good progress in the RAF, the pull of home proved too strong, and he simply could not turn his back on it – so, when circumstances conspired to present him with a chance to make a permanent return to Danville Street, the prospect was too great to resist.

On his 25th birthday, in February 1935, Tom finally inherited a £100 bequest from Grandmother Elizabeth Farnsworth's estate. It had been held in trust since her death at the age of 79 in January 1928. As she left around £3,000, the sum of £100 was, perhaps, modest, but to Tom it represented a small fortune. He felt sure he had enough to buy himself out of the RAF and launch a bookmaking venture which would make him rich!

Unfortunately, the money ran out sooner than he had planned, which, as is noted elsewhere, wasn't entirely his fault, and he was soon back to the reality of having to find gainful employment while enduring a relationship with his step-father which continued to blow hot and cold.

Mother, meanwhile, did not find the new set-up in the Jackson household to her liking. She and step-mother Amelia simply didn't get on. Initially, she looked for a way out by moving to London to live with her mother's brother, Bob Bamforth, who was then in business as a fishmonger in Ealing. Alas, she did not meet the high expectations of Uncle Bob and Aunt Audrey and failed to settle. In truth, like my father, she was only really comfortable in familiar surroundings, and, as I know from my own experiences at the same age, you can blindly, even foolishly, yearn to be back in a place which, though you may not have been happy there, is at least 'home' and spells a kind of emotional security.

Of course, an early return to Sheffield was only slightly the lesser of two evils, and her plight was desperate enough to induce a breakdown in her health. On leaving hospital, she went home to Paget Street with great reluctance. According to what mother told me in later years, she was regarded by Amelia as little more than a servant – and there was no common bond, no emotional attachment, and no instruction or example in home management. Amelia, far from being the best of housewives, preferred to play the role of the lady – and it left mother feeling she understood why Charlie Johnson had had such a low opinion of his daughter.

If there was one consolation, it was that Eliza was rather taken up with Amelia's nephew, Tom. Looking back, she always remembered him as a smart, well-dressed young man with a ready smile and a great sense of fun. Compared with most of the boys she knew, he seemed clever, lively and, well, rather special.

Over the years they were destined to share much bitterness and endure much unnecessary self-inflicted pain, spending more time apart than together; yet, towards the end of her life, my mother still remembered the Tom Farnsworth she knew at the beginning with pride and affection. She once said: 'If I could have got him away from his mother, and he'd given me the chance, it could have been so different and we could have had a marriage that worked.' How mother's relationship with my father started and developed was something she seldom touched upon in our conversations, but it evidently grew into something serious in the winter of 1936-37. This was a phase in which my father became a frequent visitor to Paget Street because his Aunt Amelia, who had never enjoyed the best of health, suddenly became seriously ill. In April 1937, after barely five years of marriage to Charles Jackson, she died. Sometime in the autumn of 1937, mother discovered she was pregnant, and there was no doubt who was responsible. The news was not welcomed by either family, and neither my Grandfather Jackson nor my Grandmother Johnstone (Farnsworth), who had fallen out during Amelia's long illness and remained great enemies to the end of their lives, wanted the couple to marry.

In fact, when my mother gave birth to me in the City (now Northern) General Hospital in late May 1938, I was initially registered as Keith Jackson, and a wedding seemed out of the question. However, in the following October, a ceremony was arranged at the Sheffield Register Office, and subsequently a special dispensation allowed my birth certificate to be amended to confirm me as a Farnsworth. My parents began their married life at 58 Danville Street, although, after father was called up into the RAF following the outbreak of war in September 1939, mother moved back to 43 Paget Street; and it was there, in March 1940, that she gave birth to her second child, Ann. Sadly, Ann fell suddenly ill at the age of four months and died. By the time my sister Pat was born in August 1941, my parents were lodging with the Claytons, George and Alice, at No.41 Paget Street – next door to my grandfather, who by now had recruited a live-in housekeeper. My father, of course, was away in the RAF, and, sometime around 1941, he and mother had a spell in Newcastle – an episode I only know about because mother often told a tale about how I inadvertently locked myself in the bathroom of the house in which we lived, and it took a couple of hours of talking to me through the door before I managed to release the latch and regain my freedom!

Later, back in Sheffield, they took rooms in a house at the top end of Rock Street, near the junction with Nottingham Street in Pitsmoor; but, by the summer of 1944, when my younger sister, Jean, was born, we were lodging with the Applebys, Nellie and George, lower down Rock Street at Number 123. In this period, I began my school career in the infants department at Pye Bank School – although, in fact, I had already tasted school life (and found it not without its attractions!) in the nursery at Newhall. It was probably in 1946 that the family returned to the East End, renting a house at 61 Newhall Road – the backyard, which was large and ideal for kicking a ball around, overlooked the infants school. This was the first home of their own my parents had had, but, for some reason, they didn't enjoy much harmony, and, although I cannot remember the circumstances, there was a phase during which they went their separate ways.

All I recall is that father wasn't there – and, when he did finally return, it meant saying goodbye to our lodger, a man called Bernard Holmes. Curiously, I can still remember the confusion and sense of loss I felt when, after travelling with Bernard as far as the end of the road leading to his new home, somewhere near Bramall Lane, we shook hands and said our goodbyes. I never saw him again. Mother and father were still together when, around 1948, we moved into 43 Paget Street after Grandfather Jackson, at the age of 67, gave up the house after deciding to marry for the third time and move in with his new wife at a house in Berkley Street at the Carbrook end of Attercliffe.

Grandfather, like my mother, was slightly built and, in his prime, full of energy and fire, but he never liked living alone. He lived to be ninety and, after being widowed for a third time, spent many years on his own – yet never stopped hoping he might meet a nice widow who could restore some feminine comfort in his last years!

Number 43 was where we spent our final years as East Enders. By late 1951 or early 1952 we had left as a consequence of circumstances explained elsewhere, and Grandfather Jackson was the only member of the family to remain in the district. He, too, eventually moved out, spending his last years in a council flat at Upperthorpe – a long way from the familiar surroundings he had known all his life. I never think of him without an image of a little man caked from head to foot in muck after a day in the moulding shop at Moorwood's, though I also remember those Sunday afternoons when he would retire to his front room and spend an hour playing the organ while encouraging me to sing.

He spent his final days in Winter Street hospital, and, the last time I saw him, he was sitting up in bed trying to eat his dinner. He was so weak, he could barely hold his knife and fork. I picked up the fork and helped him, and he said: 'Tha'll allus be able to say tha fed me the last meal I ate on this earth.' He died within the hour.

Small Boy

EARLY childhood is a phase in our lives which most of us tend to remember as a time forever wrapped in a golden glow. Some might suggest it is simply a case of distance lending enchantment to our earliest recollections, but the truth is that when we are very small we view the world in vivid technicolour and see everything with a tremendous sense of wonder, so, when we come to look back across the years, our memories emerge from a camera which seldom recorded monochrome images.

My earliest memories are of attending the Newhall nursery at three years old, and, as my mother often reminded me, it was an experience I embraced with great enthusiasm – so much so that I often wept when she arrived at the end of the day to take me home. Happiness was hammering a log with a toy mallet, drinking warm milk on a cold day, and wearing a tiny smock which, to my child's eye, was so delightfully bright green – and prized all the more because it bore my name.

The war years were hardly the best time to be starting out in life, especially in an industrial East End which was a constant target for the German bombers, but, as small kids we were oblivious to the dangers and the mood of the times. Even the regular ritual of responding to the air-raid sirens with a rush for the safety of the cellar was an adventure in which the excitement compensated for the frustration of being awakened in the middle of the night.

In Paget Street, all the cellars in our row of houses were linked by specially constructed iron doors, and climbing through to join the family next door was a novelty we appreciated. The drama and sense of mutual danger inspired added friendship and good humour among the grown ups, and the atmosphere was more about fun than fear. For some reason, at one stage there was a notion that the cellars in Canny Street were more solid and safer than those in our street, and it added to our amusement to walk out into the blackness of a night devoid of street lights and experience a 'different' cellar.

In my own case, there was added variety in that, when I was staying with Grandmother Johnstone in Danville Street, air raids meant a trip into the backyard to spend a few hours in a conventional tin shelter which, if rather crowded and illuminated within only by candlelight, had a unique atmosphere. As I remember, sing-a-longs were a feature of these occasions, but the sound of planes overhead ('That's not one of ours,' someone would mutter) and falling incendiary bombs induced sudden silence. I cannot claim to have any memory of hearing bombs drop close by, but have not forgotten once when some houses at the bottom of Danville Street were reduced to a pile of rubble overnight, and, for a number of years until they were eventually demolished, many of the surviving properties at the lower end were only prevented from falling over by hastily-erected additional wooden prop supports that extended across the pavement.

* * * *

Life was a wonderful adventure, and, even when very small, I had a compulsion to wander the local streets and beyond. With a shopping area close at hand which boasted big stores like Banners, Littlewoods and Woolworths, there was plenty to amuse a youngster, but the dusty streets in themselves held a great attraction in that one led into another and there always seemed the promise of something exciting around every corner. Sometimes we kids would seem to walk forever and end up miles from home convinced we had nearly reached the other side of the world!

I use the term 'we' because it seems I seldom embarked on those marathon adventures alone. Mother used to say: 'I wouldn't mind if you wandered off on your own, but you will insist on taking somebody's else's kid along.' More often than not, my 'victim' was Tony Clayton, son of the family with whom we lodged, and there was one unforgettable occasion when our attempts to broaden our horizons and discover new places saw landed us in police custody.

Unfortunately, at five years old I had not quite mastered the knack of reading bus destinations, and, having boarded a bus which we thought was bound for Wincobank (the next place past Brightside), Tony and I ended up in Worksop. It might not have happened had I not been so determined to ride on a single decker of the kind we seldom got the opportunity to use, and I suppose we were spared what might have been a traumatic experience because the conductress just happened to recognise us as kids from the Newhall area.

I cannot remember how we managed to board the bus and place ourselves out of sight on the back seat without being spotted by the conductress in the first place, but I do recall that, quite early in the journey, I realised we were certainly not going in the direction of Wincobank. However, it just seemed a welcome diversion to be passing through places we had never seen before, and, when we heard the conductress shout 'terminus!' and finally emerged from hiding, we were more concerned with the prospect of exploring new streets than knowing where we had ended up.

Fortunately, the conductress seemed to know we were East Enders and insisted we remained on the bus for the return journey. I think we expected her to drop us off at the bottom of Staniforth Road, so we could wander home at our own pace, but, when she invited us to ride all the way into the Pond Street bus station, we accepted it as a welcome bonus to our adventure. We probably imagined she was planning to put us on a tram to Newhall Road from the city centre. Alas, even though we insisted we were definitely not lost, she chose to hand us over to a policeman, and we ended up in the police station in the old Town Hall in Waingate.

This turn of events, of course, hardly troubled us. Indeed, we revelled in the novelty of getting so much attention, and all the more so when a kindly policewoman served us a meal of tea and cream cakes, and produced some board games for our amusement. It was only when our mothers turned up, both rather angrier than we had anticipated, that we came to the conclusion we must have done something wrong. In those days, Tony and I were inseparable, and, if we were sometimes regarded as little rascals by our parents (my mother's favourite term was 'You little varment!'), we were essentially innocents who sought simple amusements. We might get involved in the kind of mischief typical of most infants, but, apart from occasionally trying to ride on trams or buses without paying, we had no criminal inclinations. Moreover, we saw no danger in seeking the help and advice of strangers because it was a time when kids could wander far and wide without any threat of being molested or led astray.

I can recall only one instance when I found myself in any danger from a stranger, and, while the fact that I still remember the episode suggests it left a deep impression, at the time I don't recall being frightened enough to mention it when I got home. It was a summer evening when I was on my own, and, as was my habit, I walked from Newhall to Danville Street to spend a few hours with Grandmother Johnstone. The attraction of taking the route across what we called Carlisle Street 'rec' at that time of the year was that I could always drop in and watch Petre Street Cricket Club in action on their hillside pitch – an interlude which always gave me great pleasure because I was allowed to sit beside the tiny scoreboard while I watched my great hero, a red-haired all-rounder called Hancock, perform. I wish I could convey the delight I took in watching those white-flannelled cricketers, listening to their talk, and soaking in what seemed to me then such a magical atmosphere. I was a small boy among strangers, yet I felt happy and secure.

However, on this particular evening, a youth stopped me as I strode across the 'rec' and offered to show me some birds' eggs he said he had found in a nearby field. Only when he started trying to slip his hand up my short trousers did I realise he had lured me to this lonely spot for reasons I could not comprehend but which were plainly not normal or proper.

Unusually, perhaps, I didn't panic even though I smelt danger and went cold with fear, and it was my good fortune that, when someone unexpectedly passed along a nearby path, the youth suddenly ran off. I continued on my way oblivious to the implications of what had happened, and never mentioned it to anyone.

SMALL BOY

* * * *

There were some wonderful people in the old East End, but, of course, there were plenty of rogues, too. You soon learned which lads to avoid, and there were a number of families in the district who had a reputation as 'bad 'uns'. Long after the war ended, there was one house in the area that still bore a painted Union Jack on its walls and a fading message which read 'Welcome Home, Lads'. It happened to be the home of the 'B—' family, and, on a sunny afternoon, they would pour into the street and sit around on chairs on the pavement laughing and drinking. You always made a detour on these occasions to avoid passing by, for they were a rough, foul-mouthed lot and you could be sure one of the boys would grab you or taunt you just to amuse the others.

There was seldom a spell when someone in that family wasn't away in prison, and, as a small boy, I never passed their house without imagining I could see evil gazing from every window. For years whenever I had a nightmare, it was about being trapped in that house.

I think the only time during my infancy when I was aware of having a brush with serious trouble, the kind that might have led to me being identified as a kid with criminal tendencies, was once when I tagged along with a schoolpal I will call 'Ronnie' and his older sister. The experience left me too scared to ever want to repeat it again.

I have never seen 'Ronnie' since those days and have no idea what kind of life he led in his later years, but I hope he didn't grow up to be a hardened criminal, for, if he was rough and ready and full of devious tricks which fascinated me, he was a good-hearted and generous lad. He was, however, a very clever thief, and came from a family who prided themselves on getting most of the things they wanted without paying for them.

As I could never resist a wander round the shopping areas of Attercliffe, I needed no encouragement to join 'Ronnie' and his sister on an excursion, and I shall never forget the shock with which I recognised that they were stealing items from almost every stall we passed as we went through Woolworth's. When we arrived at Littlewood's and they began repeating the performance, I was only prevented from deserting them by a fear they would brand me a coward.

Fortunately, I was on the opposite side of the counter when an assistant caught 'Ronnie' stuffing a tennis ball into his pocket, and, when the brother and sister made a sudden dash for the door, I was too petrified to move, being grateful that, amid the confusion, nobody realised I had arrived with the kids now being chased.

As it was about this time that we made one of our frequent family moves from the East End, I didn't have to wait long for an excuse to stop calling on 'Ronnie', and, by the time we went back to Paget Street, he and his sister had disappeared from the scene.

* * * *

When I was six years old, we moved to live with the Applebys in lodgings at 123 Rock Street, Pitsmoor. It was here that my younger sister, Jean, was born, and this was also the phase during which I found myself at Pye Bank – a school I most readily associate with my early childhood even though my stay there probably lasted barely a year.

It is often said that the way we act when we are very small reveals much about the kind of person we will grow up to be, although, on that count, I am not entirely sure whether one incident that occurred in my time at Pye Bank reflects well on me or not. It certainly confirms that accepting defeat quietly was not in my nature, and the episode ensured my teacher, Miss Vera Fisher (she later became Mrs Smethurst), never forgot me.

Indeed, many years later, when I was established as a journalist, we renewed acquaintance when, out of the blue, she wrote to ask: 'Do you remember me?' As if I could forget someone who had once treated a cheeky urchin from Pitsmoor with such kindness.

Miss Fisher, who was then just turned 21 and in her first post after completing her studies at Bingley, found teaching infants at Pye Bank a sharp contrast with life in her native Penistone. She recently recalled: 'It was a difficult area, there were many very poor families for whom conditions were far from pleasant, and we had a lot of children who needed help. In fact, one of my colleagues, Miss Mary Cocker, had a pupil, a very small boy, who was turned out of his home every morning when his parents went off to work. The sad little lad would sit on the school steps for two or three hours waiting for the doors to open at just after eight o'clock.

'My old headmaster at Hoylandswaine had wanted me to start my career close to home, but there were a lot of people from the district who travelled into Sheffield to work, and gaining experience in a new environment was the option I preferred. I never regretted the six-and-a-half years I spent at Pye Bank. It cost me 11½d (5p) a day on the train, and, with the tram fare, it added up to just over five shillings a week to get to work. My wages, £17 a month, seem modest now, but I was better off than many of the parents of my pupils.

'We had very large classes. I had 59 boys and girls, and we were confined to a corridor classroom, but we coped very well and, despite the circumstances in which some of the children lived, the standards of conduct and discipline were high and there was a good atmosphere. Miss Poole, the headmistress, believed in being firm but fair, and, if we were not encouraged to have favourites, we seldom found it difficult to be friendly with the children because the majority were happy to be at school and responded to our efforts. The fact that there was a war on added to the gloom of the district, and I often felt it would be so nice to be able to help the children escape their normal surroundings for a few hours.'

It was in the context of this background that Miss Fisher came up with a plan to reward some pupils at the end of the summer term of 1944 by taking them, at her own expense (probably around four shillings), to spend a day on her family's farm at Penistone. She calculated she could manage five children, and decided the lucky ones would be those who finished top in a series of tests in reading, spelling and arithmetic.

I finished sixth in the list, which wasn't bad in a class of 59, but, sad to relate, let Miss Fisher know I didn't take kindly to missing the cut by a fraction. She has since insisted that I merely wore a heart-rendering look of acute disappointment over the following days, but my own memory is of expressing my dismay rather more directly. I have long since forgotten the details, but, whatever I said or did, it worked, for the party was increased to six.

The others were Irene Bates, Pat Neeley, Peter Topham, John Mercer and Graham Humphries. Sadly, I had forgotten them all until my old teacher recalled the names, and I have to admit that all except one remain no more than names to me even now. Moreover, while I happened to meet up with Pat Neeley again some fifteen years later at Newton Chambers, where she was a telephonist and a prominent member of the Thorncliffe Musical Society, I don't think either of us realised we had been in the group we might call 'the Penistone Six'. The fact serves to remind us that we forget far more than we ever remember from our past!

That July day in 1944 at James Fisher's Cat Hill Farm remains one of the fondest memories of my infancy, and I can still remember most of the details, from meeting up with the others at the school, riding into town on a tram, taking the lift to the Victoria Station from the Wicker, and savouring the experience of standing on a station platform and boarding a train for the first time I can remember.

The green pastures of Penistone were like a slice of Paradise compared with the pall of Pitsmoor, and, though the journey was in reality a short one, it seemed we had been transported into another world. Miss Fisher had organised a taxi to meet us at Penistone station, her father greeted us at the farm and led us on a tour of the animals, and, later, her mother served up a stew for dinner, which was rounded off with a dish of rice pudding served from a huge pot. To the grown-ups it was probably all very ordinary but, for we six-year-olds, what a wonderful contrast with home!

Canny Street Kid

AT DIFFERENT times during my boyhood in the old East End, we lived at Paget Street and Newhall Road, but when I reflect on those years in the 1940s I invariably think of myself as 'The Canny Street Kid' because, for me and Billy Whittingham, the top end of that short street was our Hillsborough and our Bramall Lane – and the inspiration for all our sporting dreams.

Of course, it was a different world then. Street football and cricket was commonplace in most working-class areas that didn't boast a park or a proper recreation area beyond a school yard which was out of bounds when the premises were closed. Playing in the street was relatively safe, for few folk in that district could afford a motor car (and, anyway, petrol was rationed), so there was little traffic. Apart from the occasional lorry or delivery van, the main danger probably came from the coalman's horse and cart or the ragman's pony and trap.

It was a world in which television was unknown, and making one's own entertainment was a way of life for most kids. In the case of Billy and me, with our heads filled with the names of sporting heroes picked up from the newspapers and the wireless, it was not difficult to find romance on the dusty streets simply by kicking or throwing a rubber ball and imagining we were Stanley Matthews in the winter or Len Hutton in the summer. At the time, our closest link with professional sport was when Billy's grandad worked as a scorecard seller at Bramall Lane.

Canny Street extended from opposite Newhall School on Paget Street to Alfred Road, and boasted the advantage over some surrounding streets in not being cobblestoned, so, though barely a cricket pitch wide, it was was ideal for makeshift matches involving a handful of lads.

The only time we needed to avoid it was on those Sunday afternoons when men spilled out from the nearby pubs and commandeered the bottom end (right outside Billy's house) for their tossing rings – occasions which invariably ended in high drama as the men dashed into surrounding yards and houses when the police suddenly descended on their 'pitch'.

It was not unusual for residents to be faced with an unexpected 'guest' just when they were sitting down to Sunday dinner! 'Just avoiding the coppers, luv,' he would explain to the woman of the house. 'I'll be off as soon as they've gone.' Our sporting exploits were, of course, a constant source of dismay to Ma Hitch and her family, because, as their house, number 35 Paget Street, was the last in a row of eight and boasted a gable-end facing on to Canny Street, it was perfect for our requirements.

In summer three stumps were permanently chalked on that wall, and in winter goalposts and a crossbar. All year round, for hours on end, a small rubber ball would thud against the brickwork.

Ma Hitch and her hefty sons grew tired of chasing me and Billy Whittingham away, but, when they did, if it was the cricket season we could find refuge staging a game against a garage door down an inlet further down the street. However, we preferred the top end because it offered more space in which to hit the ball – and less chance of breaking a window. There was only one drawback in playing at the top of Canny Street. On the corner opposite the gable end of the Hitch's house stood the back of St Clement's Church Hall, and, in direct line with our chalked wicket, there was an opening, barely two-feet wide, above the wall. If you happened to hit the ball in there, it was invariably lost unless you had the dexterity and daring of my pal Tony Clayton – the only lad I ever knew who could climb into and out of that tight area with the ease of a cat. Unfortunately, Tony had little enthusiasm for sport, so was seldom on hand to rescue the ball.

There was, however, one occasion when Tony was persuaded to join me in a game, and I remember it with some pain even after all these years. A cheeky kid called 'Ginger' Proctor (his family lived at 39 Paget Street, next door to the Claytons) just happened to be passing as I played a delivery from Tony towards the corner of the church hall.

When 'Ginger' picked up the ball, I expected him to throw it to Tony. Instead, he deliberately lofted it over the wall and into the dreaded hole. Then he ran off laughing, and was in their house before we could catch him. It was only later, when he emerged thinking we had gone, that we managed to give him the clip we felt he deserved. It was just a tap, a warning.

Later, I wished we had done more than that, for, at school the next morning, we were hauled before headmaster Jerry Bronks and told Mrs Proctor claimed we had bullied her son. Unfortunately, I lost my cool and said: 'We didn't hit him hard enough, the little sod!'

Only after he had caned us (six sharp strokes apiece – three on each hand), and listened as I tearfully explained what Proctor had done with our ball, did Bronks accept the boy had provoked our anger. It was no consolation when Bronks said: 'If I had known that, I wouldn't have caned you.'

* * * *

In fact, the best place to play football and cricket in the Paget Street area was just a block away from Canny Street, on what we called 'The 'Oller' – across the road from the red-bricked St Clement's Church. This had originally been a children's playground donated by the legendary Sheffield benefactor J. G. Graves in the 1930s; but, around the end of the war, when raw material for the steelworks was in short supply, overnight all the railings and swings and roundabouts disappeared – and caretaker Tom Parker, the white-haired 'guardian' of the premises, was pensioned off.

I don't remember many people mourning the loss of the children's facilities. One day it was there, the next it was gone. No more free entertainment, no more friendly chats with old man Parker in the 'den' he kept warm in the depths of winter by constantly banking up the stove with coke and wood. The only reminders of the swings-and-roundabouts era to survive were remains of the foundations jutting out of the ground – and many a cut knee was a consequence when the area became a football pitch.

'The 'Oller' was the venue for hundreds of makeshift football and cricket matches each year. These were staged every lunchtime, almost every day straight after school, and from dawn to dusk on most days during school holidays. Games would invariably feature fifteen or twenty boys in each team, and, as lads dropped out to go for a meal after two or three hours, others took their place until they came back. You had to feel sorry for the tanner ball that took so much punishment!

Elsewhere, I mention a 'real' football I was given one Christmas by Harry Allcock, the secretary of Scunthorpe United. Here it is relevant to note that the life of this ball came to a sudden and painful end on 'The 'Oller' in the gathering dusk of a February evening.

While the bottom end of the playground boasted a shed which served as an ideal and almost 'proper' goal, the opposite end, across from the church, was open to the street, so we simply used coats and jerseys as goalposts and were left to argue whether the ball had passed over or under an imaginary crossbar.

As I've suggested, there wasn't much traffic on Paget Street, but, as luck would have it on this particular occasion, a lorry was trundling past just as Maurice Salvin hit a shot wide of the pile of coats...and my lovely, if by now battle-scarred, case ball rolled with agonising slowness under the vehicle to be trapped beneath it's double back wheel.

As the ball burst with the sudden snap of a rifle shot, the pain went straight to my heart. It wasn't just the end of the match for that day. For me it was the end of a phase during which that ball had made me the most popular lad in Newhall!

* * * *

Occasionally, a group of us would walk the two or three miles to Firth Park, where we could play on grass, but, in terms of seeking a pitch boasting 'proper' goalposts (though without nets), we seldom had to look much further than a place we knew as 'The Hillock' – a stretch of wasteland between Carlisle Street and Petre Street which was a five-minute walk from Newhall Road.

It was totally devoid of grass, a stony area wedged between factories, and, even though the site of the pitch featured a public footpath which passed through the penalty area at one end, it was popular with workmen at lunchtime and with pub teams at weekends. Nobody seemed to bother about people walking across the goalmouth during a match on Carlisle Street 'rec'!

Billy Whittingham and I would often walk up to 'The Hillock' at weekends or during school holidays, for even with rusty goalposts to shoot into, daft as it might seem, in our view it took us a step closer to a brush with 'big time' football. There might only be the two of us, each taking a turn to be goalkeeper, but when we shot or headed that rubber ball 'between the sticks' we could imagine ourselves as professionals. I might be Redfern Froggatt when I nodded one in, while Billy for some reason always insisted he was Stoke's Frank Bowyer. In the role of goalkeeper, we'd dive all over the dusty goalmouth pretending to be Frank Swift, Jack Smith or whoever was our current favourite.

* * * *

Back in the late 1940s, if you had strolled around the dusty streets of Sheffield's East End, and the Newhall district in particular, you might have come across a scruffy kid in torn short trousers kicking a tanner ball against an end wall in Canny Street or in a backyard in Paget Street. The neighbours were not impressed, and, listening to the lad give a running commentary as if he were playing in a cup final, they probably concluded he was plain daft. Yet he was convinced that destiny had marked him out as one of the football stars of the future.

Of course, he never did make the grade. He lacked the natural talent, but, being one of life's great romantics, he was totally unaware of his shortcomings. Hadn't he just read *Feet First*, the autobiography of Stanley Matthews, the legendary wizard of dribble? And hadn't the great Blackpool and England winger spent hours as a boy in the Potteries dribbling round kitchen chairs to master that art? So, if 'the Canny Street kid' did the same, wouldn't he, too, reach the top?

I can vouch that it wasn't for the lack of trying that he failed, and confirm that his consolation was at least he went on to become a football writer. Some would say he didn't have too much talent for that role, either! Anyway, he got there, albeit after a struggle, and survived for a few years. It was the ideal job for a romantic.

One of the keys to my development was the way in which, even when very small, the romance of the game meant more than the reality. That was partly down to my father. He was not a consistent football follower, at least he wasn't a frequent spectator in my time, but he spent many an hour talking about when football had been his great passion, and, while I can't say he was particularly gifted as a storyteller, somehow those tales of old pre-war stars captured my imagination.

The printed word was a major influence, too. Thank goodness that if times were hard, the environment far from encouraging (few people in our corner of the East End read many books), and nobody pointed the way, at least my father's passion for gambling meant there were such papers as the *Sporting Chronicle*, the *Racing & Football Outlook* and perhaps a *Daily Herald* or *Sheffield Telegraph* to read. There was also the *Sheffield Star's* Saturday sports edition, the *Green 'Un*, which I remember greeting with great enthusiasm when it resumed publication soon after the end of the war.

It didn't, perhaps, add up to the ideal library for an impressionable boy, but at least it meant there was reading material on hand. Fortunately, perhaps, I managed to ignore the parts of the papers devoted to horse and greyhound racing and simply devoured the football. Supplementing my father's tales of players who had been the heroes of his own youth, the match reports satisfied my hunger for knowledge of the game.

After that came the discovery of the Attercliffe public library on Leeds Road. Here I found the ghosted autobiographies of the likes of Frank Swift (*Football from the Goalmouth*), Tommy Lawton (*Football is my Business*), Raich Carter (*Footballer's Progress*) as well as the Matthews book.

Incidentally, I ought to mention that, when I was staying with my grandmother in Danville Street, I used Burngreave Library in Gower Street, and it was here that a kindly assistant introduced me to Neville Cardus's autobiography – a book which, when I discovered it, fired my journalistic ambitions and was an inspiration simply because the great man had himself started out in circumstances as humble as mine.

I remember there was one occasion when I took the Lawton book to school at Newhall, and, at the end of a Friday afternoon reading session, it suddenly went missing. I was in Ken Holmes's class at the time, and when I reported the loss of the book, he sent me round the school to inquire if it had turned up in another classroom.

It caused great amusement everywhere I went when I inquired if anyone had seen a copy of *Football is my Business*, and I knew it was a waste of time. I was convinced the book had been mistakenly gathered up with the ones returned to the library cupboard in my own classroom – but Holmes was not a man to provoke by suggesting he re-open the cupboard to check. Sure enough, it turned up there when we returned to school on Monday – two days after the volume had been due back at the public library!

As for football, I knew all the theory, but the problem was putting it into practice. Playing in the backyard, shooting against the door of the outside toilet, dribbling round chairs taken from the kitchen, or practising heading against a wall in Canny Street in the company of my pal Billy Whittingham, I could make the ball do exactly what I wanted. But it was a different story in a 'real' game with other kids.

My inability to even make the list of possibles for the school team was a constant source of dismay. Everybody knew I was football daft, but nobody ever seemed to consider me a contender for a place. Yet, in retrospect, that was really a stroke of luck, for, in the end, I wangled the best position of all – that of school football reporter. In truth, the 'appointment' didn't last long, but it was enough to fire my imagination and helped shape my destiny.

I have often told the story of how I got myself that job, though I have invariably used journalistic licence to make it sound better. Previously, the credit has been given to Jerry Bronks, the old Newhall headmaster, with the suggestion that it was his master-stroke which made me a non-playing member of the team, solved my truancy problem, and inspired my ambition to be a football writer.

However, this was not entirely so.

The truancy thing had, in fact, long been solved. A year or two earlier, I went through a phase when I much preferred wandering round the Attercliffe shops or simply walking the streets to being confined in a classroom. I don't think it was the lessons I disliked so much as being trapped inside a building when there was so much adventure to be found on the outside. I mean, Banner's store was a wonderful place for a boy to explore!

Looking back, I'm surprised I was so reluctant to go to school, for in later years I honestly loved it. Yet, at the time, I was such a problem pupil, and even regular doses of the cane – and old Bronks really could make it hurt– failed to persuade me to break the habit.

Once the school even provided me with a personal attendance sheet which the teacher marked daily for me to take home to prove I had been in class. However, they stopped bothering when they found I had acquired a red pencil like the teacher's and was marking it myself! Thereafter, for some weeks, I was met at our house door every morning by two classmates, who escorted me to school.

Anyway, the notion of becoming a football reporter was entirely my own. A year or two earlier, I had seen a boy read to the school his account of a match, and I felt that was the sort of job I could do very well. When I put the suggestion to the headmaster, he was amused and probably intrigued, but he agreed to let me have a go.

Bronks could be very tough and uncompromising, and to see him in a temper was not a pleasant sight; but he would sometimes smile at you as if to say 'I think you're a silly boy, but go on, I'll let you do as you ask'. This was one of those occasions.

Thus, on the appointed day, I travelled with the team and sportsmaster Granville Twigg on the top deck of a tramcar, to a pitch somewhere in Graves Park. I don't remember all the players, but I do believe Sammy Ashworth was our goalkeeper, lanky Pete Morton was at full-back, and the half-back line comprised Graham Watson, Derek Brown and Maurice Salvin. The captain was Jack Shirley, and his front-line colleagues included Eric and Brian Hancock, Barry Day and Terry Carr.

I stood on the touchline and tried to look the part, complete with pencil and notebook; and later, at home, produced a match report which, to be honest, probably bore very little relation to the game I had seen. After fifty years, the piece has not survived, so I haven't a clue what it said, but I do remember that it contained all the cliches I could cull from every Fred Walters and Taffy Williams match report I had ever read in the local *Green 'Un*!

Bronks was not a bad chap, and he, too, encouraged my enthusiasm for the game. As secretary of the Sheffield Schools Football Federation, he was involved in a way which caught my imagination. He often talked about football, told us about an old Newhall schoolboy international from the 1920s, Harry Gooney; and I recall being very impressed when a local Sheffield and England Boys star called George Brown, who was a Meynell Road lad, arrived at our school on a visit and asked directions to the headmaster's office. A brush with fame!

I always remember that, at the end of morning assembly the day after the school match at which I made my journalistic debut, Bronks made quite a show of reading out my report, which was rather longer than he anticipated ('more *Manchester Guardian* than *Daily Mirror*, I seem to recall,' he told me many years later).

Some 500 children sat in silence absorbing my every word. It was a heady moment when old Bronks invited me to stand and the entire school applauded my effort...and if ever there was a moment when my dream of becoming a football writer was born, that was it!

After that, I remember covering a few six-a-side cricket games in the playground, but, curiously, I don't recall doing another school football match. The arrangement was never formalised. When I look back now, I often wonder why I didn't get more encouragement to continue in the role.

I remember feeling rather miffed one afternoon when I discovered the school team had gone off somewhere and old Twigg had never thought of taking the 'reporter'.

I have to admit that circumstances at home did not help, and it may be that I left Newhall shortly afterwards. My parents split up, and, after a spell when my younger sister, Jean, and I remained with my father, we went to live with my mother and elder sister Pat in Macro Street in the Woodside area.

While at Macro Street, I attended Owler Lane School for a few months, had a brief spell back at Newhall, then ended my formal education with eighteen months or so at Burngreave; and it was while at Burngreave that I persuaded the headmaster, a miserable chap called Scowcroft, to let me travel with the school football team and report the match.

Again it proved to be a one-off experience, and, once more, I found the team had left for the next match without anyone suggesting my services might be required.

CANNY STREET KID

As a boy, I was always doing something to emphasise my romantic notions.

I remember how, in one half-term holiday during my short stint at Owler Lane, I walked through Brightside and Meadowhall (the latter then filled with factories and steelworks long before the era of the huge shopping complex) and over the hill to Rotherham and the Millmoor ground, where I called on manager Reg Freeman and offered myself for trial. I didn't get one, naturally, but dear old Reg – one of the game's real gentlemen – told me I could watch Rotherham whenever I wished. He said if I presented myself at the players' entrance on match-days and announced that 'Mr Freeman says I can come in', I would be allowed on to the terrace.

I took up his offer on several occasions, and once, at an FA Cup tie with Nottingham Forest, I appeared in a crowd scene filmed for the cinema newsreels. I never saw the film myself, but a schoolpal who went to the Globe on Attercliffe Common, watched this clip of the Millmoor match, and, at school next day, told me: 'I saw a kid right at the front of the crowd who looked just like thee, Farnsy!'.

Anyway, as I was leaving Millmoor on that first day, I was spotted by the local reporter, John Piper, and, after talking to him, found my name featured in a story in the *Sheffield Telegraph* the next morning. When John (with whom I was to work many years later) discovered I had walked to Millmoor, he gave me sixpence so I could ride home!

It was not the first time I'd had my name in the paper, for there had been an earlier incident, when I was about ten years old, which emphasised my sense of romance. I spotted in the *Green 'Un* that Scunthorpe United, then in the Midland League, were seeking 'experienced' players, and I applied! The secretary, Harry Allcock, replied, told me I should write again in a few years, and, in the meantime, eat plenty of Yorkshire puddings!

I must have maintained the correspondence because, just before the following Christmas, Harry wrote again to say Scunthorpe were playing Rotherham reserves at Millmoor and invited my father and myself to the game. I think he was rather surprised when, on the appointed day, I turned up alone. Unfortunately, it was typical of my father that he didn't go with me, though I can't remember what his excuse was. Old Harry took me into the dressing room and I sat with him in the directors' box during the game; then, before I left for home, he gave me a parcel containing a ball.

It was the the first 'proper' football (we called it a case ball) I had ever possessed. It gave me and my pals hours of pleasure on the 'Oller', though it wasn't long before it was falling apart at the seams – and, sadly, it had a short but eventful history which came to a sudden and dramatic end when it was crushed by a passing lorry.

Football Daft

IN MODERN times, when top-class football is featured on television every day of the week and is so accessible to boys almost before they can walk, kids grow up familiar not only with all the stars on the national scene but a knowledge of the game on a world scale before they are out of short trousers. They watch the best players and big matches in the comfort of their own home, and with so much media coverage so readily available, they can hardly fail to be well-informed. Football at the end of the 1990s has become a branch of show business, and, with players earning the kind of money and enjoying the sort of status once reserved for film stars, there is little wonder that the game captures the imagination of the young on a remarkably extensive scale.

These days boys (and many girls) expect to have the latest replica shirts, and seldom need to wait until Christmas to get these and all the other football-related merchandise from club shops which symbolise the commercial face of the modern game. Home-made scarves and rosettes aren't as common as they used to be!

All-seater grounds have made watching more comfortable and, to some degree, changed the nature of spectating; and, if admission prices are much higher than they once were, somehow mums and dads always find the money because kids don't appreciate parents who 'can't afford it'.

Lads don't play football in the streets with a tanner ball anymore, and youngsters now not only enjoy a 'proper' pitch for matches but invariably boast all the essential equipment and facilities. It's amusing now to recall how I once got into trouble when I borrowed my sister's jumper because it looked a bit like a goalkeeper's jersey! I may have seen the real thing in the window of Wally Boyes' shop, but no way could I have bought it.

No doubt more boys than ever dream of making the professional ranks, and, among the many who fail in that ambition, those who might once have aspired to become football writers now want to go straight into television. We live in an age when the goal is to start at the top, and nobody wants to begin at the bottom.

Once we settled for keeping newspaper cuttings of our heroes in scrapbooks; now almost every kid seems to be a statistician with all the facts and figures about his favourites fed into his computer – and the Internet and news from Clubcall to supplement his quest for information.

I mention this simply to stress the contrast in circumstances between the present and a not-too-distant past in which so many of the things we now take for granted were unknown, and, perhaps, to make the point that not only are conditions very different but awareness is greater and expectations higher. The world is much more sophisticated.

We all appreciate the dramatic improvements in every area of life, but, in this age of greater equality and opportunity, it is, perhaps, difficult to relate to the limited horizons and the environment that existed, especially in working-class areas, forty or fifty years ago.

The important thing is that, if our view of things then seems rather simplistic and even quaint in retrospect, and if we were more easily satisfied with what we had, we were no less happy. It's that old 'Heaven lies about us in our infancy' syndrome. In a sense, circumstances encouraged the dreamer within the boy, and inspired the imagination to create romantic notions which, in most cases, were unlikely to ever find fulfilment.

Yet it wasn't a bad thing to dream. When I got the notion of one day becoming a 'real' football writer, frankly it was an impossible dream. But I held on to it, and, despite a very modest education, precious little encouragement, and following a few false trails along the way, I eventually got there. I can look back now and see that, with greater effort and study, I could have gone much further and achieved a great deal more. Indeed, by some standards, I haven't really come far, but, considering where it all started, to even get where I have is some kind of miracle – and it occurred because I simply kept on dreaming right into my teens and twenties!

* * * *

I was always a cheeky kid who tended to think I could begin to fulfil a dream simply by offering myself and getting close to those who were where I wanted to be. Thus, believing I could make the grade as a footballer even though I seldom made the school team, at ten I wrote to Scunthorpe United for a trial and later turned up at Rotherham on the same quest. Once I had got the idea of pursuing football journalism, at different times I presented myself to Fred Walters and Richard A. Sparling, respectively sports editors of the *Sheffield Star* and the *Sheffield Telegraph*.

When I sat in Sparling's chair at the *Telegraph*, old 'Dick' had long been retired, but I couldn't resist ringing him to say: 'I've made it!', but, of course, he had no memory of the boy who had once called in at Aldine Court to ask for some tips.

By the same token, Jimmy Hagan, the legendary Sheffield United player, was amused when, in his time as West Bromwich Albion's manager in the mid-1960s, I paid an official visit during Cup training at Lilleshall, and told him this wasn't the first time I had sought an interview. The previous occasion had been in my schooldays, when, having made an appointment with a call from the local phone box, I turned up at his sports oufitter's shop in London Road – only to be turfed out when he discovered I was just a kid!

Reference to Hagan's shop, which he ran in partnership with another United hero, Harold Brook, reminds me it was there that, some months before my aborted interview, I was gifted the only new pair of football boots I ever owned. In fact, I always claimed I was the shop's first customer, for the incident occurred on the day before the official opening.

A few months earlier, I had developed the habit of watching Sheffield FC, who were then playing up at Abbeydale Park. Typically, I got friendly with the secretary, Jim Hardie, and a committee man called Tom Brooksbank, and, amused by my interest, they invited me to meet the players. The upshot was, for a spell I got myself a job helping the trainer, Frank Fagan, lay out the kit in the dressing room, and I was soon a favourite with the players.

It wasn't long before I was joining them on away trips, and, invited to meet up with them outside the City Hall on these occasions, this kid with not a penny in his pocket found himself travelling all over Yorkshire in style – in the back seat of centre-forward Roy Benson's Rolls Royce!

Sheffield's captain was a wonderful man called Harry Parkin, who asked me if I fancied doing some odd jobs and running errands at his cutlery factory during the school holidays. At the end of the first week, he gave me a postcard to take to his pal Harold Brook. He had written on it: 'Fit this lad up with a pair of football boots, and send the bill to me.' Jimmy Hagan was looking on while 'Brookie' did the fitting!

Many years later, by which time Parkin was a prominent figure at the Sheffield & Hallamshire CFA and also a top man in local golf, I met up with him again in my role as a sports editor. He was not only a very generous man, he was one of the best examples of the genuine amateur who played for the love of the game, reached a high level in football and golf, and, though he always wanted to win, never failed to adhere to a strict code of sportsmanship.

* * * *

If I was a long way from being a half-decent player as a kid, I always fancied my ability as a football manager, and, being the dreamer I was, formed at least half-a-dozen 'clubs' and set myself up as the team-manager. The problem was not one of my teams ever completed more than a single game, and some didn't even manage that!

There were, I must admit, times when my imagination tended to push the typical romantic aspirations of boyhood to the brink of sheer fantasy, and this may have been partly due to reading volumes like *The Boys' Book of Football* and the *FA Book for Boys*, as well as the adventures of Limpalong Leslie and Baldy Hogan, fictional footballers in boys' magazines of the era like *Hotspur*. I also remember a slim novel called *The Chattertooth Eleven*, about a family of boys who formed an all-conquering team. I've never seen the book since, and have no idea who wrote it, but the impact the story had on me was remarkable.

One edition of the *FA Book for Boys*, incidentally, carried an article which suggested that a pre-match massage was guaranteed to improve a player's performance, and it gave a list of ingredients for making a suitable lotion at home. With grandmother's help, I created a concoction which, alas, not only failed to turn me into a star but left me with a serious case of body odour!

The first team I formed was Danville Street Rovers when I was ten, but I never got beyond recruiting three players – neighbourhood pals James Elmore, Chester Lowe and Terry Webster. However, taking the job seriously, I did do a bit of scouting on the Petre Street recreation ground during the school holidays, and thought I'd spotted a lad who looked to be a useful centre-forward.

Amusing as it might seem, I watched this lad playing in a kickabout with two kids half his size, and introduced myself as the manager of Danville Street Rovers. He was keen to join a 'proper' team, and I told him I'd confirm the details of his transfer if he stood outside a certain telephone box in Carlisle Street in an hour.

Armed with the number of that box, I went to another box nearer home and rang. He answered, I said I was speaking from my office at our ground on Danville Mount, and, confirming his forms had been accepted by the Football League, announced he'd be in the team on the following Saturday.

Unfortunately, by Saturday the club had been disbanded – which was probably as well because, with only five players anyway and no opponents lined up (I hadn't got round to thinking about that!), there was little hope of a game being played. Well, I did say I sometimes lived on the brink of fantasy!

Terry Webster's mother had scuppered my plans by withdrawing her son from the club – and reclaiming his subs. James and Chester then decided they would do the same, and both denied it was because, by coincidence, an ice-cream van had just turned up in the street.

When Chester, Terry and me formed the club, we had agreed we would all pay a weekly subscription of tuppence. I added 'treasurer' to my secretary-manager's title, and counted eight pennies into a tin which I placed on the sideboard at my grandmother's house.

Later that same day, I was still rather full of my telephone negotiations with my new 'signing' when there was a knock on the door. It was Mrs Webster. 'You've taken tuppence off our Terry. Can I have it back – now!' I think she feared Grandmother might put the money towards a jug of ale.

My final venture as a would-be football manager ended in similar embarrassment when, having written an impressive letter to the local vicar (I drew a fancy heading and featured a footballer above the title 'Macro Street Athletic'), he kindly arranged for my 'club' to hire a room in the church hall. Alas, on the evening of the inaugural meeting, not one player turned up.

* * * *

I saw my first professional match when I was eight years old, and, though I remember nothing of the game, I do know that Sheffield Wednesday beat Tottenham 5-1 and Jimmy Dailey, a daring centre-forward who had recently arrived from Scotland, became my first hero by scoring a hat-trick. The date was 1 March 1947.

I have not forgotten the circumstances of how that trip to Hillsborough came about. For months my father had been promising to take me to a match, but kept putting it off, and, as it was a particularly bad winter, he often used the weather as a justifiable excuse.

If I'm not mistaken, because of the snow, there hadn't been a League fixture at Hillsborough for a month, but, when our insurance man, a chap called Unwin, arrived on Saturday lunchtime and said the game with Spurs was definitely on, I decided I must go. Dad said he couldn't manage it, but at least he coughed up enough coppers for me to get to the ground and pay to get in. I can't recall the details, but, with two tram rides each way costing only a total of tuppence, I needed less than a shilling (5p) to embark on my great adventure.

The thrill of standing on the Kop behind the goal for the first time is something I have never forgotten, and, of course, I was hooked. I couldn't keep away, even on those weekends when I didn't have a penny in my pocket. It was no hardship to walk to and from the East End, and, if I couldn't afford the admission price, at least I could play in Hillsborough Park until the gates of the ground were opened ten minutes from the end of the game, then get in free.

Then, one day, I made a discovery. There was a lady called Mrs Stones who often stood outside the main entrance at the ground just before the start of a match and looked for boys just like me who had no money but wanted to see the match. She had two or three shareholder's tickets which she happily loaned out – and the bonus from catching her eye was to be able to watch the game from the luxury of the south stand!

Many years later, I discovered that the Good Samaritan in the blue-and-white scarf was, in fact, the wife of Fred Stones, who became chairman of the Wednesday Supporters Club, and, as a grown-up, it was good to be able to thank her for the pleasure her generous gestures had given me as a boy. Incidentally, I went to Bramall Lane as often as to Hillsborough, but I was never able to wangle a free ticket there!

My father was keen on football, but, in my time, never a regular supporter, and, in fact, I recall just one occasion when I went to a game with him. It was also the only time I remember playing truant from school with his blessing.

In January 1950, Hillsborough was the venue for an England-Switzerland 'B' international, and, in those pre-floodlight days when all midweek games had afternoon kick-offs, it was often a choice between football and school. I was lucky that my father especially wanted to see his current favourite, Tottenham's Eddie Bailey, and he said he would write me a note for school saying I'd been sick.

Frank Connelly, a lovely little Irishman who was my form master at the time, seemed amused when I handed him the note next morning. 'Aye, well, it's good that you're better, my boy, but, tell me, did you enjoy the game?'

In those days, the Wednesday ground was becoming a regular neutral venue for big games, and the first one I attended was the FA Cup semi-final between Manchester United and Derby County in 1948. Sadly, I recall little about the actual match, but have never forgotten the experience of rising at before five o'clock on Sunday morning to go and queue for a ticket.

I was still only nine years old, but making my way from Newhall to Hillsborough presented no problem. I had raised the 2s 6d (12½p) with which to buy the ticket, plus tuppence to cover my tram fare, and revelled in the adventure of riding across Sheffield while half the city slept. The gates didn't open until ten o'clock, but I was home before mid-day with my mission completed.

The only snag was, whilst running across Hillsborough Park in my haste to reach the ground after dropping off the tram, I lost our front door key. For some days afterwards we could only get into the house by the back entrance!

Boy on a Bike

BACK in the 1940s, a firm called Henry Wigfall's had a string of stores in the suburbs of Sheffield, and, sometime around my eleventh birthday in 1949, Dad took me to their shop in Attercliffe and bought me a bike – a brand new sit-up-and-beg model, which was not only a source of pleasure and pride but opened new horizons. For a time it encouraged my boyish sense of adventure, enabling me to explore places far beyond Attercliffe and Brightside.

In truth, it might not be quite accurate to say Dad bought that bike because, although he paid a deposit, probably as little as three or four shillings, the day we went to Wigfall's (their place was at the junction of Attercliffe Road and Kimberley Street, not far from the bottom of Staniforth Road), it would be no surprise to discover that he defaulted on the weekly instalments after a few months even though the sum involved was 2s 6d (12½p) or perhaps less.

This was not untypical of my father, for he had a tendency to be very enthusiastic about getting something on 'the never-never', especially when a win on the pools or the horses left him with a few bob to spare for the deposit, but he would lose all sense of responsibility long before the debt was cleared. Money, of course, was tight (I think he earned no more than £3 a week then, working as a clerk), other priorities no doubt intruded, and perhaps he was distracted by circumstances which eventually led to a break-up of the family.

I can well imagine that, in some way, getting me that bike enabled Dad to compensate for one of the major disappointments of his own boyhood. He used to tell a tale of how, back in the early 1920s, his step-father, 'Billy' Johnstone, had bought him a bike – then, within a couple of months, sold it after running into financial problems when he was thrown out of work.

'It was a Rudge Whitworth, a Rolls-Royce of a bike,' Dad recalled, 'but one day when I came home from school, it had gone – the old man had sold it to his brother Bob, who lived just down the street. It really hurt to watch my cousin Joe riding my pride and joy!'

Much to Dad's frustration, it took me about three months to master the new bike and learn to ride it, and, in the meantime, I suffered much indignity and a lot of grazed knees. However, once I felt in control, my ambition to use it to get to unfamiliar places knew no bounds. When I look back, I am surprised at how far I sometimes went – and what distances I was allowed to go on my own at the age of eleven or twelve. Mother would pack me some sandwiches, which would be loaded into my saddlebag ahead of another expedition into the 'unknown'.

Of course, there was not so much traffic on the roads, even on the main highways, in those pre-motorway days, especially at weekends; and certainly in the late 1940s and early 1950s the world seemed a safer place without threat from strangers for a small boy in unfamiliar surroundings.

* * * *

As the bike came into my life not long after I had made initial contact with Scunthorpe United, it was, perhaps, not unnatural that I set my heart on visiting Harry Allcock, the club's secretary, at the Old Show Ground, even though I had never been there before in my life. This was an eighty-mile-plus round journey, and I did it several times, much to old Harry's astonishment.

Harry was a wonderfully human little man, ever friendly and kind. However, I don't think he was particularly pleased when, on one occasion, I turned up at his Scunthorpe home with a puncture – and without a clue about how to repair it! Fortunately, one of his sons came to my rescue and I was able to make the trip back to Sheffield.

In fact, the first time Harry came into contact with me as a cyclist was in March 1950. Having checked the football fixtures in the local paper, I noted that Scunthorpe were playing in a Midland League match at Worksop, and, as that was only eighteen miles away, I felt sure I could get there and back without difficulty.

Happily, I arrived at the ground soon after the team, and old Harry was plainly surprised to be called to the gate, but, as always, he greeted me warmly and took me (and my bike) through to the dressing room. He only grew concerned when one of the players noticed the bike did not boast lights.

'It'll be dark before the game ends. How are you going to ride home?' Harry asked in a rich Lincolnshire accent.

That, I admitted, was something which hadn't occurred to me, and, as I sat beside Harry in the directors' box and watched the match, I gave it no thought. Being allowed to join the players in the dressing room after the game was well worth any problems I might face in getting home afterwards.

I barely knew any of them, but they were already my heroes: such men as goalkeeper George Thompson (later a Preston favourite), defenders 'Dick' Taylor and Jackie Brownsword, skipper Jeff Barker, and, my biggest hero, forward Jimmy Whitfield. The trainer, Maurice Conroy, was an especially friendly chap who, I remember from subsequent visits to the Old Show Ground, was rather fond of a new popular song called *Bewitched, Bothered and Bewildered.*

It amused and intrigued them that this kid from Sheffield had troubled to cycle to Worksop, and, when, at the end of the game, they debated how I was going to get home in the dark, I heard someone suggest putting me on a train. The next thing I knew, they were taking a collection, and old Harry came towards me with his hands full of silver. I was staggered to discover that it added up to eleven shillings (55 pence) – a sum such as I had never possessed in my life.

They insisted on loading my bike on to the team-bus and dropping me at the railway station on their way back to Scunthorpe, and I remember Harry asking the man in the ticket office to ensure I caught the train to Sheffield. By the time I reached Paget Street, I was exhausted by my walk from the Norfolk Bridge station (it was too dark to ride the bike), but exhilarated by my adventure and the unexpected generosity I had met on my travels. Naturally, I didn't arrive home without having made good use of a shilling of the money with the purchase of some sweets at a shop in Attercliffe Road!

Most of my excursions to Scunthorpe were, I recall, made in the following summer, around the time the team was in pre-season training prior to their first-ever season in the Football League. Again, I was allowed in the dressing room, and, asked to make myself useful, collected all the empty 'pop' bottles and returned them to the shop across the road. Back at the ground, the players told me to keep the halfpenny refund obtained on each bottle, so, once again, I went home with some spending money.

* * * *

It was around this time that Dad paid another visit to Wigfall's and returned with a bike for my sister Pat. She took rather less time to learn to ride it than I had, but my memory of that period is of Dad using Pat's bike to join me on a Sunday outing on which he took me to Upper Langwith – his father's birthplace on the borders of Derbyshire and Nottinghamshire.

It was the only time I ever went to Langwith as a child, and it could be said that but for the presence of that bike in my life I might never have become aware of our family's history. Certainly without that solitary visit, I would not have known where to begin looking for information when, nearly thirty years later and long after father's death, I elected to trace our family tree.

However, on that topic, there was another significant bike trip, on which my father sent me alone, with a family connection that was to prove a starting point for research I began around 1977.

The place I visited in 1950 was East Drayton, a village just off the A1 beyond Retford. How I found it I shall never know, for Dad gave me only the most basic directions, and I didn't possess a map; but it was here that Annie James, my grandfather's sister, lived in a property known as the Old Vicarage. (For some years I believed that living in a former vicarage suggested a link with the church, but, in fact, her husband had been a steelman and worked in Sheffield.)

Annie James was then in her seventies and a widow, and, in truth, at the time I didn't have much of a clue about exactly how she was connected to the Farnsworths of Paget Street. She was just a kindly old lady dressed in dark clothes who readily admitted me to her home once I had introduced myself.

Knowing what I know now, I can imagine she was staggered to see her great-nephew turn up her doorstep. According to something I remember my grandmother telling me, at that time I very much resembled Grandfather Tom Farnsworth as he had been as a boy – and old Aunt Annie must have thought I was a ghost from her distant past.

Of all my Grandfather's brothers and sisters, she was the closest to him, and, as she had lived for some years in Sheffield, certainly the one with whom he had had most contact after he left Langwith. My unexpected call must have stirred many memories of family dramas dating back so many years. She probably knew better than anyone the full circumstances which led to Grandfather's ill-fated trip to Canada and the United States shortly before the Great War.

She no doubt asked me some questions, but I have no recollection of what we discussed as I ate a boiled egg and some bread. I only remember being enthralled to discover a shelf full of cricket books, which apparently belonged to one of her sons. When I looked back in later years (I discovered Annie had died within a few years of my visit), I regretted not having had the wisdom to have asked her about my Grandfather. But, of course, I was too young to be aware of the knowledge she possessed, or to appreciate the significance of what she could have told me.

The consolation, of course, was my bike had at least enabled me to meet her and enjoy a trip which lived on in my memory with enough impact to eventually prompt me to delve into old Tom Farnsworth's background and history.

* * * *

However, for a number of reasons, the bike eventually started to lose its attraction and was neglected so much that it grew rusty standing in our backyard. I think the novelty began to wear off after a frightening experience when I got the wheels caught in some tramlines in Newhall Road and a motor car coming up behind sent me flying over the handlebars.

I was left with badly gashed legs which needed hospital treatment – and the motorist never even stopped.

Once fit again, I preferred to walk or use public transport in my quest for adventure, and, anyway, I found that, if I wanted to continue my trips to Scunthorpe,

I could ride in a motor car – for a local man, Wally Boyes, had signed for them, and he was happy to give me a lift. So much better than pedal power!

Boyes was a former Everton and West Brom winger (he had played against Sheffield Wednesday in the 1935 FA Cup Final), and, after the war, he had opened a sports outfitter's shop in Barnsley Road. Me and my pal Billy Whittingham used to spend hours gazing in the window of Wally's shop, wishing we could afford to buy some of that lovely football kit.

I think old Wally was rather taken-aback when I asked him if I could have a lift to Scunthorpe, and he probably thought I was a cheeky little chap, but he always made me welcome. En route we used to pick up two other players, Harold Mosby and Jackie Brownsword, and, on the way home afterwards, they used to treat me to tea and cakes.

I was always sorry Wally didn't live to see me make the grade as a football writer, but, happily, both Harry Allcock and Jackie Brownsword did, and they never forgot the youngster they called 'the boy on the bike'!

Gambling Man

A N ABIDING memory of my father is of the countless hours he spent sitting at the kitchen table studying racing and football form. Our kitchen table was invariably littered with such papers as the *Racing & Football Outlook*, the *Sporting Chronicle*, and the *Daily Herald*, plus a few thick yearbooks containing details of every horse that ever raced.

The edges of every newspaper which came into our house were filled with father's notes on doubles and trebles and likely winners – and, if you left a school exercise book, notepaper or even personal letter around, it would invariably go missing and end up converted into form analysis sheets or betting slips. I once treasured a letter from the legendary Peter Doherty, who was then manager of Doncaster Rovers, and came home from school to find it covered in my father's racing notes!

Of course, there was no television or teletext service then, and many was the time when Dad would jump up from the table after tea and dash into town to get a late edition of the *Star* containing the results of the later races in the stop press of the last edition. In the days when the local paper produced a racing special called the *Early Bird*, it proved to be the only thing guaranteed to get Dad out of bed before eight o'clock.

In later years, I was always amused to watch him poring over the racing pages for hours on end, looking very studious in a pair of Woolworth's spectacles which I don't think he really needed but liked to wear for effect. He never seemed to look through the lenses, but wore the spectacles on the very end of his nose while peering over them.

As a betting man, father had his moments, but, like most punters, he certainly lost more than he won. No wonder mother often said that, if only he could have devoted the same amount of time and effort to a 'proper' job, the old man might have made a lot of money.

A place on the racing desk of the local paper would have been an ideal position, but the nearest he got to such a role was when, late in his life, he had a spell as a messenger on the *Morning Telegraph* – ironically, just after I had joined the sports department.

On those occasions when he enjoyed a sudden windfall from the horses or the football pools, he could be very generous, especially if the sum was slightly out of the ordinary. In those days, anything around £20 was considered a fortune, and there were times when his winnings, from the pools anyway, topped £100.

He would celebrate by buying himself a new suit or overcoat, or perhaps a pair of shoes – whatever his faults, father always loved to dress well and look smart. Moreover, he would buy me and my sisters some item of clothing, even if sometimes it was nothing more than something he'd spotted in a second-hand shop. Unfortunately, as the bulk of the money was spent in the pub, it seldom lasted for more than a few days, so the new suit or whatever quickly found its way into the pawnshop pending another bit of luck.

As he knew, the only people who always made money from gambling were the bookies, and one of his most oft-repeated 'what might have been' stories concerned the time he became a bookmaker – and failed because he 'backed a loser' in his choice of bookie's runner.

Elsewhere I have mentioned how, on his 25th birthday in 1935, my father inherited £100 and used part of the money to purchase his discharge from the RAF. Once back home in Danville Street, he put the rest into a bookmaking venture.

Those were the days, some thirty years before the legalisation of off-course betting and the emergence of betting shops, when backstreet bookies operated in every district. When Tom's step-father, 'Billy' Johnstone, who showed great enthusiasm for his venture, offered to act as his runner, he seemed the ideal choice. After all, he was known in every pub in the area, and it was, anyway, an operation best kept within the family.

The punters wrote their selections on slips of paper (which they marked with a code name to identify themselves), which they either brought to the house or gave to father or 'Billy' Johnstone in the pub. Father would then do the totting up later at home, and he and 'Billy' would each deliver the winnings to their own 'customers'.

All went well for a while, then, suddenly, father suffered a long and puzzling losing streak which, within a few weeks, wiped out all his funds. He could hardly believe his bad luck, and knew he would have to admit defeat.

That evening in the Brunswick pub in Grimesthorpe Road, father just happened to bump into a punter who had won rather a lot of money from him – or, at least, he believed that was the case.

'Tha'rt a lucky blighter, how does tha manage to find so many winners?' father said.

'What's tha mean? I'm out of work and haven't had a bet for months,' he replied.

Only then did the penny drop. It transpired that the winning slips bearing the man's code had all been passed through 'Billy' Johnstone. What 'Billy' had been doing was to wait while he knew the racing results, then write a betting slip, put it in with the others, and later pocket the winnings for himself while purporting to deliver them to the lucky punter.

I imagine the atmosphere at 58 Danville Street was charged with ill-feeling for the next few weeks at least, and, of course, father soon had to get a 'proper' job and revert to being on the other side of the gambling fence.

Curiously, although father's penchant for gambling was a dominant feature of our home life, it was something which never appealed to me. Of course, I often looked at his books and papers, and I frequently took his weekend betting slips to the local bookie, 'Dobbie' Dobson, on Friday nights – Dobbie's wife always rewarded me with an orange or, sometimes, a sixpence.

Yet, apart from enabling me to learn by heart all the Derby and Grand National winners since the year dot, father's racing books failed to influence me – and never inspired me to take up gambling.

However, knowing how to write out a betting slip and how to read a racecard, I was tempted to have a bet – but only once. I must have been about eleven years old when I selected a horse called Big Bill, wrote out a slip with a sixpenny each-way bet and my father's 'TF58' code, and delivered it to 'Dobbie' Dobson's house. The horse won at 100-8, and, though my winnings amounted to only a few shillings, I savoured the thrill of being a successful punter.

All the same, I had the sense to know it was simply a case of beginner's luck. I could never see myself spending hours studying form like my father. There were better things to do with my time, and, when I had any money (which wasn't often) I preferred to waste it in other ways!

Grandma

MY GRANDMOTHER Johnstone was a tiny, grey-haired woman, barely five-feet tall. Unfortunately, no photographs of her survive, but I have an abiding image in my memory of her dressed in a long brown overcoat and black boots, and, on her head, the familiar black beret without which she seldom went outdoors. I can see her now struggling up Danville Street with her shopping bag, swaying slightly and stopping for breath every few yards as she battled to climb the steep hill.

As a small boy, on a Saturday afternoon I often sat on the doorstep of her house, number 58, awaiting her arrival. She might have started out to 'settle up' her 'strap' account and get groceries from Lily Bell's shop on Grimesthorpe Road, then buy the weekend joint from 'Butcher' Booth at Talbot's in Gower Street, before calling at the fishmonger's. She probably also had to drop into the pawnbroker's in Ellesmere Road to reclaim Grandad Johnstone's best suit or pocket watch and chain. She was soon overloaded with baggage.

However, once these calls were completed, before heading for home she invariably rewarded herself with a couple of hours in the Brunswick pub (opposite Lily Bell's), where, having met up with Grandad, three or four glasses of bitter were enough to make her slightly tipsy. If I grew impatient of waiting on the step at Danville Street, I knew I could deposit myself on the step outside the Brunswick – and, with luck, Grandma might nip out with some crisps and a bottle of pop.

Soon after landlord Tommy Thompson had called 'time!' at three o'clock, Grandma would stumble home. When I spotted her at last at the foot of the hill, and ran down to greet her and help with the bags, I sometimes sensed her slight sway was not significantly related to any tactical ploy designed to negotiate a gradient which presented a challenge to someone of her age. The way her eyelids kept flickering told me it was the drink that had made her unsteady on her feet!

One memory of those Saturdays at 58 is the smell of beer and fresh fish, and watching as the main meal was cooked, after which my grandparents would either retire to bed or fall asleep in their fireside chairs. By the time they awoke, tea was due, and afterwards Grandad would get ready and disappear back to the Brunswick for the evening.

Grandma, meanwhile, would put on her coat and nip to the pub across the road, the Star Inn, for a jug of beer, while I would be dispatched to the beer-off at the top of Clun Street to get her a tin of Top Mill – her favourite snuff. A glass of ale and a sniff of snuff was a nightly ritual on those occasions when she didn't join Grandad at the pub; and together we would listen to *Henry Hall's Guest Night*.

The wireless, a small, home-made black box attached to a large horn-shaped loudspeaker which stood on the sideboard, was a great source of pleasure and comfort to her. She especially liked to listen to Tommy Handley's *ITMA* show and Jimmy Jewell and Ben Warris in *Up The Pole*, but, if there was nothing on which she considered worth listening to, she was content to sing quietly to herself – *You Are My Sunshine* is the once-popular song I most associate with her.

Incidentally, sometimes if she didn't feel sufficiently recovered from her Saturday lunchtime session to fetch her own evening beer from the Star Inn, she would send me across the road. As I wasn't old enough to buy beer, the landlord would fill my Tizer bottle, then put a paper seal across the top of the cork to satisfy the law. Alas, the seal, being light on gum, invariably fell off before I got halfway home, but, the walk being a very short one, there was little risk of bumping into a policeman!

As I spent much of my childhood at Grandma Johnstone's, she was a major figure in my early life, and, whatever her weaknesses in the eyes of others, I loved her because she was kind, sympathetic, and, like most grandmothers, tended to spoil me. Her humble back-to-back house was always a haven where I was not only sure of a welcome, but a few pennies from the handbag she always kept under the cushion in her fireside chair for some sweets (she called them spice).

In truth, she didn't always have a few pennies to give me, but, like many of her neighbours, she had an account at the local shop. In Grandma's case, it was at Lily Bell's that she obtained her midweek groceries 'on t'strap'. She would send me to Mrs Bell's with a list of her needs, and always include 'two ounces of spice' among the items.

It was Grandma who introduced me to the pawnbroker with her twice-weekly visits to his premises. I spent many a week at her house, and, if I wasn't schooling, the ritual on Monday mornings was always the same. After our breakfast of Blakey's Malted Oatmeal (for some reason I have never forgotten that the meal invariably coincided with listening to *Lift Up Your Hearts* on the wireless!), she would say; 'Well, we're skint, so I've got to go to the 'pop' shop. Are you coming with me?' Of course, I always said yes, because I knew that, once in funds, Grandma would give me tuppence to buy a Maytime iced joy-stick from Mrs Gallacher's shop on the way home!

It was not uncommon for my grandparents to sell some item of furniture to ease the strain when financial circumstances were especially bad, and I have never forgotten the Sunday evening when they parted with a beautiful mahogany-cased gramophone which had long been a great source of pride.

On this particular evening, it never occurred to me that there might be some reason other than the pleasure of playing music when Grandad decided to stage an impromptu record recital. Alas, it transpired he was simply checking everything was in order, for, halfway through the session, we had a visitor whose arrival was not unexpected – and he had come to buy the gramophone and records as a job-lot following negotiations in the Brunswick earlier in the day.

The man had no sooner disappeared out of the door with his purchase before Grandad pocketed the money, and he and Grandma put on their coats and went off to the pub!

'Billy' Johnstone

ILLY' Johnstone, my father's stepfather, cut a sorry picture in the last years of his life. Seldom sober for long, invariably careworn and unkempt, he gradually lost all his old pride and self-respect after my grandmother's death. It was painful to witness his decline, but, sadly, there was a certain inevitability about the way he lost his grip on himself.

I never knew much about his early years, other than that he came from the Woodside Lane area and was the youngest of the four children of Robert Johnstone. His brother, Bob, lived only a few doors further down Danville Street when I was a boy, but I don't remember there being much contact between them. They were different types who had created sharply contrasting worlds for themselves. Bob always seemed to have made something of his life and enjoyed a stability and sense of purpose 'Billy' lacked. As for his sisters, Lily and Polly, I never saw nor heard anything of them.

'Billy' seems to have met my widowed grandmother sometime after serving in the Great War, but their marriage was delayed because, for some reason, it took rather longer than expected to prove that Grandfather Farnsworth was really dead. Until she wanted to re-marry, Grandmother had never possessed a death certificate for her late husband. It seems to have complicated things that he had died at sea.

'Billy' and my grandmother appear to have launched a second-hand clothing business in the early 1920s. They may have rented a small shop, but he often talked about the years when they owned a pony and trap which they used to gather and sell their wares. According to family legend, the operation failed because of a tendency to booze away the profits almost as soon as they had made them.

That was a pattern which continued all through his life. Like so many people of modest means and limited education and ambition conditioned by circumstances in which poverty was tempered by occasional periods of comparative wealth, when 'Billy' had a few bob the money burned a hole in his pocket. He lived for the present.

However, the 'Billy' I remember from my earliest years was not a man without character. He was well-built, handsome and, in the eyes of a small boy, friendly and dependable. I don't suppose much of what he ever said to me was profound or significant, but, curiously, he always seemed strong and wise, and one felt secure in his company.

'Billy' always seemed generous, because, while my other Grandad only gave me a Saturday penny, he would give me a threepenny bit, or, sometimes, a sixpence. Moreover, he brought me gifts from work – one of my proudest possessions being a sledge he made in the bad winter of 1947 when I was able to spend so many hours speeding down the steep incline of Danville Street.

There was also a pedal motor-car which I assume he acquired second-hand from a workmate. I must have been five or six years old when he bought this, but I still remember how he painted it bright red before I took it home to our lodgings in Rock Street. What pleasure and adventures I enjoyed with that car.

I should mention that Rock Street was on the route of the Shiregreen buses, numbers 150 and 151, and, crazy as it might now seem, I used to ride my little car along the road all the way into the Bridge Street bus station in the city centre – then load it on to the platform of a Shiregreen bus which brought me home. It never occurred to me that I needed bus fare, but, for some weeks anyway, I was allowed to ride free after admitting to the conductress that I had no money!

I imagine 'Billy' was a popular workmate at the Vulcan Road premises of Edgar Allen's, where he supplemented his labourer's income by setting up as the workshop hairdresser – something he had picked up while serving in the Royal Pioneer Corps. He kept his shears in a box in the sideboard at home, and, naturally, for years nobody else ever cut my hair. A number of his Danville Street neighbours also made use of his service, though, to be honest, I believe there were some who only came once, and left complaining about being scalped!

His was a world in which, with no hobbies or interests outside of work other than a regular flutter on the horses, all social activity evolved round the public house. He was never happier than when in the tap room of Ernest Makin's Buckenham Hotel or Tommy Thompson's Brunswick. When 'Billy' was in funds, he was one of the most popular customers in those pubs.

* * * *

A turning point in his life occurred on Good Friday 1948. I have never forgotten the date because it was the day I watched Rotherham United for the first time, and I always remember arriving home full of excitement, ready to tell my father about the game, only to find a sombre group sitting round the kitchen table.

The moment I spotted Grandmother Johnstone in the house, I knew something dramatic had occurred. She hadn't visited 43 Paget Street since the day her sister Amelia was buried, but, in this instance, she put aside her reluctance to call on my mother because she needed to tell my father that Grandad Johnstone had suffered a serious accident at work.

It transpired that 'Billy' was fighting for his life in the Royal Infirmary after his leg had been trapped in the jaws of a crane. Grandmother had been warned to expect the worst, and for the next few days spent most of her time at his bedside.

It's curious the things one remembers. I must have spent some time up at Danville Street in the following days, for I recall being left alone in the house while the grown-ups went off to the hospital; and, in a corner of the living room, I came across Grandad's bloodstained overalls. I picked them up, and two threepenny bits and a few pennies fell out of the pockets.

'Billy' spent about six months in Ward Five at the Infirmary, and, though his recovery was slow and he was handicapped for a long time, he survived to outlive my grandmother by several years. However, the quality of his life after the accident was seldom high, and, following Grandma's death in 1954, his last years were far from happy.

Not long after he came out of hospital, he collected £750 compensation. That was a lot of money in those days, and, had it been invested wisely, it would surely have ensured my grandparents of comfort and security for at least a few years.

In the event, 'Billy' chose to go back into the second-hand clothes business, and opened a shop in Grimesthorpe Road. Alas, the venture failed in under twelve months. The property just happened to be situated exactly halfway between the Buckenham Hotel and the Brunswick – and Grandad spent more time in those pubs than in his shop. The Johnstones were probably the most popular customers while they were drinking themselves silly and treating all their friends.

Once the money had gone, 'Billy', still handicapped from his accident, had to find a job again, and, over the next few years, he was reduced to all kinds of menial work. He seemed a deeply dispirited man even before Grandma's sudden death, but after she went (he came home from work one night to find her dead at the foot of the stairs), he seemed to lose all heart and sought escape from reality by spending as much time as possible in the pub.

His final years coincided with a curious and troubled phase in my father's life. Father spent much of this period separated from my mother and living with 'Billy', and, while they developed much more mutual respect than had ever been the case before, it was a far from ideal existence. To say it was a rough-and-ready carry-on would be overstating the case.

In fact, immediately after Grandma's death, it did at first look as if the bereavement might induce a reconciliation between my parents. I remember that, at the time, I found the prospect rather frustrating because, some months earlier, I had joined the army to escape a way of life in which we didn't have a 'proper' home. Now it looked as if we might have one. However, in the event, the proposed 'reunion' was delayed for several months.

It was during this phase that, because of the imminent demolition of the houses in Danville Street, the local Council offered to re-house 'Billy' Johnstone on the

Shiregreen estate, where they would have had a home with an indoor toilet and bathroom, plus a nice garden.

Not surprisingly, neither he nor my father wanted to leave the Pitsmoor area – an attitude which, while it said much about them, was not uncommon. Many families were in the habit of 'doing a swop' to avoid having to quit a district in which they were comfortably settled and among friends. 'Billy' managed to negotiate a 'swop' with some people in Bramber Street, and so he and my father ended up moving from one old back-to-back to another!

Exactly when my mother joined them there, I am not sure because I was then at the Army Apprentices School at Harrogate, but the fact that we had a family home again did have the effect of unsettling me. Here it is sufficient to say that I didn't rest until I was able to obtain my discharge and return to Sheffield permanently. Ironically, I hadn't been back long when it became obvious that my parents' 'reunion' was a mockery and unlikely to survive much longer.

They never stopped fighting, and some of the scenes I witnessed are still painful to recall. Pots and pans as well as furious words flew around the kitchen. As we all lived in one room, it was impossible to escape an atmosphere of anger and bitterness compounded by the sight of 'Billy' huddled in a corner, drunk and filled with despair as he tired of trying to intervene. Within a few months, I decided to look for 'digs' and leave.

A few days afterwards, my mother and sisters also departed, so my father and 'Billy' were again left on their own. 'Billy' did not live long after that. His funeral was a strange affair in that my father and I were the only mourners, and no tributes were paid to him before he was laid to rest alongside my grandmother in an unmarked grave at Shiregreen.

He may have lived in obscurity and had many faults, but I remember him with affection and prefer to associate his memory with the time when, to me at least, he seemed handsome and wise – and only got drunk at the weekends!

Goodbye to Paget Street

I DON'T recall the circumstances that prompted my mother to walk out of our Paget Street home in 1950. All I remember is returning from Newhall School one afternoon to find the house deserted and in darkness. Later it transpired that Mother had taken my sister, Pat, with her to wherever she had gone to live, leaving me and my six-year-old younger sister, Jean, with my father.

It was winter, and I have a fairly clear memory of that evening. The kitchen fire had gone out, and Jean helped me clear out the dead ashes as we attempted to re-light the fire. We packed newspaper and sticks into the grate, laid a few pieces of coal on top, and, to ensure a strong draught, I wedged a shovel on the top edge of the grate and covered the hole with a sheet of newspaper.

Unfortunately, the newspaper kept catching fire and had to be replaced. When this happened for the third or fourth time, Dad's precious racing page from the *Daily Herald* suddenly disappeared up the chimney – and, within a few minutes, burning soot was puthering into the room. Ethel Yuell, who lived across the yard, arrived to announce that all the street could see the chimney was on fire.

The upshot was a visit from the fire brigade, a dramatic if minor episode which attracted scores of curious neighbours into our backyard, and no doubt inspired a few muttered comments from some about kids being left on their own. What they might have said had they known mother had walked out is not difficult to imagine.

People didn't particularly take pleasure from the misfortunes of others, and some of our near-neighbours obviously knew enough about the situation to show some sympathy and understanding. However, there were plenty of critics who viewed walking out on a marriage as taking the easy option, and considered leaving children behind as something unforgivable.

Those were the days when, if marriage break-ups were not uncommon, the general view in most working-class districts was along the lines of 'you've made your bed, so you must lie on it'. Many couples survived together in circumstances much worse than existed in our house, and sticking together through thick and thin 'for the sake of the kids' was a philosophy widely embraced – though, in a lot of cases, as there probably wasn't much choice but to stay, that was the easy option.

All this is invariably outside the understanding of children, and my sister and myself were unaware of the reasons for the development, or its implications. We might feel that these things didn't seem to happen in most other families, but thought nothing of just accepting it. We were, however, conscious of the neighbours' perception of the situation, for many a look or a glance expressed something which told us our family had somehow gone beyond the pale.

There came a time, long before I left school, when I began to consciously resent an attitude I found in some people which suggested that, because we had a less than harmonious home background, everyone in the family was written off as losers. This anger probably benefited my sisters and myself in the long run, for we had to good fortune to channel it into a determination to rise above our circumstances, and I think we all succeeded.

However, for a long time, in my case anyway, it created a chip on my shoulder which, until I was old enough to know better, caused me to blame my parents for all our childhood misfortunes.

Curiously, I was reminded of this, and the false perception of outsiders, only a few years ago, when some research for a book project brought me into contact with an old insurance man of ours. He happened to be a distant relative of the founder of a major local company whose history I was writing, and, not having met him since my early teens, I anticipated he might be quite pleased to see how well I had progressed since those days.

Alas, he made it plain he couldn't believe someone with my early background had been entrusted with such an important task, and I was shocked at the evidence of a prejudice which seemed so unreasonable. At least it proved that, as a youngster, I hadn't misinterpreted the look of disdain I saw in the eyes of people like that insurance man.

To return to 1950 and the day my mother left, I have only vague recollections of how my father, my sister and myself managed over the following weeks. I know I was given responsibility for doing the shopping at Rosie Skillington's beer-off in Alfred Road (when Dad remembered to leave some money!); and, with school dinners from Monday to Friday, and Sunday dinner at Grandma Johnstone's, we didn't starve.

More often than not, there was little food in the house at tea-time, and, if Dad forgot to leave some pennies for the gas meter, we couldn't even make a cup of tea until he came home. However, if there was any Nestles milk or Tate & Lyle Golden Syrup around, we could stave off any pangs of hunger with a few spoonsful of one or the other!

I mention these things simply as matters of fact, for, at the time, we didn't really give the situation too much thought. Jean was too young, anyway, and both of us accepted things as they were without complaint and adapted accordingly. I cannot imagine what we did about clean clothes and such things that children take for granted, and no doubt at times we looked a couple of scruffs in school. But it didn't trouble us.

Then one evening after school, my mother arrived to take Jean away with her, and I was left alone with Dad for a few months. Mother later returned again, and, when she invited me to join her, I didn't hesitate – even though Dad was disappointed when I announced my decision, and I didn't have any idea where Mother was taking me, or what her circumstances were.

My departure on that occasion coincided with another incident that has stuck firmly in my memory. The same afternoon, after school, I'd got involved in a street fight with a classmate called Alan Rowley. When my sister, Jean, knocked on the door and said my mother was at the end of the road waiting to talk to me, I was sitting in the darkened kitchen nursing my bruises. Rowley might have been smaller than me, but he was much tougher and more streetwise – and he'd given me quite a thrashing.

Don't ask me how the fight had come about. Fisticuffs was not my forté, for, in terms of physical strength and aggression, I was definitely bottom of the class and would normally have run a mile rather than join in a fight. I wasn't a coward, I just knew my limitations.

In this instance, I think I got provoked during a classroom dispute and, with a rashness that was not untypical, foolishly vowed to 'sort it out after school'. The irony was that Rowley and I were good pals, but I ended up facing him in a ring formed by a circle of boys baying for blood and not caring whose it was. It proved to be mine.

A couple of pals carried me home, where they left me alone to contemplate the shame and pain of defeat. My sister's knock on the door within the hour, and my mother's offer of a refuge with her, could not have been better timed. It meant escaping the indignity of facing my Newhall classmates the following morning. Mind you, I probably would have left anyway, for while I wasn't really unhappy living with Dad, I was attracted by the prospect of starting a new life in another part of the city.

However, I didn't know what I was letting myself in for at my new abode – 78 Macro Street.

Macro Street

MACRO Street, which disappeared in the huge Woodside redevelopment which started in 1960, was situated at the lower end of the Pye Bank hillside just above Bridgehouses – the first turn on the left after Rock Street. It ran parallel with the Sheffield to Manchester railway line which, since the mid-19th century, had passed along the full length of the street's bottom side behind a stone wall that climbed higher as the street increasingly inclined downwards from Pye Bank. Where the street ended at the junction with Woodside Lane, trains sped over a bridge going towards or coming from Neepsend and Wadsley Bridge on the famous Woodhead route. In the shadow of the bridge stood a police box.

Except from the top end of the street, at pavement level you were unable to see over the wall and on to the railway, but you were always aware of the trains. Familiarity with the constant rattle of goods waggons and the regular thunder of the passenger expresses roaring to or from the Victoria Station enabled the locals to turn a deaf ear. By the same token, the smoke and incessant falls of soot from the old steam engines were environmental hazards accepted as a normal part of everyday life. Hanging washing on a clothes line in a Macro Street backyard was invariably necessary, but not to be recommended if you wanted shirts to be Persil white!

The house to which my mother took me for the first time on an evening in the autumn of 1950, and where we were to spend the next four years, was close to the bottom of the street, being the largest of a small group of old properties situated between Fowler Street and Birley Street. Number 78, which boasted nine rooms, including a box room, a tiny kitchen, plus two attics, was the house with the big double gate, and had once been the Wellington Inn pub.

Like its near-neighbour, the former Locomotive Inn at the foot of Fowler Street, it had long since reverted to domestic use, though evidence of its former status could still be seen. For instance, the corridor door leading to the cellar had clearly once been the serving hatch of the off-licence; while it was obvious that the large wooden cellar door in the pavement outside had been made with barrels of ale rather than bags of coal in mind. It was not difficult to imagine that the large living room had once been the pub's main lounge, where customers had sung round the piano while warming themselves in front of the huge fireplace.

Now number 78 was a lodging house run by a widow called Ma Easy, and, I always assumed, she had been the landlord's wife in the Wellington's final years. However, what is relevant to mention here in discussing its location is that its largest upstairs room, the main attic, had a skylight which offered both an excellent close-up of the railway tracks across the road and a splendid panoramic view towards Sheffield's city centre.

To the left and east you could see beyond the Royal Victoria Hotel and Victoria Station; to the right and west you could make out the towering Bradfield Road flats at Owlerton along the Upper Don Valley. Beyond the railway lines in the foreground, a mile or so to the right stood Neepsend, dominated by two huge gasholders (we had some relatives whose house in Farfield Road was in the shadow of these giants, and they could seldom see in their kitchen without the aid of the electric light!). Looking the other way, you could observe the hillside on which stood such familiar city centre landmarks as the Old Town Hall, the Cathedral, the *Telegraph & Star* offices, and other well-known buildings.

Somewhere in the middle distance you could pick out the brewery of William Stones, Samuel Osborn's Rutland Road steelworks, the same firm's large white-painted box-shaped tool factory, the famous soot-blackened Cornish Works of James Dixon's, the silversmith's, and the Royal Infirmary.

Although the valley, from Lady's Bridge to Hillfoot Bridge, invariably seemed enveloped in the smoke and steam of industry, except on Sundays and Bank holidays, the distant hillside, which extended from the Upperthorpe and St Phillips districts to Crookesmoor and lower Walkley, was often clearly visible. In those days it was filled with a mass of tightly-packed housing, and, on a good day you could see what seemed toy-sized buses climbing or descending some of those steep streets.

At night, of course, the darkened panorama presented a vast backcloth illuminated by thousands of street and house lights, with occasional neon signs from cinemas and pubs lending a touch of romance and even enchantment to the view. Briefly, finding entertainment in simply gazing at the scene from that rooftop window, one could forget the realities of life at Macro Street; though there was always the risk of being choked by the soot and smoke from the passing trains if one didn't close the skylight quickly enough as they approached!

* * * *

Life at 78 Macro Street was, to say the least, a culture shock – so much so that, although I was to remain there for three or four years, my initial stay lasted barely two weeks because the surroundings were so unlike anything I had experienced before, and at first I found it difficult to adapt. One day I just walked out, returned cap in hand to Paget Street, and begged my father to take me back.

If we had never boasted much of anything, and if our circumstances had often been less than ideal, at least we had previously had our own hearth and some privacy as a family. Here at 78 we were thrown among an odd assortment of strangers with whom we would not have willingly lived given the choice. It was almost impossible to avoid their company. Everybody 'mucked in' as if we were one large family, and everything, apart from the sleeping arrangements, was communal.

Even at bedtime you could not enjoy your own space. On my first night, I found I had to sleep with two of the other lodgers, and later shared an attic with a couple of old guys while sleeping in a double bed with a younger lodger.

I don't know what I expected when I started out with Mother and Jean from Paget Street, but I probably imagined us living in rented rooms. The reality didn't dawn on me when, after entering the front door of this big house and walking down a dark corridor to be greeted by two barking Alsatian dogs, we emerged into a large, well-lit room full of people.

This room, I soon learned, was the focal point in the house, the only place the lodgers used when they were at home and not sleeping. It served as the lounge, the dining area – and the landlady's bedroom! It contained a large sideboard (with mirror) on which sat a big wireless; a single bed; a commode; a rocking chair; and a large dining table with four or five dining chairs. Washing invariably hung from a four-bar airing rack suspended from the ceiling.

The pots having been partially cleared from the table after the evening meal, there must have been about ten grown-ups sitting and standing around. Two men in working clothes were perched on the guard in front of a huge fire burning in the grate, and two or three others were playing cards, while several women stood watching the game. They all fell silent and gawped when we appeared.

The major figure among them was clearly the old woman in the rocking chair alongside the table. She was the landlady, and I soon came to know her as Ma Easy, although she had started life as Beatrice Brookes and her first husband had been called Nelson. Aged about sixty, she was a large woman with straight silver hair and a big, round face. In her prime she must have been very strong, for her arms were huge, though now the skin on them hung loose.

I soon discovered that both her legs were swollen and heavily bandaged. Later, Mother explained that, except when she wanted to use the commode, Ma Easy only climbed out of her chair to get into the bed which stood against the back wall. She had been confined to her rocking chair for some years, and while it prevented her from using the outside toilet, her immobility didn't stop her managing the house and keeping tabs on her lodgers.

It transpired that my arrival raised the number of lodgers to sixteen, and, in addition, Ma Easy's two daughters and their husbands and children were in residence – plus Peggy and Judy, the Alsatian dogs. I calculated there were 23 or 24 humans on the premises, and, although there were subsequent changes as some lodgers left and others came, a breakdown of the accommodation arrangements in those early months, plus some memories of the personalities, will give you some idea of the environment in which I found myself.

* * * *

The front room on the ground floor was the bedroom and living quarters of the Buckleys – Ma Easy's elder daughter, Gertrude, her husband Ronnie, and their young children, Jean and George. Ronnie, who was in his thirties at the time, was quite a character; a devil-may-care type who only seemed to want to be serious when pursuing his great passion for the pigeons he kept in a cote in the backyard. However, the thing I remember from that first night was the shock of seeing him strutting about the house stripped to the waist – not so much because of his semi-nakedness but the fact that his upper body was extensively scarred. It transpired that he had once been involved in a fire, presumably at work.

On the opposite side of the ground floor, shooting off from the lounge at the back was the kitchen, which was the living quarters for the Cowlings, Lol and Annie, a young couple with two very small children. As there was no bathroom in the place and everyone was constantly trooping in and out to either wash under the cold tap at the sink, or to re-fill the kettle, the Cowlings seldom had any privacy. All the cooking was done on the ring in that kitchen, but Lol and Annie endured the situation for several years until their name came to the top of the Council housing list. In the meantime, no doubt at the end of every evening they were grateful to be able to escape to their sleeping quarters in the first-floor front room above the yard gate.

The next bedroom on the same landing was occupied by Ma Easy's other daughter, Jean, her husband, 'Jock' Borg, and their baby daughter, Molly – plus Judy the Alsatian. 'Jock', of course, was a Scot from Glasgow, a slightly-built man in his twenties who seems to have arrived in the area while doing his National Service in the Pioneer Corps.

The Uptons were probably the most intriguing of the lodgers. Johnny and Sarah, who were then in their fifties, occupied the third bedroom on the first floor. This was at the back of the house, and, on the night I arrived, it was something of a shock to learn that, to reach my bed in the boxroom above the kitchen, it was necessary to walk through Johnny and Sarah's bedroom. However, though Johnny stood in his nightshirt and Sarah sat at a dressing table in her underclothes, neither seemed embarrassed by my appearance.

Johnny was a small, thick-set man with greying hair and spectacles. Like several of the other men at number 78, he worked at Samuel Osborn's steelworks in Rutland Road, where he was a labourer-cum-errand boy. A dullard of limited intelligence, he was a silent type who seldom engaged in conversation. Apart from when he and Sarah went off on an occasional visit to relatives, he spent all his evenings sitting in an almost permanent doze at the dining table.

Except at bedtime, he would never change out of his working clothes, and he exuded a permanent odour of dry sweat and dust. After his evening meal, he would take off his boots, remove his false teeth, sit on a straight-backed chair and, once comfortable, quickly drop off to sleep. Sometimes, old Ma Easy would shout him awake and persuade him to have a game of cards with her, and, as they played, it was amusing to see him keep nodding off and starting to snore before suddenly shaking himself back to consciousness – invariably taking a sly look over the top of his spectacles to see if anybody had noticed.

During my initial spell at the house, Johnny was the main character in an amusing episode which occurred during a card game. Ma Easy kept complaining about a smell which, she insisted, was getting stronger, and, after a while, she stopped the game and ordered the other players, including Johnny, to get down on their hands and knees to try to locate the source of the offensive odour.

Suddenly, someone announced from under the table: 'I've found it – it's coming from Johnny's socks. Hey, Johnny, has tha' been walking in some shit?'

Sarah Upton, a thin, white-haired woman with a long face and a slight stoop, always struck me as being a sad figure – a victim. Somehow, I always felt she deserved something better, and yet she was such a simple soul, so naturally kind, that she never seemed less than content.

Every day she used to change the bandages on Ma Easy's swollen legs, washing and treating the wounds with great care. It was a task Sarah seldom allowed anyone else to undertake, and, according to the gossip among the other lodgers, this was because she felt responsible for the accident which had caused Ma Easy's original injuries. It seems that one day Sarah had absent-mindedly left an upturned bucket in a place where Ma Easy walked straight into it and suffered a heavy fall in which she severely gashed both legs.

I never did learn anything about how and when Johnny and Sarah had ended up at number 78, and the curious thing was that, in my time, they never seemed to want to leave and find a place of their own. There was a spell when Ma Easy helped her younger daughter, Jean, buy a house just up the hill at Fox Street, and I recall a phase during which Johnny and Sarah moved up there as lodgers. However, they still spent more time at number 78 than anywhere else, and it was as if Sarah was utterly dependent upon Ma Easy and didn't want a life of her own.

Johnny and Sarah had a son, Jackie, who, sadly, grew into a young man with the mental age of a boy. Jackie, who was probably in his early twenties at the time, was harmless, but he cut a strange figure. If you didn't know him, he was not someone you would like to meet in the street on a dark night. Hunchbacked, with a heavy, jutting jaw exaggerated because he had no teeth and refused to wear his dentures, he had greying curly hair, dark eyes, and a sunken face which always looked in need of a shave.

Regarded as the house simpleton, Jackie was at the beck and call not just of Ma Easy but most of the other grown-ups in the place. He had a full-time job as a labourer at a local factory, but, instead of handing over his wage packet to his mother, every Friday night he always delivered it into the hands of Ma Easy, whose reward was to supply him with spending money.

Jackie was the house errand boy, and, on my first Saturday at number 78, it was a novel experience to be sent with him to the local beer-off to collect the weekly rations. He could carry two boxes containing a dozen loaves and twelve bottles of milk with ease, while I struggled with a bag containing a large quantity of tins of beans and tomatoes. He was a heavy smoker, and seemed to spend most of his time smoking and eating sweets.

He was never happier than when he had a packet of fags, a bag of 'spice', and a few bob in his pocket; but, when penniless and skint, he would sit and sulk, and, on those occasions, his ugly and sorrowful face was a picture of dejection and misery. Yet it didn't take much to put a smile on his face, and, as Ma Easy used to say, when he was in funds he was like a dog with two tails.

Jackie loved Saturday nights, when he could go off to the Roscoe or the Don picture house and gorge himself with spice while watching a film, then, contrary to Ma Easy's wishes, pop into a pub on the way home to have a glass of beer. A special occasion he appreciated was when, perhaps once a month, his parents took him to a variety show at the Empire.

As I have mentioned, when I first arrived at number 78, I shared a bed with two other lodgers – and one of them was Jackie Upton. From the beginning, Jackie didn't strike me as an ideal bedmate. Fortunately, my other sleeping companion was a chap called Ernest Thornhill, who at least seemed much more 'normal', and I was grateful when he offered to sleep between me and Jackie.

Ernest Thornhill, I should mention, was my mother's partner, a man destined to spend most of the rest of his life in that role. At the time of my removal to Macro Street, he had known my mother for only a few months, and this was the first time I had met him. Like Mother, he was separated, and they met when Mother was persuaded to make up a foursome one Saturday night. Ernest introduced her to Macro Street when she decided to walk out on my father.

Two other 'guests' at number 78 were a couple of old men who were also unusual characters – Walter Hallam and 'Billy' Lodge. They both turned out to be likeable chaps, people you would describe as victims. They were probably widowers who had fallen upon hard times, but, if they were not men with habits you would consider exactly pleasant, I don't remember that they were a problem once you learned to accept them for what they were.

Walter, however, was not someone a young boy was likely to take to at first sight, for it was his misfortune that he was one of the ugliest men you would ever expect to meet. I cannot describe his face other than to say it appeared to have at sometime been flattened by a hammer. He had hardly any nose, and, with this and a pair of sunken eyes with which he could only see when wearing steel-rimmed spectacles, he wore an expression of permanent curiosity. Moreover, his bottom lip was somehow always turned outwards, which meant he was continuously slavering.

It sounds cruel to say it, but, frankly, when he was eating he had to stoop so close to his plate to be sure of seeing what he was doing that he ate like a pig. I think he boasted only two teeth in his head, and made such a meal of masticating that it was safest not to sit too close to him at the dining table. When, having finished his food, he decided to light his pipe, I soon found it was wise to make a quick retreat because burning tobacco and lighted matches went anywhere but where they should...and if they didn't catch you, Walter would get you with his spittle!

In truth, at the outset the adults and children in the house invariably ate separately – that is, the grown-ups had their food first – but the experience of eating at the same table as Jackie Upton and Walter Hallam in my first week was an ordeal I found so uncomfortable that I barely pecked at my food. Perhaps, as Ma Easy was quick to point out, I was stuck-up and considered myself superior when I had no right to do so, but, somehow, I couldn't help myself wanting to weep to think we had to live in these circumstances. It put the top on it one night when the old girl chose to use her commode just as I was finishing my supper.

In later years, Mother never wanted to talk about the Macro Street phase, and, no doubt, it was a low point in her life which she preferred to forget. I'm sure she didn't want us to live in those surroundings, and probably felt trapped by the pattern of events which had taken us to number 78. When I look back, I feel far more sorrow than anger about the situation in viewing it from my mother's viewpoint. It is, perhaps, too easy to suggest that she, with Ernest Thornhill's help, ought to have found something better, for that is to forget how handicapped they were, without the money or resources to do other than accept what was available and conscious that temporary arrangements could soon become a permanent trap.

As an adult, I cannot recall our time at Macro Street without a sense of deep dismay, and I still cringe at the memory, but, if it was a place where we felt we didn't belong and which showed how easy it was to fall below what many would consider a reasonable level, it is only fair to stress that our fellow residents were honest and decent by their own standards. They were as much victims as ourselves, though, in many cases, the difference was they did not aspire to anything much better because that was all they had known.

As a family, our good fortune was that the Macro Street experience failed to bring us down to their level, and, indeed, it made my sisters and myself all the more determined to try to rise above it and one day enjoy a better life.

Penny in the Slot

I T WAS in that initial brief spell at Macro Street that I first started to recognise there was a sense in which our lives were going out of control. The stability had gone, and I knew there was nothing a boy of twelve could do about it. It seemed then that, as a family, we would never again have a 'proper' home where we could live happily together and shut out the rest of the world, and I felt as if I had suddenly found myself stranded in a foreign country without the means of getting back to familiar surroundings. I felt vulnerable, exposed, lost.

You might wonder how I could feel homesick when I was living in the same house as my mother and sisters, and the only alternative was to return to my father at Paget Street, where the circumstances were far from ideal and unlikely to improve. Yet going back to the East End looked much the lesser of two evils, and there came a moment of blind and childish panic when my feet couldn't get me there quickly enough because my heart told me I didn't belong at Macro Street.

I little knew then that, within a couple of months or so, I would gladly swallow my pride and come to terms with the reality of having to adapt to life at number 78. When you have no choice, it's surprising what you can get used to, and I did; but it was a while before I recognised the situation for what it really was.

Father, I have to say, welcomed me back with open arms, and, for a time, we lived in harmony and comparative comfort. Whatever the problems in terms of the two of us sharing the practicalities of managing the day-to-day essentials of cooking, washing, cleaning, etc., what mattered to me was the sense of security and privacy being at Paget Street gave me. How does one describe the feeling you have when, walking down the road on a cold winter night, you finally see the welcoming lights of the house you call home, a place you know as 'our's' and where you don't have to live among strangers?

As my father was out at work all day and I was out at school, the time we could devote to housework and suchlike (what little got done!) was limited. So Dad eventually decided to advertise for a cleaner. He put a postcard in the window of a newsagent's shop at the top of Newhall Road – and such was the response that he spent every evening of the following week conducting interviews.

During the many periods when our parents were living apart in the years when we were growing up, I don't remember one instance when my father brought another woman home. I cannot say whether this was by accident or design, and have no idea if the opportunity ever arose. When I look back, I often think nobody could have blamed him for finding someone else. I don't mean it as a criticism of my mother when I mention that she found it difficult to survive without another man at her side; and, as I recall, there were three other men in her life.

During our time at 61 Newhall Road, when she and father were living apart, there was a man called Bernard Holmes, whom she met while working in Firth Brown's canteen. Well-built, with broad shoulders and a rugged face, he was employed in one of the workshops, and, when he moved into our house, my sisters and myself, being very young, accepted him as a substitute dad without a murmur. In fact, some fifty years later, I still remember him with affection, for he was a very gentle and kindly sort of chap, and I have never forgotten how, on the night he left and disappeared from our lives, I travelled part of the way with him and said a final farewell at the end of the street where I assumed he was now going to live.

On another occasion, in the early years at Paget Street, Mother had a relationship with a younger man called Keith Nelhams. He was a Londoner whom she met while working as an usherette at the Globe cinema in Attercliffe. I don't remember much about Nelhams other than that he was a projectionist, and perhaps it was typical of the ignorance and blind acceptance of we children that we thought it was wonderful one night when Nelhams and my mother arranged for us to get into the Globe free to watch the film *Pinnochio*.

Now, in what we might describe as the Macro Street era, Ernest Thornhill had come into my mother's life, and, as I have mentioned, their attachment was destined to continue until his death some thirty years later. For some reason, however, they never married. Forty years ago divorce was not as easy as it later became, and there was probably a very understandable explanation why Ernest could not get his freedom at that time. It was only partly down to cost, for I believe his wife would not contemplate divorce even though the marriage was at an end.

Curiously, in later years when you might have expected Ernest and my mother to marry, the question does not seem to have been seriously considered. Ernest was an easy-going guy who was obviously a source of strength and comfort to my mother, but, if he was loyal and dependable, he was never the type to set a lead in improving their situation. Mother was always the one who sought fresh lodgings, and who, ultimately, found them the house where they were to spend their last years together. I never heard her utter a single word of criticism of Ernest, yet there was a sense in which I am sure she felt disappointed by the way their relationship drifted into something much less fulfilling than it ought to have been.

As for my parents, when they were finally divorced in the late 1960s, the step was prompted by my father's unexpected decision to re-marry. Ironically, his second marriage lasted little more than a couple of years before he died suddenly at the age of 59.

Back at the start of the 1950s, I cannot imagine what his views were on the possibility of starting again with someone else. He wasn't given to talking to me about such matters, and, even in later years, never discussed the subject. Once, not long before I left home myself to get married, I witnessed yet another fierce argument between my parents and afterwards asked him why he seemed to have given up on their marriage. His only comment was: 'You'll understand when you're older.'

At that time, I must admit, I tended to blame him more than my mother for the breakdown, and it was only much later that I came to see there had been faults on both sides – faults which neither could help or should have been blamed for. For better or worse, they were what they were and did what they did because they felt it was what they had to do at any particular moment. Sadly, by the time I learned to understand this, it was too late to tell them.

It was as a consequence of a comment my father made during the phase when he was interviewing candidates for the cleaning job at Paget Street that I had a feeling he might be hoping for something more than an employer-employee relationship if the opportunity arose. He asked me what I would think if he found me another mother, and, as kids will, I shrugged my shoulders and said it might be nice.

In the event, if he did have any aspirations in that direction after he had appointed a cleaner, I was the person responsible for scuppering his plans within a few weeks.

The situation in the house was such that I would often get home from school and find there was nothing to eat in the place. In normal circumstances that meant waiting for my father to arrive to provide the money for me to fetch bread, milk and whatever from Rosie Skillington's beer-off in Alfred Road.

On this particular day, I arrived home just as the cleaner was leaving. She was a pleasant woman but, in my eyes, a bit bossy. She told me not to make the place untidy now she had 'fettled' it, and, as she walked out of the door, said to remember to tell my father the gas man had been.

Those were the days when you paid for your gas through a penny-in-the-slot meter in the cellar. Every so often, the gas man came to empty the meter, and, after counting the pennies, he usually left ten or twelve by way of rebate – along with a receipt. On this day, I found the rebate and receipt in the kitchen cupboard.

As there was no bread in the house and Dad would not be home for another hour-and-a-half, I decided to take a couple of pennies and use them to treat myself to two penny cakes from Cousin's shop on the corner of Paget Street and Sanderson Street. I was so hungry, I had scoffed both cakes long before I got back home. Foolishly, perhaps, I decided to return to Cousin's and buy two more cakes.

The mistake I made was not to tell my father what I had done. When he arrived, I said nothing, and, after we had had our tea, I went out to play football on the 'Oller with my pals. By the time I returned, Dad had discovered the gas rebate money – and found four pennies missing.

The sin of having used the money to buy four cakes seemed much greater by this time, and, when Dad asked if I knew what had happened to the missing pennies, I denied all knowledge that the gas man had even been.

Nothing more was said, but, of course, I knew I would be found out. Fourpence may seem such a pittance, but it might just as well have been four pounds, so great was my guilt. And, anyway, the following day it transpired that my crime had been compounded when my father tackled the cleaner about the missing pennies – and, believing him to be accusing her of theft, she stormed out of the house in a huff.

Of course, when my father confronted me, I told him the truth. Alas, my pleas for mercy fell on deaf ears. I was ordered to my bedroom, where, a few minutes later, Dad arrived to deliver a thrashing which left my backside stinging with pain.

Later, after he had disappeared to the pub, I dried my tears, collected my coat, and ran out into the street. Only then did I decide to start walking towards Macro Street. An hour later, by which time it was after ten o'clock, I sat under the bridge in Woodside Lane trying to pluck up the courage to knock on the door of number 78.

As fate would have it, I suddenly spotted my mother and Ernest Thornhill walking towards me. They were on their way home from the pub. Mother saw me emerge from the shadows. 'Is that you, Keith?' she asked. 'Yes,' I said, 'Can I come back to live with you?'

It was, I suppose, a case of any port in a storm, but, whatever my previous reservations, this time I didn't have any doubts I would make the best of things in the big house. In any event, it soon transpired that there could be no going back to Paget Street ever again, for my departure prompted my father to give up number 43 and return to live with his mother in Danville Street.

With hindsight, I can see that my decision to walk out on him precipitated a chain of events which added to my father's woe over the following three or four years. He had no sooner settled back with my grandmother when my mother took him to court for non-payment of maintenance to his children. Now he couldn't even use the excuse that he had me to look after, and, unfortunately, he ended up being sent 'down t'line' – and he experienced several subsequent spells in prison on the same count.

I have to admit that only in much later years did I appreciate the extent of his misfortune and come to regret what was another example of the pain which my parents always seemed to be inflicting upon each other. It was all very sad, and it is even sadder to think that, at the time, I never gave a thought to my father's imprisonment. By the same token, I was also totally ignorant of what it really meant when Ernest Thornhill suffered a similar fate for failing to help his estranged wife support their daughter. The memory, however, gives me pain.

Expelled from Newhall!

THE last two or three years of my schooldays constituted a curious phase as a consequence of the circumstances of my home life, and, looking back, perhaps it was not surprising that my formal education suffered.

When I first went to live at Macro Street, I saw the opportunity to move to another school as a novel bonus – at that age anything new is a welcome diversion. However, though the nearest school was Burngreave, for some reason I don't now remember, I insisted on switching to Owler Lane despite the place being about three miles away. As I had failed my eleven-plus exams a couple of years earlier, I knew I couldn't get into the part of Owler Lane reserved for the really clever kids, but perhaps I thought attending the premises next door would enable me to feel as if I was getting a superior education by association!

Ironically, I had no sooner settled at Owler Lane when I walked out of Macro Street and ended up living back at Paget Street – just across the road from Newhall. However, I decided against returning to my old school at that moment, but then, illogical as it might seem, when, within a couple of months, I found myself once more a resident of Macro Street, I suddenly had the notion that I really ought to be attending Newhall!

Why I wanted to return there, I can't explain other than to say it was an instinctive, spur-of-the-moment thing inspired by a mixture of sentiment and a longing for familiar surroundings. I may also have been finding Owler Lane more testing than I had expected, for there were certain lessons – French was one – in which I was at a disadvantage because I had never previously studied the subject, and the rest of the class were two years ahead of me.

Bronks, the headmaster at Newhall, knew me well enough, and, if he could be a fearsome sight when on the warpath, I liked him and believed he not only liked but understood me. He had spent just about all his teaching career in the East End, so he knew something of the environment in which his pupils lived; and, while he was very much of the 'spare the rod and spoil the child' philosophy, his bark was often worse than his bite. He may not have always shown it, but there was a warm, human streak in his make-up.

For instance, aware that the parents of many pupils might not be able to afford to send their children to the annual pantomime, he always arranged a free Christmas outing to Attercliffe Palace, where an interval ice-cream was laid on – paid for out of the headmaster's pocket. I also recall that once, when he learned I had never been to the seaside, he made sure I was on the next school trip to Cleethorpes.

He was also keen on organising educational trips for the kids, and had a system by which parents could pay the fare in advance weekly instalments. If he had a fault it was that he didn't show much sympathy when, as happened to me once, a pupil's parents abandoned plans to send their son or daughter on an outing and asked for a refund. The money may have been needed to pay the rent, but Bronks somehow seemed to view the decision as a personal slight.

It was not difficult to get the wrong side of Bronks, and he never left you in any doubt when you had displeased him. He was a solidly-built man with the frame of a heavyweight, and, when he was angry, just to see him pounding across the school hall, swatting his cane against his thigh, was enough to strike fear in your heart. He walked with a limp which somehow always seemed more pronounced when he was on the warpath, and there was nothing more frightening than to be the focus of the fury reflected in the dark eyes behind his steel-rimmed spectacles.

When someone upset him, he had a way of silently glaring at them, as if to suggest his expression should be enough to show how bitterly disappointed and let-down he felt. When I met up with him again in later years, I experienced this 'treatment' after a minor misunderstanding.

Just before he retired, sometime in the late 1960s, I arranged an interview and promised to write a piece in the *Morning Telegraph*. However, as I had not consulted my boss on the subject, and he chose not to use my article in the paper, Bronks felt I had deliberately let him down. When we next met in the street, he never spoke a word and just glared as I explained what had happened.

* * * *

Yet I have many fond memories of the man. I recall only being able to afford one major school trip, to the Festival of Britain in London in 1951, and the interest Bronks showed in me on that outing is something I have not forgotten. He loved sport, and, knowing of my enthusiasm, when the train was about to pass through Nottingham, he called me out of the carriage and into the corridor, where we stood as he pointed out where Trent Bridge, the City Ground and Meadow Lane were. On the journey home that evening, he talked for an hour about football in general and an old Newhall 'wonder boy' called Harry Gooney in particular.

As secretary of the Sheffield Schools Football Federation, he always encouraged a good turn-out from Newhall whenever there was a schoolboys international staged in the city. He was always telling us 'If you can't cheer, don't boo!', and, while he wanted us to be good sports as spectators, I think he was disappointed that the school never produced another Gooney – someone who would play for England Boys, go on to become a professional footballer and bring fame to Newhall.

He hated any form of cheating, or attempts to put one over on him or a teacher, and was so keen to catch culprits that many a lad was declared guilty when he was really innocent. I recall a sports day when I was myself a victim of this tendency to see the worst in a situation.

Once a week, we used to travel on the tram up to a sports ground off Stubbin Lane, near Sheffield Lane Top. The way it worked was that one party of boys would attend the first session, then, as they were leaving, another batch would arrive for the second session. I was in the first group, but, just as we were about to board the homeward tram, I realised I had left my kit in the changing rooms. The teacher, a man called Brown, was convinced I had done it deliberately in order to enjoy another game of football – and, later, Bronks took some persuading that this hadn't been the case.

One highlight which caused Bronks great pride came when Newhall finally went all the way to the semi-final of a Sheffield schools football tournament. The team that year was made up of boys a couple of years older than my own group, and all I remember of the game was that it was staged at the Atlas & Norfolk ground at Roe Lane, and we lost to a Meynell Road side which included a lad destined for football fame – Albert Quixall.

Morning assembly was a daily ritual in which Bronks was in his element, and there was nothing he enjoyed more than conducting the hymn singing on those occasions. The Halle Orchestra's Sir John Barbirolli had nothing on this other JB in terms of energy or range of physical contortions with his baton! No other headmaster in Sheffield can have attacked the task with such passion, and, to see Bronks taking time off to wander among the pupils and root out and remove the children he described as 'groaners' (and there were plenty) was to see a frustrated perfectionist at work.

He would always round off these sessions by calling a senior boy called Peter Law to the front. Law had a beautiful soprano voice, and old Bronks' face was a picture of sheer delight as he listened to his star pupil sing *O For the Wings of a Dove*.

It was against the background of some of these memories that I felt my heart pulling me back to Newhall, and, one Monday morning, I simply turned up there and asked Jerry Bronks if I could come back. It amazes me now to think I was able to do so without any parental note or backing, and I often wonder what I would have done if Bronks had said no and sent me packing. Certainly, I would have been rather late reaching Owler Lane!

Fortunately, Bronks agreed to take me on, though, knowing how far I had to travel, he warned that if I didn't get to school on time, or if I provoked any problems, I would have to leave and go somewhere else. Perhaps he knew it was an arrangement that was unlikely to last.

I was put into the class of a stern-faced old spinster called Florence Coupe, a fearsome little woman (she was about 5ft 2in) who wore her hair in a huge bun. She boasted a very large bosom, and, always walking very upright, had about her an air of superiority in the sense that she seldom showed any hint of humour and invariably wore a pained expression. She gave the impression she would have preferred to have been in charge of a better class of pupil and was wasted in the rough East End.

In truth, she wasn't always as stern as she seemed, but, talking to her face-to-face, she made one feel inferior. Of course, those were the days when discipline was the keynote, and the slightest hint of disrespect for your teacher was to invite an instant dose of physical punishment. There was seldom room for intelligent debate, and certainly it did not pay to disagree with Miss Coupe even if you were in the right.

Unfortunately, one Friday afternoon I got the wrong side of her – and did so in rather spectacular style.

She had a visitor, and while they were talking together in whispers at her desk in front of the classroom, we pupils were instructed to occupy ourselves and keep quiet. All went well until I let out an almighty yelp. This was prompted by the flick of a ruler against my neck by a boy in the desk behind. When I turned round, the occupants, David Law and Brian Hancock, were smirking, which, of course, added insult to injury, and provoked a few sharp words from me.

Once Miss Coupe's visitor had left, she called me out, and, ignoring my attempts to explain why I had yelped, told me to hold my hand out to be caned. I refused. 'You're not caning me for something that wasn't my fault,' I said. She kept insisting, I kept refusing, and the upshot was she sent one of the other boys to fetch Bronks. Within a few minutes, by which time I was shedding tears of frustration and still pleading my innocence, my favourite headmaster burst into the room – and his face was like thunder.

He, too, refused to listen to my explanation. By this time, I suppose the yelp that had launched the incident was no longer the crux of the matter. The issue now was that I had refused to accept my punishment, and done so with a vociferous show of disrespect. My initial feelings of injustice were purely incidental.

Bronks invited me to hold out my hand for him to cane, but again I refused. 'You can't cane me for something that isn't my fault. No! No! No!' I shouted.

In the end, of course, he did cane me, and the episode, prolonged by my resolute stance, could hardly have been more entertaining for the rest of the class. However, the cruellest blow came when, as I stood there weeping at the pain he had inflicted and the sheer disbelief at what seemed undeserved punishment, Bronks said: 'Now, I want you out of this school, and, on Monday, you will find another place.'

Not surprisingly, perhaps, the boys whose actions had sparked the incident remained silent, and I don't recall either of them saying anything to me afterwards. No doubt they were as surprised as anyone at the way the situation developed. Miss

Coupe, too, was lost for words. Between the time Bronks left the room and the school bell at four o'clock, she carefully avoided looking at me, and I walked out of the premises without hearing one word of regret.

Looking back, I can well imagine I was regarded as a rebellious kid, a problem pupil, and I doubt if Jerry Bronks or Miss Coupe held out much hope for me in terms of achieving anything in life. I wasn't normally bad-tempered, and respected my elders in much the way that most boys did then, but, when I was under fire or felt myself the victim of unfair treatment, I did have a tendency to react with great passion and emotion.

The irony was that, many years later, by which time I was first a reporter and then sports editor of the *Morning Telegraph*, nobody took greater pride in my success than Jerry Bronks. If I met him in the street and he was with someone, he would introduce me and boast that I had been one of his star pupils. We had many conversations in this period, but he never hinted at remembering the circumstances in which he had thrown me out of Newhall. I often wish I had broached the subject.

As for Miss Coupe, I only met her once after I left Newhall, and the occasion was not without a touch of humour. By now I was in my late twenties, married and respectable, and making good progress in my career. I was walking down Chapel Walk in the city centre when I spotted her walking towards me. As we drew close and I started to speak, she affected interest – until I mentioned my name. Suddenly, her half-smile became a frown, and she scurried away with a speed that took me aback. I had only wanted to inquire how she was, and, perhaps, to say I bore her no ill-feeling for what had happened all those years earlier. I wanted to tell her what I had done with my life, and to ask what had happened to her. As I watched her disappear from view, I wondered whether the mention of my name had pricked her conscience. Perhaps not, but I would have liked to say it didn't matter.

Burngreave

AFTER Jerry Bronks kicked me out of Newhall, I completed the final eighteen months or so of my formal education at Burngreave, a secondary modern school which had the convenience of being only a fifteen-minute walk from Macro Street. Once I settled in, I often wondered why I had been so reluctant to move there in the first place, for it was pleasant enough, and I enjoyed it. Indeed, this was a phase in which I really enjoyed going to school.

We used to joke that ours was the highest school in Sheffield, for it stood atop of a hill from which the red-bricked building could be seen for miles around. The school overlooked the distant industrial Lower Don Valley on one side and a cemetery on the other, and someone once said that, as most of the pupils expected to work in the one place and be buried in the other, the limitations of our hopes and expectations were evident in the horizons we could see from the classroom windows.

My time at Burngreave proved eventful and sometimes enlightening, but I left in 1953 without any formal qualifications, and lacking even a final report which might have identified my strongest and weakest subjects for the benefit of any prospective employer. For some reason, the last term of that final year did not conclude with the usual examinations – although, at the time, I don't think any of us in old Jasper Holdsworth's 4A class were too upset about that!

As you might imagine, having left Newhall in circumstances which did not reflect well on my character, I was not accorded the warmest of welcomes to Burngreave. Old Scowcroft, the headmaster, was a slightly-built, stern little man who had a habit of peering at you over his spectacles with an expression which always seemed to me to be a mixture of disdain and disgust. Almost from the start, he made it clear he did not have much time for me, and only much later did I realise the first thing he must have done when I turned up at the school was to telephone Jerry Bronks.

If Bronks marked Scowcroft's card in the way I suspect he did, perhaps there was no wonder my new headmaster saw me as a pupil to be endured rather than encouraged. That first impression coloured his opinion of me all the time I was at Burngreave, and his attitude was illustrated on the day towards the end of my final term when I approached him for advice about how to go about seeking a career in journalism.

He was a man who always seemed devoid of a sense of humour, and this was the only time I ever saw him smile. Indeed, he actually chuckled, but, unfortunately, he saw me as the joke. 'Journalism? You? I shouldn't think you ought to look for a career like that – it's far beyond your capabilities,' he said. Some teachers in the same situation might have suggested that, while I seemed to be setting my sights rather high and would have to work very hard to attain such a goal, it might be possible to get there in the end if I studied English and shorthand, read widely, and showed the desire to succeed.

He was not only convinced I was a hopeless case, but wanted me to know that was his opinion. Yet I'm sure I was not totally lacking in promise. True, living at Macro Street ensured I was hardly likely to dress in the best of taste, and maybe the ragged clothes I wore made me look poorer than many; but I was enthusiastic, and, faint though it may have been, there was at least a semblance of talent.

With the benefit of hindsight, I suppose it is too easy to be critical of one's teachers, but I often wonder why there was so little genuine concern for the welfare of pupils, and never the slightest attempt to encourage boys to persevere and seek further progress in subjects for which they showed some natural flair. Only when, in later years, one met up with some of those teachers did one appreciate they were not the all-knowing and super-intelligent beings one had once imagined. They were ordinary people like the rest of us, and, as such, the man who considered his duty anything more than simply teaching was the exception rather than the rule.

When I arrived at Burngreave, Scowcroft placed me in the third-year 'B' form, and seemed rather amused by my protestations that I had always been in an 'A' stream at my previous schools. It might seem trivial, but I was genuinely upset about what seemed a deliberate demotion, and, in the subsequent end-of-term examinations, I took much pleasure in proving my point by finishing top of 3B by a substantial margin despite appalling marks in my two worst subjects – woodwork and science.

Ironically, my moment of triumph was marred by an episode in which I was caned for celebrating my success with too much enthusiasm. At morning assembly, all the boys who had finished top in their classes were called on to the stage, where they were invited to step forward to be applauded when their names were called. At the sound of my name, I raised my arms in a gesture of victory normally reserved for the boxing ring, and our form master, a man called Guyler, took exception to what he interpreted as an act of defiance. He could not understand why I was so delighted and angry at the same time, but, then, as usual, I was guilty of wanting to make a point and express my feelings – and in those days pupils were not expected to have minds of their own!

If I felt I should not have been in Guyler's class in the first place, I have to say I did not regret the experience, for he was different from any previous teacher I had worked under, and it was an enlightening phase. Guyler was not really all that much older than the boys in his class, and this may have been his first appointment. He had a misleadingly light approach to the job in that he invariably walked into the classroom grinning; but, if you saw it as a cue to try a bit of humour, he would lose his temper very quickly.

There was one boy who arrived at the school just after me, and to say he brought out the worst in Guyler would be an understatement. This boy, called Parrott, was already six-feet tall, and he clearly resented being confined to a school desk which was several sizes too small.

Once, Parrott's back-chat got too much for Guyler, who yanked the boy from his desk and caned him on his backside. A physical struggle between the pair ensued, and the upshot was that someone was despatched to fetch Scowcroft. For the rest of us, it had been an entertaining diversion, and, when the drama was over, I penned a short piece of verse about Parrott's painful bum. Alas, Guyler discovered the offending poem – and promptly gave me three strokes across the backside!

Scowcroft was not won over even when, at the end of the following term, I finished fifth in the school's senior class. Frankly, I was disappointed to discover that I could have finished top but for further flops in science and woodwork. Alas, you could always guarantee me finishing bottom in those subjects.

At least the form master, Holdsworth, was impressed that a boy fresh from the 'B' class had done so well; but he was confused when I tried to explain I should never have been in the lower grade in the first place.

Holdsworth was one of the best teachers I ever had. He had a knack of making everything seem interesting, and I can't recall being bored for a moment when he was discussing or explaining a subject. He had a genuine talent for his job, although, if one had seen him away from school without knowing how he made a living, one might have thought he was a bank manager. Well-built and balding, with sharp features and small, dark eyes, he invariably wore a suit when most other masters preferred sports jackets and flannels; and his manner was that of a man who was dealing not with boys but mature students.

He was certainly not soft, and there were times when his discipline and authority were rather frightening; but he talked about history, geography and current affairs in a way that made you want to listen. He was one of the few teachers I had who didn't speak down to his pupils, and, within reason, he encouraged intelligent debate.

Yet, even in his case, there was a certain remoteness when it came to dealing with his pupils as individuals; and, like Scowcroft, he did not seem to want to know more than the necessary minimum about his boys. I once wrote an essay (we called it a composition in those days) about Macro Street, and was sure it would shock him; but he simply marked it with the note 'very realistic' and never said anything to suggest it had made an impression on him or provoked his curiosity.

You felt he was unlikely to give any of his pupils a moment's thought once he was away from the school. So, perhaps, it was hardly surprising that he, like Scowcroft, did not respond to private inquiries intended to induce advice on how one might pursue a career in journalism.

Curiously, when, some ten years or so after I left Burngreave and had finally achieved my ambition by becoming a reporter on the *Sheffield Telegraph*, I was sent to cover the funeral of a prominent local businessman; and Holdsworth happened to be one of the sidesmen on duty at the church in the Millhouses district. When I spotted him, he was handing out hymn books, and I was sure he would be pleased to see me. To my dismay, he showed no sign of recognition when I introduced myself, and my reference to the old school provoked little response. I had half expected some comment along the lines of: 'Oh, you did it in the end, then?'

But, no, he didn't even remember me. Indeed, once he knew I was from the local paper, he seemed more intent on ensuring that I included his name among the mourners. I felt it was the least I could do, and made a point of placing him high on the list that appeared in the paper; but, reflecting on the incident later, I felt there was a certain sadness about his anxiety to be seen to have figured alongside the industrial leaders who attended that funeral. All those years earlier, I had placed him on a pedestal, and it was a blow to find he was an ordinary mortal.

There were many things at Burngreave which were different from Newhall. One novelty was the system by which each class was divided into four house groups. I cannot now remember the names of those 'houses', but have not forgotten how much I enjoyed the weekly house meetings. Indeed, before I had been at the school a month, I ended up taking on the duties of house secretary – no doubt seeing it as an opportunity to develop my writing.

Taking notes and compiling minutes was right up my street, and a pleasant bonus was reading the minutes aloud at the subsequent meeting. Those minutes, I must admit, were unlike anything anyone could have expected. I turned them into essays which included touches of humour and a range of details such as would normally be considered superfluous in something supposed to be formal. However, rather than prompting a rebuke from the house master, my novel reports induced a look of amusement. 'Well,' he said one day, 'they are certainly different from the usual run of minutes.'

I often wondered whether the house master mentioned those minutes to old Scowcroft, and, if so, how he reacted. It is the sort of thing you would have thought might merit a mention in the teachers' common room, but, if anything was said to the headmaster, he probably responded with a grunt.

It was with a grunt that Scowcroft reacted to my request to be allowed to act as school football reporter. He said I could do it if my form master and the sports master were both agreeable, but, when I read my first report to the school at assembly a week or so later, he sat stony faced and obviously unimpressed. I was not encouraged to continue in the role.

The Kid from 78

URING my early weeks at Burngreave, there was one incident which probably confirmed headmaster Scowcroft's view that I was a 'wrong 'un'. However, it was an episode in which I considered myself an innocent victim, and, if I was guilty, it was only by association – though, unlike in a similar episode at Newhall, this time I didn't refuse to be caned!

Burngreave drew its pupils from a number of districts in the area, and, living in Macro Street, I belonged to the contingent from Woodside. Naturally, I was keen to be accepted by the new colleagues with whom I walked up Fowler Street every morning on the way to school. In the beginning they called me 'the kid from 78', and I was never sure whether this had anything to do with my home being the best-known lodging house in the district.

I recall getting involved in forming a football team (yes, yet another!) with a group of lads of my own age plus several of their older brothers, and, for a short time, we knocked about together. I desperately wanted to 'belong', and, as kids will, we got up to all sorts of pranks – including one which went tragically wrong on Bonfire Night when, for a dare, a lad held a banger in his hand too long, it exploded in his face, and he ended up losing the sight in one eye.

We were always doing something daft, but, while I might have preferred to find somewhere to kick a ball about, I joined in and enjoyed escapades which, for the most part, were harmless. However, I drew a line when it came to joining in the fights and tests of physical strength which seemed so important to most of the others, and, if they thought I was a coward, at least I avoided the unnecessary punishment and bruises that would have been inevitable.

The school gate we used was at the top end of a short terrace called Sun Street, off the top of Danville Street. One day as 'our gang' left school together, a boy at the front of the group grabbed a bottle of milk from the window-ledge of one of the houses. He ran off, and, wanting to be matey, when everyone dashed after him, I joined them as they ran down the hillside, along Melrose Road, across Burngreave Road and up to Pitsmoor Church.

In the churchyard, the lads took turns at swigging the milk. I watched, and no doubt hoped to be given a turn, but never got the chance to have a drink before the empty bottle was slung behind a gravestone.

The next morning at school assembly, Scowcroft announced that a local housewife had been to see him to report the theft of a bottle of milk. When he ordered the culprits to turn themselves in by lining up outside his office at the end of assembly, I felt I didn't really qualify. But, of course, it was no good claiming I'd had nothing to do with the decision to nick the milk, and hadn't drunk any. My mates insisted I shared their guilt and should join them in owning up.

When Scowcroft appeared, I was still pleading my innocence, and telling him I hadn't touched the milk not only failed to save me from getting six strokes of the cane like all the rest, but, naturally, it hardly endeared me to the others. It was not entirely by mutual consent that I retired from the gang the same day!

We were all instructed to visit the woman whose milk had been stolen and deliver an apology. When we went along at lunchtime, she received us with an apologetic smile and admitted that, had she been asked to identify us, there was only one boy she had seen when she looked through her window at the time of the incident...me! Talk about adding insult to injury.

* * * *

I doubt if I missed the gang when they threw me out, for I palled up with a lad in my class at school called Terry Cain, and, within a few weeks, we had enrolled as members of the Hillsborough Boys Club. It was a fair step to the club's premises in Langsett Road, but this proved an enjoyable phase in which I discovered snooker and table tennis. I even got into one of the club's football teams as a regular!

It was one of the best boys' clubs in Sheffield, and several leading professional sportsmen, including Henry Hall, a national boxing champion, and Dennis Woodhead, the Wednesday footballer, had been members. It's association with so many people who had gone on to enjoy sporting success certainly inspired me to believe membership alone would boost my chances of making the grade.

It was here that I met Captain Stanley Royle, the club's warden and one of the most respected figures in his field. Royle had been a soldier, but what first impressed me was being told that he had played for Manchester City as a winger. Only many years later did I discover he had, in fact, managed just one Football League appearance, playing against Sheffield United at Bramall Lane three decades earlier, in April 1922. However, that knowledge did not detract from my appreciation of him as an ideal warden and a wise and kindly man.

Royle spent most of his life running Hillsborough Boys Club and, over the years, hundreds of lads had cause to be grateful for his guidance and influence. Like Sheffield FC's Harry Parkin, whom I mentioned earlier, Royle was always an amateur sportsman and prided himself on a code of conduct on and off the field which ensured his boys never lacked a good example. He was a chirpy, enthusiastic little man, and if he seemed rather posh to a boy from Sheffield's East End, he was, in fact, very down to earth and well aware that many of his members came from less than perfect backgrounds.

The club had a large membership, and I recall being impressed by the way he knew the name of every boy. If you happened to enter the lounge, he always had a word and would break off to speak even if he was entertaining an important visitor. What seemed remarkable then was the way he spoke to you as if you were an adult. Somehow, he made me aware that there was a different kind of world, full of possibilities, beyond Macro Street.

He was the first man I ever heard suggest there was nothing a boy could not achieve if he really wanted, but he made it plain that the only way anyone succeeded at anything was by working at it.

He had a good team of helpers who ensured the club was run properly, and, like old 'Pop' Bennett down at the YMCA, Royle was passionate about the cause of helping young people get a proper start in life. Nobody enjoyed the success that the various HBC teams and individuals achieved more than him, but he always said sportsmanship mattered more than winning, and he had a genuine repulsion for boastfulness and unfair tactics.

As kids, of course, we were always looking for something different, and one novel experience which attracted Terry Cain and myself was the local branch of the Army Cadet Force. We turned up at Norbury Hall one evening, met Captain Steele, and, within a few weeks, found ourselves parading in full uniform. The outfit was certainly better than the suit I usually wore, and the pity was I couldn't go to school in khaki!

I don't think I stuck with the ACF for more than a few months, but I did well and impressed old Captain Steele in that spell; and it was probably during this phase that I first started wondering whether a career in the army might prove a way of escaping Macro Street.

However, I didn't take that step for some time, and, meanwhile, I had a few ups and downs at number 78.

The Club Trip

TWO or three of the male lodgers at number 78 were long-time members of the local working men's club at Pitsmoor in the early 1950s. Old Walter Hallam, who was nearly blind, spent almost every evening up there, and, though I seldom saw him the worse for drink myself, we often wondered how, with his poor sight, he managed to negotiate the long walk back home down Fowler Street in the dark after a night on the booze. He was always falling in the street on these occasions, and many was the time he arrived home covered in dust and muttering oaths. Once he suffered cuts to his face, and was not amused when Ronnie Buckley suggested they had improved his looks!

There was one memorable episode after a night at the club when, in the company of little Billy Lodge, Walter walked straight past the house in Macro Street and had reached the bottom of Harvest Lane before realising they had gone too far. Walter's excuse, when he finally made it home, was it was raining heavily and he'd had his head down – and he complained that little Billy, being rather intoxicated, hadn't been much help.

Billy, staggering in behind Walter, was soaked to the skin. Honest, he looked as if he had just been dipped in the Don. Water was still dripping from his hair and off the bottom of his overcoat, and I remember how everyone laughed when he emerged from the dark passage and into the brightly-lit room and said: 'It's a bit damp out there.' What made it funny was the fact that he didn't intend his remark to be humorous.

Anyway, he promptly collapsed into a chair, and what we didn't realise was it marked the beginning of the end for old Billy, because he went to bed that night and never got up again. A week or so later he was carried out in a coffin, the victim of pneumonia. At the time, I was sleeping in the same attic as him, and, for several days, he kept everyone awake with his coughing and spluttering and repeated cries of 'Oh, dear!'

The thing I have never forgotten about the night he died was the smell. It was my first experience of death at close hand, and, frankly, I didn't realise how seriously ill old Bill was, for nobody in the house seemed to be paying him much attention.

Billy, who was probably in his late sixties, hadn't been at the house long, and I don't think anybody knew much about his background. He had simply turned up one evening with old Walter and begged for lodgings. He was still working somewhere, though I don't remember what he did, and my impression was that, after being

89

widowed, he had given up his home and gone to live with either a daughter or a niece, then been thrown out following some dispute.

Anyhow, one of the highlights of the year with which Walter and (on this particular occasion) Billy were involved was the Pitsmoor club's annual children's excursion to Cleethorpes, for which each member was allocated seats. These may have been free, but, if not, the sum involved was nominal.

In those days these trips were an essential part of the WMC scene all around Sheffield, and, early on the morning of the chosen day, hundreds of coaches would line up outside all the city's leading clubs to collect thousands of excited children – for many of whom these outings were their only visits to the seaside. Every child was given a pink five-shilling (25p) voucher for 'Wonderland' – it cut up into a dozen or more small coupons which ensured the kids of participation in all the amusements.

One year, the weeks immediately ahead of the trip coincided with one of those frequent phases when I was out of favour with Ma Easy. Unfortunately, I had a habit of answering her back and insisting that, as she wasn't my mother, she couldn't boss me about. Well, I did admit I tended to be a cheeky kid.

I don't recall the incident which prompted the latest dispute, but the matriarch's proposed punishment was to ensure I was left behind when the other children in the house went to on the club trip to the seaside.

If Ma Easy had not made such a meal of repeating my 'sentence' every time I was within earshot, I might well have simply accepted it, but when, some days before the outing, she was still seizing every opportunity to tell everybody I was staying at home while the others were off to Cleethorpes, I decided I would use any means I could to confound her by getting myself on that trip.

It was one of those occasions when I had cause to be grateful for my ability to compose a decent letter and prove the pen was mightier than Ma Easy's authority!

It was little Billy, who was totally oblivious of Ma Easy's ban, who suggested the idea of appealing to the secretary of the Pitsmoor Club. However, it was my own notion to write, and to explain in my letter that, as usual, those members of the club who lived at number 78 had arranged for the children to join the outing, but, unfortunately, owing to the restricted allocation, there was no place for me.

As Billy suggested, I mentioned his and Walter's names, but insisted I didn't want to make an issue of my omission, and stressed I was anxious not to embarrass the committee's friends who were my fellow lodgers. But was there, I wondered, a late vacancy I could fill?

Whether I really expected a response, I don't remember, but, remarkably, I received a prompt reply in which I was invited to attend a committee meeting on the evening before the outing. When I turned up, those gentlemen asked me a few questions, told me what popular old chaps Billy and Walter were, and said it wouldn't be fair to two of the club's most respected veterans if I were prevented from joining the other children on the trip.

By the time I got home, the other kids at 78 – all, of course, younger than me – were being packed off to bed to ensure they would be up and able to make an early start to catch the 'chara' for Cleethorpes next morning. Ma Easy asked if I didn't now regret having been 'a bad lad' and wished I were going.

'But I shall go!' I responded, waving my ticket in triumph. 'The club have found me a place.' How I savoured telling her how I had beaten her ban, to which she responded: 'I don't believe you, you defiant little sod.'

She believed me the next morning when I was up with the others and joined them on the long walk up Fowler Street – and all the more so when I returned home in the evening with the makings of a sun tan!

I don't remember much about the outing, though I do recall delighting in regaling Ma Easy with details of 'a lovely day' during which I'd had a double helping of dinner at the specially-arranged mid-day meal at a fish-and-chip cafe near the coach station, and all the kids had enjoyed a good sing-a-long on the homeward ride.

In fact, I did take a promenade snap home with me to show the old girl, but, unfortunately, it was one of those cheap photographs which start to fade within the hour – and, by the time I reached 78, you couldn't tell the difference between my face and the candy floss I was holding, because both were just a blur!

Incidentally, not wanting to get Billy in trouble, I didn't mention that, on hearing of my successful appeal to the club's committee, he'd given me a shilling for spending money.

A Lost Pen – and a
Brush with the Law

A T THE bottom end of Macro Street, a few yards above the railway bridge which marked where Woodside Lane ended and Harvest Lane began, there used to be a police box. It was often lit up late on a Saturday night, and, more than 45 years later, I never think of that box without recalling a painful incident which didn't turn out quite as I had anticipated when I sought the aid of the constable on duty after being thrown out of number 78. In precipitating a midnight visit to my attic bedroom by two detectives, it proved a rather chastening experience.

When I re-joined my mother and sisters at the big house, I had done so because there appeared to be no alternative, and, although it never felt comfortable or seemed the right place for us, I suppose I adapted pretty well. However, if I tried to settle and fit in, there is a difference between accepting your lot while letting your environment change your perceptions and aspirations, and taking circumstances in your stride while vigorously rejecting their influence.

There was a sense in which I knew I would never settle. I couldn't help it because something inside me resisted everything the place represented, and, in truth, this was a piece of good fortune because, had I willingly embraced that environment, I might have been lost. The people were not cruel or criminal, and, indeed, I never suffered any physical or mental ill-treatment, but, all the same, I didn't want to be like them – I dreaded being caught in the same trap. Let them live as they wished, and good luck to them, but let me go a different way – this was my philosophy even though I was still considered a child. Perhaps it explains why I was regarded as a rebel. I couldn't wait to grow up and escape.

Fetching a dozen loaves or half-a-dozen bottles of milk at a time from the shop round the corner in Fowler Street, was an ordeal at the outset, because I believed it advertised to everyone in the shop (which always seemed full) exactly where one lived. However, I gradually became less self-conscious – except once, when one of Ma Easy's daughters, Gert, sent me into a crowded shop to ask, in all innocence and to the amusement of the other customers, for 'a packet of ST's' (it was years before I knew what sanitary towels were!).

I admit there were times when I made my dismay at living at 78 obvious to anyone who would listen, but, on the whole, Ma Easy regarded me as a cheeky young rebel who could and would be moulded into conformity. Perhaps even she recognised that there were spells when I yearned for acceptance and simply wanted to enjoy a sense of belonging, if only until I was old enough to get away.

Those periods in which I set out to please often succeeded in making me a favourite with the silver-haired old matriarch. When she chose, she could be kind, and, though there was often friction in the air when we conversed, sometimes I think we quite liked each other.

Then, alas, came a day when a double errand turned into a kind of nightmare which led me to that police box at the end of the street.

One means of escaping 78 for a few hours came on Saturday afternoons when I visited the home of Ma Easy's married son, Walter, and his family. They lived just across the other side of the city centre, in that part of Park Hill where, at the time, there was a huge sprawl of ordinary housing before the redevelments which created the famous high-rise flats in the district. Walter, a coalman, was a friendly chap, while his wife always made me welcome. Being with them was like being back in an ordinary household.

The calls at Walter's house came about because one of the regular errands I undertook was to a Duke Street chemist who produced a home-made concoction of soothing mixture popular with mothers whose babies were having teething problems. The children at 78 for whom this was bought were Ma Easy's youngest grand-daughter, Molly, and one of Annie Cowling's kids.

On this particular day, having been given two shillings (10p) for a double supply of soothing mixture, I was also asked by Ma Easy to call at a city-centre shop to get a refill for her new ball-point pen.

More than forty years later, it is difficult to imagine what a cherished instrument such a pen was in a working-class home at the start of the 1950s. Ball-points had only been widely available for a few years, and this particular one was a fancy little thing which, courtesy of a simple adjustment, boasted the novelty of writing in both red or blue ink according to one's choice. If I saw one now, I would probably consider it rather cheap, but, with its imitation gold plating and decorated beading, and having a top or cap bearing a small chain, it was regarded as a treasure by Ma Easy.

To cut a long story short, soon after leaving the shop where the refill had been fitted by an assistant, I was walking up Duke Street swinging the pen by its chain when, to my dismay, I suddenly noticed that the important bit, the bottom half which contained the refill, was no longer there. With increasing panic, I retraced my steps back towards the town, but no missing part did I find; and, all but in tears, after calling to buy the bottles of soothing mixture, I arrived at Walter's with a sorry story to tell his wife.

Perhaps I was more preoccupied with my tale of woe than hanging up my jacket properly on the overcrowded peg behind the door in Walter's kitchen, but it never occurred to me to remove the bottles from my pockets. Sure enough, a few hours later, when I was ready to get the bus home (the now-forgotten Inner-Circle route, bus numbers 8 and 9, was ideal for getting between Park Hill and Woodside), I discovered that the jacket had fallen to the floor – and its soaked state bore testimony to two shattered bottles of soothing medicine.

Returning to Macro Street at after ten o'clock with only a useless pen top was bad enough, but arriving without the soothing medicine as well, and with only a tame explanation by way of compensation, added up to an ordeal I did not relish. However, I did anticipate that, after the inevitable initial anger and strong words from Ma Easy, there might be some sympathy for my double misfortune.

Unfortunately, the living room was full when I arrived, for most of the lodgers were back from their evening out, so I had a captive audience as I related my misadventure. Ma Easy, who seemed to revel in 'playing to the gallery', produced a torrent of self-righteous abuse and invective followed by a stream of accusations.

It was her claim, that I had never bought the refill or the soothing mixture and pocketed the money, which prompted a change in my stance from defensive to offensive – and after that the whole situation got completely out of hand. I think I must have said something to the effect that the worst thing my mother had done was to bring us to this den of iniquity and thieves, for suddenly Ma Easy shouted: 'Get out!'...and I found myself charging from the house and into the street.

It was a cold, starry night, and I didn't have a clue what to do next, but, spotting a light in the police box, I felt salvation was at hand. I was soon telling the constable about being thrown out, and, when he took me back to the house, with right and the law on my side I was sure Ma Easy and the others would be put firmly in their place with a few short, sharp words from the man in blue.

Of course, it didn't turn out like that. I cannot remember now how long I had then been back living at 78, but in that time I had, on several occasions, been guilty of speaking my mind about the place – certainly there had been a few 'incidents', most of them quite minor. However, as harmony had been restored between me and the landlady in recent months, I assumed they had been forgotten.

Not so. Ma Easy, recalling some of the things I had said and done with a selectivity and bias I could barely believe, created such an image of me as a foul-mouthed and violent boy with criminal tendencies that the policeman said he didn't wonder she had told me to leave. I had walked back into the house on the offensive: within minutes I was on back on the defensive – and lost for words.

What hurt me most at the time was that my mother sat at the other side of the room throughout the episode without saying a word. With the benefit of hindsight, many years later I came to understand her silence. We might have all ended up in the street that night if she had come to my defence. Unfortunately, her failure to speak damned me in the eyes of the constable.

It is not difficult now for me to imagine how he must have viewed the situation, He cannot have been impressed with the surroundings in which he found himself, and perhaps he felt it was just the kind of environment ripe for breeding the tendencies of a petty criminal. It would be interesting to know exactly what he said when, returning to his box, he reported the episode to his superior.

In fact, the policeman persuaded Ma Easy to let me at least stay the night, and she put on the resigned look of a long-suffering but kindly old woman and said I'd better get off to bed before she changed her mind. I still felt the victim of an injustice, but, weary and overwhelmed with woe, I was glad to get my head on the pillow and go off to sleep.

That, however, was not the end of the matter. I was sleeping soundly when I was suddenly shaken awake. The attic was without electric light, and all I could see was the glare of two torches and the shadows of two men at the side of the bed. They were detectives, obviously following up the constable's report, and wanted to know where I had been all evening.

It never crossed my mind that I might be being sized up as a possible petty criminal, but, long afterwards, I could imagine they fancied I might have been up to no good somewhere. However, I was so concerned to tell them about the pen, the soothing mixture and my allegations of ill-treatment on my return home that they must have realised they had merely walked into a domestic dispute without wider implications.

It was probably as early as the next morning when I first appreciated that Ma Easy must have said something to the constable which prompted him to refer me to his colleagues in CID. Moreover, after breakfast on that Sunday, by prior arrangement mother took me up to West Bar Police Station, where I was interviewed again. I thought I was there merely to explain my dilemma and lodge a formal complaint, but found myself cast in the role of a potential wrongdoer.

I know I came away puzzled by the episode and bitter at the turn of events. However, things at 78 returned to normal within a few days, we put that spot of trouble behind us, and what you might call an uneasy truce prevailed. It wasn't the last time Ma Easy threw me out, but the later incident belongs to another chapter in the story.

Dreamer

IF I FOUND the situation at Macro Street far from ideal, the circumstances did not detract from my tendency to walk about with a head filled with dreams. Even in the last months before I left school, I could find romance in simply exploring the humble streets of Woodside and Pitsmoor. Most of those streets no longer exist, and, if they did and I were able to visit them again now, I would probably wonder what it was that so captured my imagination.

About this time I discovered grown-up fiction and a number of books which came into my life at just the right moment to feed my imagination and lend added credence to my dreams. An incidental benefit at that stage was that they also started to gradually improve my knowledge and stimulate awareness, and, albeit very slightly at the outset, point me in the direction of self-education.

I had been a reader from an early age, but most of the books I borrowed from the public library as a boy were about sport. It is not without irony that it was at Macro Street where I came across something which opened up fresh horizons, and it happened because Ernest Thornhill, my mother's partner, just happened to be one of those people who devoured acres of pulp fiction. This was something new to me then, for my father was not a great reader of any kind of literature, and though I have always thought of him as being more intelligent or cleverer than Ernest, I never remember him reading a book.

Ernest was essentially a passive reader who was unlikely to read anything of great depth, but every week he went through perhaps a dozen of those American comics and picture-strip type novels which enjoyed such great popularity in the early 1950s, and he also bought lots of cowboy books plus detective fiction of the type churned out by Mickey Spillane and Hank Jansen. Most of these didn't appeal to me, but one day Ernest left lying around a paperback copy of Howard Spring's *My Son, My Son*. When I picked it up and started reading, I found I couldn't put it down.

Howard Spring is all but forgotten now, and the kind of novels he wrote, while they enjoyed immense popularity and huge sales, were not considered anything other than popular fiction. However, if not rated as great literature, they were very well written by an excellent storyteller who knew his subject – and they exerted a significant influence on me. There came a time, much later, when Spring's autobiographical books made a significant contribution to my development, not least in prompting me to emulate his own exercises in self-education. He, too, had a very humble start in life, and was largely self-taught, and one of his examples I followed was to seek to improve my English by studying the letters in *Cobbett's Grammar*.

In truth, it was to be a few more years before I got really hooked on reading and was inspired to consciously embrace self-improvement, but discovering *My Son, My Son* and finding I could relate to the characters and background not only lit the first sparks of ambition, but probably did more than anything to make me aware of 'literature' and send me to the library in search of more of the same kind of novel.

Of course, for a long time I was reading at random and without any sense of direction or purpose, so many of the books were without merit. But at least I'd got the reading habit, and I could only benefit from having a new world opened up to me.

It was with images from the novels of authors like Howard Spring stamped indelibly on my mind that I roamed the local streets and found romance round every corner and in every building. For instance, on my way from Macro Street to visit the Coliseum picture house in Spital Hill, a stroll along Railway Street, up Oborne Street and over the steep banking which led to Spital Street, was as dull a walk as you can imagine, but it would leave me enraptured and imagining these places as scenes from fiction. It was almost as if I believed myself to be a character in an L.S. Lowry painting, though at the time I probably thought I was William Essex out of *My Son, My Son*!

When I look back, I feel the flaw in the pattern of the development prompted by the reading I did in my teenage years was that while books increased my knowledge and improved my ability to write, there was a sense in which the choices I made had the effect of separating literature from life. Does it make sense to explain what I mean by saying I tended to see my ambitions to write as something purely literary (with a capital 'L') rather than something related to the world in which I lived? This, of course, was down to a lack of guidance or any facility to discuss what I was thinking with someone who might have adjusted my viewpoint.

In truth, my education didn't really begin until I was 25 and first joined the staff of a newspaper, for that was when, working alongside other journalists, I entered a world which was my university, and where I began to appreciate the art of writing plain and unpretentious English.

Of course, in the Macro Street phase, books took second place to other distractions which, providing one could raise the money, were more instant. Of these, the major attraction was the cinema (we called it 'the pictures'). A ninepenny visit to the Coliseum or the Roscoe transported one into another world in which those figures on the silver screen overcame all odds and invariably lived happily ever after.

Those were the days when the inside front page of the local *Star* newspaper was filled with what seemed an endless list of suburban cinemas, and, when funds were available, I would study the films being shown around the city and think nothing of travelling to a distant district to see a particular picture.

Who now remembers such cinemas as the Walkley Palladium, the Crookes Palace, the Roxy, the Hillsborough Kinema, the Phoenix, the Roscoe, and the Sunbeam, or recalls the sense of adventure inherent in visiting places with such exotic names? Even the sight of those names on posters on the hoardings which were so much a part of the scene then was enough to generate enthusiasm, and, just spotting a newly-posted advertisement for a film sufficed to inspire an excited sense of anticipation.

In my East End days, the cinemas of Attercliffe like the Adelphi, the Globe and the Pavilion always seemed so sophisticated and the epitome of luxury, what with the way the lighting emphasised the colour and pattern of the proscenium curtains, the plushness of the seats, and, of course, the wonders of the the the images we watched on the screen. Who can forget what a let-down it always seemed when one came out of the cinema and into the chilly, gas-lit street?

The Coliseum, the nearest cinema to Grandma Johnstone's Danville Street home, was probably my earliest favourite because of its accessibility, and I remember how I used to aspire to graduate from my seat in the sixpenny pit to one in the ninepenny stalls. How one yearned for the day when one might be old enough to actually sit on the back row of the stalls and enjoy the company of a girl! As it was, we kids could only get into 'U' category films, and had to be accompanied by an adult to gain admission to 'A' films – always being relieved when 'yes' was the response of a stranger whom one asked 'Can you take me in, Mister?'

The one disadvantage of the 'Coli' was it operated two houses nightly, while some cinemas ran continuous showings and, if you timed your arrival right at these places, you could see the same films at least twice. Indeed, during school holidays, I often entered the Wicker Picture House, the Capitol at Sheffield Lane Top, or the gods at the Hippodrome at two in the afternoon, stayed in my seat until they had played *God Save the King* at half-past ten, and emerged physically and mentally numbed after watching the same picture (and full supporting bill) three of four times!

Incidentally, it is amusing now to reflect that when certain cinemas started opening on Sunday evenings, as a boy it always seemed the height of sophistication to join the inevitable long queue outside and persuade some stranger to take you in. Once, the news spread rapidly among a group of my pals that the manager of the Sunbeam at Fir Vale was given to letting a few under-sixteens into his cinema on Sundays, and we enjoyed several weeks of unrestricted Sabbath cinema-going until one evening we arrived to find a bobby standing by the ticket kiosk to watch for for under-age patrons.

I liked musicals best, be they a black-and-white film biography of songwriter Gus Khan, *I'll See You In My Dreams* starring Danny Thomas and Doris Day, or the technicolour *Jolson Story* and *Jolson Sings Again*. I doubt if any films I saw as a boy gave me more pleasure than those Jolson bio-pics, and, on more than one occasion, I watched one or the other half-a-dozen times in a single day! Nearly fifty years later, I can still recite sections of the script from memory, and have never forgotten how I wept on my bed at Macro Street when I read that the real Al Jolson had died.

You may recall that, in the first Jolson film, the highly-fictionalised story had the young Asa Yeolson running away from home, being picked up by a policeman, and ending up in a boys' home where he joined the choir and delivered a beautiful rendition of *Ava Maria*. It was typical of the effect the scene had on my imagination as a ten-year-old that I was inspired to join the Sunday evening congregation at St Clement's, Newhall, because I believed I, too, could follow Jolson's route to showbusiness fame if I began by singing in church. The fact that I couldn't sing didn't seem to matter!

Incidentally, when I first saw *The Jolson Story*, afterwards I dashed from the cinema to read the poster outside advertising the picture, and went home convinced the voice which had so enthralled me actually belonged to Larry Parks, the actor who had played Jolson. How, you might wonder, could I be so ignorant? Perhaps it said much about the world in which we then lived.

When television began to arrive in working-class homes in the first years of the 1950s, it marked the start of an era in which even a boy from the backstreets could acquire a lot of knowledge and information which had previously been largely inaccessible. Had it arrived ten years earlier, I might have known who Jolson was – and much more. However, initially, while stimulating awareness of another world, TV was essentially a novelty and a new source of entertainment; and at that stage I don't think 'the box' was as influential in my life as books and the cinema.

It is amusing now to recall the time when old Ma Easy first had a TV set installed at number 78, and reflect on how the room curtains were closed and the lights switched off while the lodgers sat in darkness to watch black-and-white figures on the ten-inch screen of a piece of furniture which resembled a miniature wardrobe. The first big event we watched was the 1953 FA Cup Final, in which the legendary Stanley Matthews starred in Blackpool's famous defeat of Bolton; but the highlight of that summer was, of course, the Coronation. Walking out into the sunny backyard after three or four hours in a darkened living room was just like coming out of the pictures!

Curiously, although I was then approaching the time when I would leave school and start working, my cinema trips were never made in the company of a girl. Of course, I dreamed of having a romantic attachment, but opportunities were limited, and, anyway, my funds seldom stretched to entertaining a female partner. Moreover, in that context, I lacked confidence and sophistication, and no doubt I was younger than my years.

My sister Pat had a pal called Sheila Garfitt, who lived just round the corner in a yard off Fowler Street, and I remember being told that this girl had taken a shine to me. She was a bonny lass, full of laughter and always merry, and I carried a torch for her for several months. However, although she was the same age as me, she always seemed older and more worldly, and, while we often spoke, I never plucked up the courage to ask for a date. Any hopes I might have harboured were finally shattered when I discovered she had started courting. In fact, she surprised everyone by marrying at sixteen, but I think the reason she has stayed in my memory is that when, a year or two later, I inquired what had become of her, someone told me she had suddenly fallen ill and died.

Starting Work

I LEFT school at the age of fifteen in July 1953 without any formal qualifications and with no real idea of what I might attempt by way of a career. Given the choice, I would have plumped for a menial job in the editorial department of a newspaper office in the hope that it might eventually lead me into journalism, for, even then, I felt that was my destiny. However, as I have already intimated, there was nobody at school with whom one could discuss these things or seek guidance, and, anyway, my headmaster seemed to have marked me down as a failure.

In fact, a couple of weeks before I was due to say goodbye to Burngreave, I did try one newspaper office, the weekly *Rotherham Advertiser*. Taking a morning off school, I turned up there without an appointment, and, unfortunately, within a couple of minutes, the editor, a man called John Dickinson, halted our impromptu interview in the front entrance and sent me packing after finding I couldn't spell 'parallel'.

In reality the only sort of work I was equipped for to begin with was something in the clerical line. I was obviously aware of this because, on the way home from that aborted interview, I made a spur-of-the-moment decision to drop in at the Savile Street premises of John Holding & Co. to see if they had a vacancy for a junior clerk.

I chose this firm (I think they made steel forgings) because my father had worked there a couple of years earlier, and I remembered once having met his boss, Mr Lumb, when I was collecting Dad's wages. Lumb received me warmly even though I had no appointment, said if I was half as good a clerk as my old man there would always be a job for me at Holding's, and asked when could I start.

Alas, on the appointed day, I didn't turn up, because, in the meantime, I had allowed myself to be persuaded to begin my working life as a trainee scale mechanic with a firm called CWS (Scales) Ltd – a remarkable choice for someone who had not the slightest inclination towards anything remotely mechanical.

It happened because Ma Easy felt I ought to learn a trade and promised to have a word with her nephew George Brookes, who lived in nearby Percy Street. She sent for George, he arranged for me to meet his boss, Clem Ambler, at the firm's Matilda Street workshop, and I was offered a job after the briefest of interviews. I wasn't entirely convinced I'd done the right thing by accepting it, but after Mother bought me a pair of overalls it was obviously too late to change my mind without hurting someone's feelings.

When I look back, it is intriguing to recall that, at the interview, I was given no practical test, and I wasn't even asked if things like metalwork and woodwork had been among my better subjects at school. Moreover, there was no talk of a formal apprenticeship, and no mention of attending evening classes on subjects related to the trade. No doubt if I had shown a natural flair for the job, I would have picked up a lot of things very quickly, but I worked for CWS (Scales) for about six months, and it was wasted time for everybody.

The firm, which occupied a small portion of a larger CWS building that has long since disappeared, provided a maintenance and repair service for all the weighing machines in the wide range of Brightside & Carbrook and Sheffield & Ecclesall Co-operative Society shops and depots which then existed in the region. They serviced everything from small shop scales to those huge platforms on which lorries weighed their loads.

At that time, there were a couple of other firms which did similar work and had branches in Sheffield – Pooley's and Avery's. Indeed, Pooley's workshop was just across the street from CWS (Scales).

I seemed to spend most of my time doing little other than heating up small pieces of metal that fitted into a weighing machine, dousing them in water, and then attempting to file the edges to a point. Initially, it was amusing using a piece of equipment operated by a foot-pedal to get the metal red-hot, but I soon grew restless and bored.

Occasionally, George and the other mechanic, a happy-go-lucky chap called Colin Hanson, would take me with them on jobs, but even as their labourer I was pretty useless because, on the heavy work, I hadn't the physical capacity to be of much help.

However, I did enjoy the company of Colin Hanson, for he had a lively sense of humour which contrasted with the dour manner of old Clem. When Colin was in the building, he invariably sang as he worked, and the words of the songs amused a kid like me because they were invariably rude. One included these lines:

It was on the bridge at midnight,

Throwing snowballs at the moon,

She swore she'd never had it,

But she swore too bloody soon.

I think my pay was less than twenty-five shillings (£1.25) a week, but being a wage-earner slightly raised my status at Macro Street. Indeed, I even qualified to have beans on toast for my evening meal like the grown-ups instead of bread and treacle! Moreover, it made me feel quite mature to leave the house each morning carrying an old shoulder bag containing cheese sandwiches, a tiny medicine bottle filled with milk, and small quantities of tea and sugar wrapped in newspaper.

About this time, incidentally, I developed a short-lived passion for physical culture, and had some notion that I might benefit from a course in bodybuilding. At home in the attic at Macro Street, I started performing a routine of exercises from a booklet loaned me by Ma Easy's son, Walter; and, during lunchtime at work, I would run the length of Eyre Street and spend nearly an hour kicking a small rubber ball about on some waste land off Bramall Lane. I would often feel knackered when I got back to the workshop, but felt sure I was well on my way from being a seven-stone weakling!

Clem, the boss, was a decent old guy even if he did tend to be rather serious and a bit unimaginative. A well-built man with thick grey hair, he was the first man I ever met who chain-smoked, and I was always intrigued at the way, when he was working at the bench, he never removed a cigarette from his lips – the burnt part of his fag just grew longer and longer without the ash ever dropping off. When I tried to emulate him, I couldn't stop coughing – and I was on Park Drive while he smoked Capstan Full Strength!

It didn't take Clem long to recognise my unsuitability for the job, and he was soon viewing me with a resigned look that combined amusement and despair. Fortunately, he was a kindly and patient man, and I think he might have persisted with me much longer than he did but for the fact that I grew increasingly restless and was soon expressing a frustration he couldn't fathom.

Once every couple of weeks a man who I presumed was the area manager visited the workshop, and, compared with Clem, to me he seemed rather posh and important. I always felt the grown-ups were desperately keen to impress him, and his presence invariably made me suddenly very self-conscious. He and Clem usually had lunch together at a local cafe, or, perhaps, at some nearby pub, and they would leave me to eat my sandwiches alone, expecting me to be making myself busy by the time they returned.

The beginning of the end came one afternoon when they walked in and I was on the telephone. They weren't pleased when they caught me making a private call, and would have been even less impressed had they known I had looked up the name of a freelance journalist in the directory and rung to ask him how I might get into newspapers. I have long since forgotten who it was I called, but the poor fellow must have been mystified when I suddenly rang off before he'd finished talking!

A few weeks later, Clem said things weren't working out and asked me to leave. Frankly, I was more relieved than disappointed, but, by the time I ended up at the Youth Employment Bureau in West Street on the following Monday, I felt tearful as I admitted to the shame of having been sacked. However, the man who saw me, a kindly chap called Tom Coates, said the only mistake I'd made was to have taken a job for which I clearly had no aptitude. He suggested I should become a junior clerk – and, giving me a green card to take to my prospective new employer, sent me to the Arundel Street branch of the Sheffield Smelting Company.

Arundel Street

IN THE first ten years after leaving school, I went through a dozen different jobs as well as having a short spell in the army. Before finally graduating into newspaper journalism at the age of 25, I worked in the offices of six or seven firms whose activities spanned a range of trades from selling coal to manufacturing steel, and I also had brief periods as an hotel porter (twice), a shop assistant and a door-to-door salesman.

My first clerical post is one I recall with affection, for although I spent barely eight months at the Sheffield Smelting Company's Arundel Street branch, it was a mostly happy, eventful and enlightening phase in which it was fun to go to work.

The firm, which already dated back nearly 200 years at the time of my arrival, was in the business of treating gold, silver, platinum and other precious and non-ferrous metals. Their headquarters were at Royds Mill, near Norfolk Bridge, and what they called the 'A' Street branch had been a town mill and sales office since the 1890s, before which the property had belonged to a scissor manufacturer called Hobson.

Number 95 Arundel Street, which stood at the corner of Howard Street (close to what is now the entrance to Sheffield Hallam University) until the premises were demolished in the early 1960s, was a weary-looking building from the outside, typical of so many factory properties in the central part of the city at that time. However, it boasted an oak-panelled main entrance and reception area which, with its Victorian-style dignity, certainly impressed the boy who arrived for interview on a cold January day in 1954. After the CWS workshop, this was definitely a step up!

I happened to be wearing a blue-and-white Wednesday scarf that afternoon, and, though I never felt Tom Knowles, the office boss, was much of a joker, he often jested that I only got the job because I supported the right team. Of course, it didn't influence the decision, for I later learned that Denys Bryars, the branch manager, was the brother-in-law of a Sheffield United director.

Bryars and Knowles were looking for a junior clerk to replace a lad called Alan Kyte, who was due to start his National Service in a couple of months or so, and they felt it would be beneficial if I spent a few weeks in the warehouse before moving into the office. The idea was to familiarise myself with the firm's products, and I didn't mind even though I had wanted to avoid another manual job. However, it was disappointing to discover my role meant clocking in (the machine was a quaint old wheel with an arm you punched into a hole bearing your works number) for a 7.30am start instead of arriving with the office staff at nine o'clock.

Moreover, I knew that, unlike people in the office, the manual workers didn't get paid when they were off sick! I also soon noticed that while the workmen used a rather dingy and barely furnished attic room at lunchtime, some of the clerks dined at Mary Gentles' fish-and-chip cafe in Howard Street – and I considered that kind of eating out the height of sophistication. I knew I couldn't afford it every day, but for 1s 3d (6½p) you could get a decent meal complete with a pudding and a pot of tea.

A few weeks in the warehouse turned into nearly three months, and it might have been longer if I hadn't kept badgering old Bryars, insisting that I desperately wanted to be a clerk. Bryars, a tall, distinguished-looking man, was one of the most decent people I ever met, and always seemed to view my pestering with kindly amusement. It is intriguing now to reflect that our paths were destined to cross again some twenty-five years later when, as President of the local Chamber of Commerce, he confirmed my appointment as editor of *Quality*, the Chamber's journal.

Bryars was perceptive and thoughtful in his dealings with his staff. He had been with the firm since leaving school, and urged me to be patient and try to learn all I could in the warehouse because, he said, that was how he had started – and look where he was now. He was then only halfway to becoming the company's top man, but epitomised the rewards of an ideal that was common in that era when boys were encouraged to devote their entire working lives to one firm and told that hard work and loyalty would ensure security and success.

Success, of course, was relative. Jim Gregory, under whom I worked in the warehouse, had started out at the same time as Bryars, but he never had the opportunity to aspire to achieve the same progress. Yet Jim was dedicated, intelligent, and very good at his job.

In fact, it was good fun working under Jim's supervision, for he was friendly, likeable and something of a father-figure. He had been wanting a warehouse lad for years, and was dismayed to discover that not only was I just temporary help, but I was determined to make it as temporary as possible!

The people who knew me at Arundel Street remember a cheeky youngster who, while enthusiastic, capable and quick to learn, too often tended to be disrespectful to his elders and had a mind of his own. I was seldom slow to say my piece, but perhaps it was mostly a case of growing increasingly anxious to join the collar-and-tie brigade. Moreover, I was still having problems at Macro Street, and it obviously didn't help that I sometimes brought my troubles to work.

In this context, the only woman in the department, Clare Armstrong, became my confidante, and I benefited from her kindness and generosity. She was a good listener, and would slip me a sixpence or give me a mashing of tea or a cake if I hadn't brought any 'snap' to work. She and her husband, Harold, were childless, and many was the time I told her I wished she'd adopt me!

I was a gregarious boy, and before I'd been at the firm more than a few weeks, I had made myself known to just about everybody on the premises. There were often long spells when I was left with nothing much to do, and I must have spent hours roaming the building, talking with anyone who would give me the time of day. It was educational, for many of the workmen were amused by my curiosity and enjoyed the novelty of being asked what they were doing and why.

Naturally, I went through the experience of being sent for the 'long stand' by one of the foremen in the mill, and the incident caused great hilarity in the warehouse; but, if it was meant to be a hint that I was making myself a nuisance, the lesson went unheeded. Jim might urge me to stay at my post, but I preferred to wander. Sometimes I would slip into the office and ask Alan Kyte: 'How much longer is it before tha'll be joining t'RAF?' (Alan, incidentally, returned to 'A' Street after National Service and spent the rest of his working life with the firm.)

My imagination turned most of the men I met in the works into 'characters'. Typical of these were a pair of middle-aged warehousemen called Ernest Blackwell and Arthur Hilton. Ernest, who had apparently worked on the buses before joining the firm, was a thick-set chap with grey hair and glasses, while Arthur was slim and balding. I don't think they were too pleased when I suggested that, with a couple of bowler hats, they could double as Laurel and Hardy.

Arthur had been a professional musician. He amused me with yarns of his days as a cinema pianist in the silent era, but his only tale that I still vividly remember concerned a man who worked in the rolling mill. I had noticed that this chap, whom I remember only as Percy, had no fingers on one hand, and, in response to my curiosity, Arthur said: 'Aye, he got his fingers caught in a moving roller, and saved himself by yanking his hand free and breaking the fingers off. He went round showing everybody his fingerless hand, and five people fainted before someone recognised he was in shock and urgently needed treatment.'

The office at 'A' Street was not very large, and, situated at the front of the building, alongside the main entrance and the counter at which local silversmiths collected their orders, it housed six or seven desks plus a small switchboard. An area in one corner was designated the stock control department, the rest was known as the sales section.

Tom Knowles, the boss (his title was Town and Country Sales Manager), was a distinguished-looking but rather dull man with a moustache and spectacles and a somewhat superior manner. I always considered him unimaginative and insensitive, lacking a sense of humour and seldom seeming to take more than a nominal interest in his staff. He was impatient with the failings of others, and never warmed to me. When I met up with him again in later years, he remained as critical as ever, and seemed to delight in reminding me that I was a very rough boy when I worked at 'A' Street.

By contrast, the younger Bill Stroud, who headed the stock control department, always appeared much more human. A slightly-built, balding man in spectacles, he and his junior colleague, a slim teenager called Ivan Priestley, took their jobs very seriously while sharing a sense of fun. Their work, especially at stocktaking time, often took them into the works, and, when one or other returned with a joke they had picked up, it would be repeated amid gales of laughter – with old Bill always seeming rather embarrassed to be seen to be enjoying himself.

Bill, whose father had worked in the firm's rolling mill for fifty years, was what even then one would describe as of the old school. Sober in dress and manner, he was totally dedicated to the firm and devoted to his work, but if at times his respect for his superiors seemed 'over the top', there was invariably a twinkle of humour in his eyes – and he always had time for other people.

He could take a joke, too, as I found early in my spell in the office. One of my jobs was making mid-morning tea, and, on one occasion when he was late back from a works department, I sugared his cup twice and sat back to await his reaction when he took his first drink. Remarkably, he simply smacked his lips, drank the lot in two gulps, and was quite amused when I admitted I'd given him four spoonsful of sugar instead of two.

His colleague, Ivan Priestley, was then about eighteen. Although slightly handicapped, Ivan was a bundle of energy and enthusiasm, and, to see him work his way through a pile of Twinlock ledgers, carefully entering columns of endless figures, was to understand the true meaning of patience and diligence. Such work is now much easier thanks to modern technology, but then it was a long, hard slog – and Ivan revelled in it.

Ivan became my pal. Like me, he was a football fan, and, as a Sheffield United supporter, he once invited me to join him on a rail excursion to watch a match at Tottenham. The advertised fare was twenty shillings (£1), which was beyond my means at the time, but, typically, Ivan came up with a way of raising the money.

Over the years, Ivan has given countless hours of service to a wide range of sporting organisations, and is well known for his part in helping his father-in-law, Ben Jessop, promote the cause of junior cricket. In 1954, he was secretary of the recently-launched Beck Road Youth Club.

One of the club's fund-raising schemes was a threepence-a-go 'lottery' which involved pushing paper tickets out of a packet. If the right ticket emerged, you won a few bob, but each packet was guaranteed to raise 30s (£1.50). Ivan persuaded me to invest in one of these, supervised my tour of club members (who didn't know I and not the club was the beneficiary), and I ended up with enough money to go to Tottenham and get into the ground.

I must digress briefly and explain that this trip was partially inspired by the fact that, at the time, I had got myself a pen friend called Ted Wallace, who lived in St Albans. Without going into all the details, when I first had contact with Ted, he sent me a photograph of a teenager whom he described as himself. It later transpired that Ted was, in fact, a man of about forty, but this didn't dissuade me from taking on board his suggestion that we ought to meet up if I could arrange to visit London when one of the Sheffield teams was playing there.

Naturally, I had told Clare Armstrong and Ivan all about Ted, who was so keen for me to correspond that he sent me a regular supply of stamps. I think they were curious about the man's motives and imagined all sorts of potential dangers, and, though in the event it was all very innocent, they decided that, should I go to 'the big, bad city' as planned, I ought to have Ivan as my protector.

That day, we met Ted, and not only had the benefit of being taken across London by someone familiar with the capital, but, as we weren't travelling home until the midnight train, Ted offered to pay for us to go to a show. Ironically, during our tour of the West End, I spotted an advertisement for something at the Plaza called *Red Garters*, starring Rosemary Clooney and Guy Mitchell, and only when it was too late did I discover it was not a 'live' show but a film we could have seen in Sheffield within the month.

The 'A' Street office, like the warehouse, was full of 'characters'. There was, for instance, a colourful, white-haired little man called Edgar Naylor. Then in his seventies and officially retired, he came in two or three mornings a week to help Austin Redman and the stern Miss Trickett in the wages department. Old Edgar captured my imagination because, in his bowler hat and pin-striped three-piece suit, he seemed a throwback, like a figure from Dickens. One could imagine him sitting on a high stool and using a quill pen.

I was intrigued to discover that his brother, Bill, had a humble job somewhere in the works; and, seeing them together, the contrast in their attire and manner made me wonder about the differences that had shaped their careers.

One of my duties involved costing London and Birmingham branch delivery sheets, which involved learning how to ascertain current gold and silver prices. I surprised a few people in the way I mastered this task so quickly. In truth, I was mad keen to show I could do any job they gave me, and it is amusing now to reflect on how reluctantly impressed old Knowles was when I had no trouble picking up the knack of using a rather complicated new mechanical adding machine which represented a giant technological step for the firm.

There was a shy but attractive young girl called Kathryn Wild on the switchboard, and one of my jobs was to help her carry parcels to the post office in Charles Street. I was also urged to learn how to use the switchboard so I could deputise for Kathryn when she was at lunch.

I so enjoyed that job, for a while I would gladly have spent all day doing it, but my keenness to be helpful and informative did rather tend to get the better of me. Once I upset old Knowles when he heard me take a call from an important customer and ask the man if he'd mind holding on because the person he wanted, Denys Bryars, was on the toilet.

There was another time when my sense of fun got me into hot water with Jack Horner, a foreman in the wire department. One day Jack got a personal call from his wife, and I used the internal phone to ask him to come to the private booth in the corner of the office. While awaiting his arrival, I mumbled the words of the nursery rhyme about Little Jack Horner, not thinking anyone could hear. When a red-faced and angry Jack came bounding out of the booth and headed in my direction accusing me of insulting his wife, I didn't know where to put myself.

Many of the customers who came to the front counter to collect small items of silver were also among the memorable characters from this phase – not least a silversmith called Cyril Plant, who was a typical veteran craftsman of that era. His workshop, in a tiny room on Howard Street, was cluttered with tools and bits and pieces of work in progress, but he was a master of his trade. However, the attraction for me was in having the opportunity to sit with him in Mary Gentles' Cafe (he never removed his trilby when eating) and listen to his tales of old-time football. I was never more impressed than when he told me he had once written a regular dialect column on football in the *Green 'Un.*

Goodbye to Macro Street

WHEN I went into the army at the age of sixteen in September 1954, it was not because I wanted to be a soldier. I was simply seeking a way out of Macro Street, and joining up seemed to offer an escape which, because I opted for an Army Apprentices School, promised the bonus of extending my formal education. The irony was that, in the end, the decision to accept the Queen's shilling and sign on for twelve years was one of those spur-of-the-moment things that happened two months or so after I had sat and passed the entrance examination but meanwhile gone cold on the idea of a career in khaki.

In that first year after I left school, I never ceased to hope that something might turn up to give me a fresh start in new surroundings. I longed to live in a 'normal' home again, to enjoy some security and stability, and, especially, to feel comfortable and content in a one-family environment which might give me the opportunity and encouragement to make something of my life. Of course, the situation I was in meant there was always the danger of acting in haste out of sheer desperation.

At work, I was amongst people without much knowledge or understanding of my domestic circumstances, and I don't think they ever appreciated how deeply I envied their ordered and settled lives. I couldn't wait to grow up and begin to emulate them, and, in the meantime, longed for someone to come to my rescue – which, of course, was an impossible dream, though I was too much of a romantic to accept that it couldn't happen.

People like Jim Gregory, Clare Armstrong and Ivan Priestley were good to me, and certainly showed some sympathy when, as happened many times, I arrived at work with another tale of trauma from the previous evening. However, there was a limit to what they could do. They had their own lives to live, and there was no way they could offer me an escape from Macro Street.

Most of the episodes which I then saw as traumas were probably fairly minor. Indeed, I have long forgotten the majority. All I remember is the accumulative effect of a succession of disputes which induced an increasing mood of rebellion that was seldom far from the surface even during brief periods of calm. I had a chip on my shoulder as high and wide as the Wicker Arches.

The episode which first prompted me to look seriously at the possibility of joining the army occurred one weekend at a time when my mother was in hospital. I cannot remember what was wrong with her, but don't think it was anything particularly serious because she was only away for a few days. However, in her absence, something happened which prompted Ma Easy to have another go at me, and, though I have completely forgotten the details, I know the incident ended with me walking out of number 78 – again!

One abiding memory of the lowest points in my childhood is of the times when I was walking the streets on nights that always seemed cold and wet, and either being afraid to go home because I had done something wrong or simply having nowhere to go. That is how it must be when one is on the run – ever on the outside looking in, and acutely conscious of the warmth and comfort within those brightly lit houses you pass in the street.

I ended up on the doorstep of Clare Armstrong's Machon Bank, Nether Edge home late one Saturday night. It was wrong to impose myself, but Clare and her husband, Harold, recognised my desperation and took me in. For me, the rest of that weekend was an exercise in luxury and good living – excellent food, a hot bath, a warm single bed in my own bedroom, and the novelty of wearing pyjamas and being given what was probably the first toothbrush I had owned. Was there any wonder I wished a miracle could occur so Clare and Harold could adopt me!

Of course, it couldn't last. When we went to work on the Monday, my escapade was reported to Messrs Bryars and Knowles, and an inquest duly followed. This was one of the occasions when I recognised what a poor opinion Knowles had of me, for, perhaps not unnaturally, he was impatient with my constant personal problems and felt they should not intrude into my workplace. I overheard him telling Clare she was a fool to allow herself to be involved, for it was obvious I was 'a waster who would always be trouble'. Fortunately, Denys Bryars was much more sympathetic.

As I have noted, this wasn't the first time my domestic situation had come to the boss's notice. There had been one occasion, for instance, when, having talked to Clare and Jim Gregory about running away to London to seek the aid of my pen friend, Ted Wallace, I suddenly found my threat taken so seriously that it was mentioned to Bryars – and he went as far as to have Wallace checked out through his Salvation Army contacts. I don't know what he learned, but he warned me I would be jumping out of the pan and into the fire if I used that particular escape route.

In this latest instance, Bryars, in his wisdom, got in touch with what I think was the Children's Department at the Town Hall, and the upshot was I reported there and repeated my weekend story. What inquiries they had made, I'm not sure, but, anyway, it was arranged for me to spend that Monday night in a foster home on a distant council estate. All I can recall now is having salmon paste sandwiches for tea! The following day, my mother, having come out of hospital, collected me after I had finished work, and we returned together to Macro Street.

It was soon afterwards that I went to the Army Recruiting Office in Ecclesall Road and made inquiries about joining the Army Apprentices School, and, within a few weeks, I had had a medical and sat the entrance examination. News that I had passed duly arrived by post, along with confirmation that a place had been reserved for me as an apprentice clerk at a Harrogate camp, plus details of when and where I should report to sign on and collect a rail voucher.

In my heart, I knew I didn't want to be a soldier, and it soon began to seem to me that the advantage of getting away from Macro Street didn't really justify committing myself to the army until I was 26 years old. The more I thought about it, the more I felt there had to be better options. I put soldiering out of my mind, and looked for other alternatives.

In an ideal world, there would have been someone within our immediate family circle who could have given me temporary lodgings at least. Unfortunately, while for many years I had been a regular visitor to Aunt Charlotte, my mother's sister, at her pre-fab at Stannington, and Aunt Mary, my grandmother's sister, at Southey, I knew there was no prospect of moving in with either. Moreover, with my father serving yet another sentence for failing to keep up his maintenance payments for Pat and Jean, I didn't feel it a good idea to try Grandmother Johnstone. There were other relatives at Neepsend and Grenoside, but I knew they would not appreciate being troubled.

Aunt Charlotte, however, came up with one suggestion which, for a while, seemed to offer some hope – she said Uncle Bob Bamforth, the same relative who had once accommodated my mother when she had been a teenager looking for a home, was prepared to consider my case. Bob, my late grandmother Jackson's brother, and his wife, Audrey, were now living at 23 Brunswick Street in Sheffield, and I was invited to look them up.

Uncle Bob was a thick-set, bespectacled man of about sixty. I had met him when I was a small boy, but, as he had no time for the Jacksons, and had never forgiven my grandfather for the way he had treated my grandmother, he wasn't on our visiting list – and we certainly weren't on his. He maintained a casual contact with Aunt Charlotte, but had more or less cut my mother off after she rejected his attempts to help her when she was a girl.

Mother used to say Uncle Bob considered himself too good for the likes of us, and she was probably right, for, nearly twenty years after the period I am now discussing, I did meet up with him again through his links with local amateur boxing. As long-time secretary of the Referees and Judges Association, he was impressed when I turned up again in his life as sports editor of the *Morning Telegraph*, and, when our association coincided with his Golden Wedding, he duly invited me to attend the party. Unfortunately, he made a point of asking me not to mention it to my mother, for he did not intend to invite her. He changed his mind only when I said if she didn't come, neither would I.

Back in 1954, of course, I knew little about him or his feelings about our branch of the family, but, all the same, I have to admit I found him rather intimidating and was aware that, if I hoped to persuade him to offer me an escape from Macro Street, it would be on his terms – and those terms would probably be somewhat uncompromising.

The fact that he was even considering taking me in showed that at least he cared, and, in truth, I don't think he was a bad sort; but he was a cautious man, very serious, somewhat stern, with, perhaps, a tendency towards the kind of superior attitude you sometimes find among those in a family who have 'got on'. In truth, while his circumstances were reasonably comfortable, he was really just an ordinary working man who was not particularly well off but would never let anyone else think so.

To me at nearly sixteen, there seemed something Victorian and austere in his manner, I felt inhibited and 'on trial' in his presence, and, from the outset, doubted whether I could match his expectations.

He and Aunt Audrey, unable to have children, had adopted a boy, John, who was now married with a child of his own and lived nearby. John, learning I might soon be living with his parents, agreed Uncle Bob was strict, but insisted I would be comfortable at Brunswick Street.

The idea was for me to pay a few visits and spend some time with them ahead of any formal decision, and all went well for a few weeks. Indeed, I felt it a happy omen when Uncle Bob allowed me to practice typing on his portable machine, and, keen to show he wanted to encourage my journalistic aspirations, he took me with him to a boxing tournament and suggested I might write a report. Much later, I learned he devoted some sixty years to serving amateur boxing in Sheffield even though he had never thrown a punch in anger in his life, and, moreover, I discovered he was known among his friends as a wise and amiable colleague.

Up at Brunswick Street, his typewriter became a big attraction on my visits, and I found myself happily pounding away for hours at a time. Unfortunately, one day disaster struck. I broke it – and to say he wasn't pleased would be an understatement. The damage was something trivial like a hook coming loose, and if it cost much to repair it can only have been a few shillings, but, though he may not have intended to do so, Uncle Bob made me feel as if I had committed a violent act of sheer vandalism.

I left his house that evening in tears, and vowed never to go back. If I had returned just once, perhaps I might have found he had forgotten the accident, and who knows what course events may have taken. Instead, I slammed another door shut.

It can only have been a few weeks later that I arrived home from work one Friday evening to find my mother excited about a man who had called at Macro Street that afternoon. This was the Army Recruiting Officer, and he had clearly made a big impression on her. Indeed, she seemed to think I had let him down very badly by not having shown up to start as a boy soldier on the date appointed.

According to what she said he told her, my marks in the entrance examination had been so good he felt I had a great future in the army. He convinced her I would be turning down the opportunity of a lifetime if I rejected the vacancy that awaited me at Harrogate, and appeared to have suggested that in keeping a place open he was doing me a very special favour.

It is easy now to see that it was all sales talk certain to have a huge impact on someone for whom a visit from an army officer was a major event. Mother probably saw the hand of fate in his call, and I must admit my judgement was influenced by her obvious enthusiasm. To her it was as though this was a happening comparable with winning the pools or some similar stroke of good fortune.

If I had had to spend the following few days going through a medical, taking tests, and filling in application forms, the delay might have been long enough to help me see clearly what I was doing. In the event, all I had to do was turn up at the Recruiting Office on Saturday morning and sign – then make myself available to catch a train on the Monday.

There are times in one's life when one does not so much make a crucial decision as allow oneself to be swept along by the circumstances of the moment – and this was the case now. The nagging doubts and negative thoughts which had prompted a change of mind some weeks earlier were now forgotten, and, typically perhaps, I could only see the novelty and attraction of an instant opportunity to walk out of Macro Street and start a new life.

I signed up on the Saturday morning, spent the afternoon watching Wednesday play Tottenham, and presented myself at the Recruiting Office at 9am on Monday. By lunchtime I was kitted out and eating my first meal as an Army apprentice.

Mother undertook to call at 95 Arundel Street and announce my news. According to what I learned later, the people at the Sheffield Smelting Company seemed to think I had actually signed up some weeks earlier and the army had sent Redcaps in to haul me away. It was entirely in keeping with their impression of me that my exit should have been with a bang rather than a whimper!

One minor regret was leaving behind in my desk at the firm a number of small but sentimental personal belongings which I never saw again – including a collection of cigarette cards of old footballers, and a scrapbook of football match reports I had been using as models for writing practice. However, in turning my back on Macro Street, I also forsook several treasured souvenirs of my schooldays which I suppose ended up in a dustbin, though, at the time, I probably didn't care.

GOODBYE TO MACRO STREET

The train to Leeds, where I would change for Harrogate, was taking me away from a world I imagined I would soon happily condemn to the past. I remember as if it were yesterday how, when the train sped over Norfolk Bridge and I looked over to the hillside on which Burngreave School proudly stood, I saw that red-bricked building as a symbol of a phase in my life I thought I would readily forget. When we passed through Newhall and Brightside, places which had once meant so much to me, I said a silent farewell, and felt convinced my Sheffield days were over. How wrong I was.

Soldier Boy

I SPENT exactly one year and 116 days as a boy soldier before being discharged in late November 1955 at the age of seventeen. My Certificate of Service states my release was because I 'ceased to fulfil Army medical requirements', but, in truth, the only thing physically wrong with me was my heart wasn't in the job. Indeed, some might suggest I 'worked my ticket'.

It was a phase which could, and probably should have been a major turning point, but I couldn't settle and, once I decided this wasn't the career for me, there was no way I would be content until the army had been persuaded to let me go. Had this been National Service, no doubt I would have served my time whether I liked it or not, just as thousands of others had all through the era of conscription; but I had voluntarily committed myself for twelve years, and there came a moment when the prospect of remaining in khaki until I was in my mid-twenties suddenly seemed like a life sentence.

Curiously, there was much about the life that I enjoyed, and, looking back, I remember it as a period which did me far more good than harm. I accepted the discipline, was comfortable with the drills and routine, and appreciated a situation in which I had three good meals a day and plenty of healthy exercise. Taking a daily shower was certainly an improvement on my weekly visits to the Corporation Street slipper baths in Sheffield.

Moreover, as an apprentice clerk I revelled in the study of shorthand, typing and office procedure; and, at the Army Apprentices School and later at the ROAC Boys' School, I was encouraged to attempt early journalistic exercises with the one-man production of some duplicated magazines. I even grew two inches taller, to stand 5ft 4½ins when I returned to civilian life!

In 1996, some forty years after my thirteen months at Harrogate, I returned to the camp to attend the final passing-out parade before the place ceased to be what had become an army college, and the thing that struck me was how very young the apprentices seemed. Frankly, it pained me to see lads of fifteen and sixteen, many of whom appeared too small for their ill-fitting uniforms, giving themselves to the army at such an early age. It was chastening to reflect that I had once done the same.

In other circumstances, I might well have taken to the life, but there was a sense in which I felt imprisoned and believed I had relinquished my freedom – and, although it didn't happen immediately, once I was aware of where I was and the implications of remaining in the role for twelve years, I was overwhelmed by a blind panic. In later years I recognised that, all in good time, even a military career could have given me the opportunity to be myself and pursue my ambitions, but in 1954 and 1955 I couldn't see beyond a present in which I appeared to have given up something I felt I would miss more than anything – the right to choose what I did and when.

Of course, like any other recruit, in the first weeks I endured bouts of homesickness, but, initially, I took to my new surroundings more readily than might have been expected. Having arrived some weeks after most of the other boys starting out in the HQ Company at the Uniacke Barracks, high on the hills above Harrogate, I had some catching up to do, but, happily, in a barrack room of about twenty boys I found myself in the company of a decent group of lads who helped me find my feet.

When I arrived at Harrogate on that bright September day, I was met by a veteran Northumberland Fusiliers sergeant who took me to the Penny Pot Lane camp by bus. Once there, I faced the CSM, a man named Cole, for the first time, before being passed on to a kindly old sergeant called Tommy Blades (Royal Signals), who guided me through the process of kitting out and delivered Apprentice Tradesman No.23220382 Farnsworth K to the barrack room which would be his sleeping quarters for the next few months.

The event which sparked my first serious bout of homesickness occurred within a few weeks with a bombshell out of the blue in the form of a letter from my father in which he reported the sudden death of my grandmother at Danville Street. What made the news all the more poignant was the knowledge that, until he had called at Macro Street in search of me, Dad didn't even know I was in the army, and, according to what he now wrote, it took him several days to ascertain where I was based. As a consequence, grandmother had been buried before I learned how she had been found dead at the foot of the stairs at home.

At that moment, because I had missed the funeral anyway, Tommy Blades suggested application for compassionate leave would be inappropriate. My consolation was that a 72-hour pass was due within a few weeks.

With the benefit of hindsight, it is easy to see that the weekend leave I took in October came too soon, and had the effect of sowing the first seeds of doubt about having joined the army. I had arranged to sleep at Aunt Charlotte's while in Sheffield, but, naturally, one of my first calls was at Danville Street. There I found Grandfather Johnstone, my father... and, unexpectedly, my mother.

At that stage, it did look as if my parents were going to get back together, and it suddenly dawned on me that I would never have joined up if I had known this might have been on the cards. I had only signed on because we didn't have a 'proper' home. In the event, their 'reunion' was delayed for another seven or eight months, but the signs I saw that weekend left me wishing I hadn't become a soldier, and I returned to Harrogate with a heavy heart.

Ironically, my confusion was complicated over the next couple of months when a letter from my mother revealed that, contrary to what I had been led to believe during my spell at home, there was now no prospect of my parents patching up their differences. And, just to add another twist to the tale, Mother and Ernest Thornhill had unexpectedly left Macro Street and found new lodgings at Swallownest.

This was a phase during which, frankly, I wore my heart on my sleeve and succumbed to emotions which were a mixture of despair and frustration. One minute I longed to be back home, the next I felt as if I never wanted to see Sheffield again. In truth, I couldn't get home out of my mind, even though I knew that, just then, there was no place for me with either of my parents. Indeed, I discovered to my dismay that my father was back 'down the line' for failing to keep up his maintenance payments.

I must have been a pain to many of my colleagues, but people like Tommy Blades and our barrack room boy sergeant, George Ient, were good and patient listeners. I also had good friends in the Revd Percy Moffatt, the camp chaplain, and a man called Wilmore, the Regular Army warrant officer who was in charge of the clerk's department where I was learning my trade.

Ient was no more than two years my senior, but he was wise and mature beyond his age, and talked to me for hours on countless occasions. I think he came from an army family, and he and his brother both embraced soldiering with enthusiasm. George, fresh-faced and always wearing a cheeky smile, was a lively lad who enjoyed life, and he probably got into a few scrapes in his time; but he was obviously a natural leader destined to go a long way in the army.

Tough and self-reliant, George probably found it difficult to relate to my problems, and, when I reflect on our conversations, it is not hard to imagine he was not particularly impressed by what he saw as a lack of steel. At least he took the time to try to help with a few words of sympathy and encouragement, and I remember him with great affection.

Padre Moffatt was a jolly, round-faced Yorkshireman whose sessions in religious instruction were invariably occasions of light relief and laughter. He allowed us to smoke in class, and I remember how once, when the camp was plagued by a flu epidemic, he told those of us who were still fit enough to attend his meetings that a cigarette would help ward off the germs!

Moffatt soon became aware that a preoccupation with what was happening at home was preventing me from settling to soldiering, and did his best to lift my gloom. Learning of my interest in writing, he spoke of having been a schoolpal of Kenneth Wolstenholme, the sports broadcaster, and talked of his progress into journalism. I think Moffatt knew I was not cut out to be a soldier. One day he said he believed I would make a career in newspapers – and, by way of encouragement, told me to use his office to study and write at any time when I was free of army duties.

Moffatt, incidentally, persuaded me to attend confirmation classes, and, when I was confirmed, suggested I might consider taking a second Christian name. I chose 'William', and have not forgotten the Padre's reaction when he wrote out in full 'Keith William Farnsworth' and said: 'Yes, I think that will look very good on the dust jacket of your first novel'!

I am sorry I cannot now recall Wilmore's Christian name, and in recent years have never ceased to regret I never saw him again after I left Harrogate, for he proved an especially good friend and no doubt would have been pleased to know I finally made something of my life after failing as a soldier. Responsible for instructing us in army office procedure, Wilmore was one of those natural teachers who have a knack of imparting knowledge with humour. You seldom left his class without a smile on your face, and he made learning fun.

It was Wilmore who, spotting I could write a decent essay, encouraged me to produce a magazine, the *Clerk's Gazette*, and provided the paper and duplicating facilities. Unlike me, he was neither surprised nor saddened when, within hours of receiving our first edition, the lads used the magazine's pages to protect the freshly-polished central aisle of our barrack room – probably without having read a word!

Wilmore's concern for my welfare was such that, with Christmas looming, he offered to accommodate me in his family home in the married quarters if I decided not to spend my leave in Sheffield. At the time, I had resigned myself to the prospect of having nowhere to stay if I went home, and, as the holidays neared with still no hint of a solution, I more or less agreed to accept Wilmore's kindness.

Then, unexpectedly, I got a letter from my mother in which she said there was room for me in her Swallownest lodgings after all. When it came to the crunch, I couldn't resist the lure of Sheffield, and, unfortunately, my late change of plan did not go down well with Wilmore. In truth, I think he understood, but was confused that one minute I had been so adamant about not going home and the next I felt it was the only place I wanted to be. CSM Cole made it plain he was not pleased at the way I had apparently snubbed (he used a much stronger word) his friend.

Ironically, a couple of days before we were due to start that leave, I became one of the last victims of the 'flu epidemic which had swept through the camp, and, instead of packing my kit bag to go home, I was confined to the MRS (Medical Reception). I remained in bed for five or six days, and didn't make it to Sheffield until Christmas Eve.

Alas, I hadn't been in my mother's lodgings at Swallownest more than a couple of hours when it became obvious I wasn't welcome. Mother had been glad to see me, but it transpired that either she had omitted to mention my impending arrival to the woman who owned the house, or there had been some misunderstanding.

The couple in whose house my mother and Ernest Thornhill were lodging had previously lived at Macro Street. I cannot now remember their names, but I had known them at number 78, and, as they were a cut above the rest and plainly only in temporary difficulties, I wasn't surprised they had got out and found a house of their own at the earliest opportunity.

I have forgotten their story, and probably never knew much about them anyway, but recall the man as a big, friendly chap who had taken me on a few trips on his motor bike. The woman was not unkind, but she was a serious type who, quite properly perhaps, resented being taken for granted.

I seem to remember that my younger sister, Jean, was the only one of us living with Mother and Ernest at the time, for memory suggests my older sister, Pat, turned up at the house around the same time as me. This meant that instead of three lodgers, the woman was faced with five – and she made it plain one of us would have to go. As it was late, I was allowed to sleep on the sofa that night, but the next day the debate about the need for my departure was resumed. Christmas Day or not, there was no charity in the woman's heart. My only option seemed to be to return to Harrogate, but how, I wondered, could that be arranged when pubic transport was shut down. The woman suggested seeking the advice of the village policeman.

Mother and I went off up Worksop Road to visit Police Constable Brookes, a huge chap who turned out to be one of the kindest men I ever met. When he learned the details of my plight, he said I needn't go back to camp if I didn't want to – I could spend the rest of my leave as a guest in his home.

I had a very comfortable and happy ten days or so with 'Bobby' Brookes and his wife, and, remarkably, he wouldn't take a penny for my accommodation and food. When I raised the subject, he kept saying we would sort it out later, but, in the end, insisted he wanted nothing.

During my stay, he encouraged me to talk about the circumstances which had taken me into the army and led me to turn up in Swallownest for Christmas; and, in the course of one conversation, he asked me how much pay I had brought home – and particularly wanted to know if I had tipped up anything to my mother. In fact, I had paid her some 'board' on the day I arrived, and hadn't thought to ask for it back when I was thrown out. 'Bobby' Brookes said I couldn't be expected to pay twice.

I have met many good and generous people in my life, but 'Bobby' Brookes was one of the best. I knew him for less than two weeks, and never saw him again after that holiday, but he has always had a place in my heart and mind as the man who most epitomised what is meant by a Good Samaritan. To take in a complete stranger and treat him like a son was a wonderful gesture.

Like so many other people I met along the way in those years, he responded with enthusiasm to my talk of wanting to be a writer; and even put his portable typewriter at my disposal. Happily, in this instance there was no repeat of the earlier Uncle Bob episode and I managed to avoid damaging any keys – and also had the bonus of having the pieces I wrote read and commented upon.

I was encouraged to come and go as I pleased while staying with the Brookes family, and I called on various friends and relatives, saw a couple of football matches, and visited one or two cinemas. It is intriguing now to reflect that during this spell I patronised the local Pavilion Cinema in Swallownest for the only time in my life – little knowing that the manager was Allan Lax, the father of Linda, who, thirty years later, would become my second wife.

I remember how, on the day I left to return to camp in early January, 'Bobby' Brookes uttered his only criticism of my mother and then gave me some advice. He noted that, since leaving me at his house, my mother had not been back once to inquire if everything was all right. 'It's not my concern what you do, son,' he said, 'but, from what I have seen and heard, my advice to you is to go back to the army and forget Sheffield – there doesn't appear to be anything to keep you here.'

When I wrote to thank Mr and Mrs Brookes, I promised I would think long and hard about his suggestion, but I must admit that as time passed I knew I could never forsake Sheffield. The place never seemed to stop tugging at my heart.

Many years later, when I began to get a regular by-line in the local *Morning Telegraph*, I often wondered whether 'Bobby' Brookes might see it and recognise it as belonging to the 'Christmas orphan' to whom he had once given shelter. Sadly, when I eventually elected to try and track him down, I discovered he had long since died.

For many years after leaving the army, I used to have nightmares in which I somehow found myself hauled back into uniform, and it was always a relief to wake up and realise it was just a bad dream. The fact that my phase as a reluctant soldier remained close to the surface of my subconscious for so long probably serves to emphasise the impact the experience had on me, although an expert in mysteries of the mind might say I was plagued by guilt at having failed to complete my 'sentence' and fear that I might yet have to finish it.

Curiously, I have more happy than unhappy memories of the period. The officer who penned the testimonial I was given on my discharge described me as 'an intelligent boy capable of making a success of any job he puts his mind to', and what I wanted to do I invariably did well. I wasn't a bad soldier, my military conduct was recorded as 'very good', and I easily kept pace with the other lads in most activities.

However, my heart wasn't in it. Unfortunately, this was not like any other job, where you could simply hand in your notice and quit if you found it unsuitable. It was possible to buy yourself out, but, as that cost £50, a sum well beyond my means, the only option seemed to be to take every opportunity to press for my release.

Yet it wasn't all tears and despondency. In between the spells when I was desperate for a way out, there were plenty of times when I became so engrossed in what I was doing that I forgot my frustrations and enjoyed the moment. Once, for instance, when I was chosen as one of the boys who would line the route when the Queen visited Bradford, I was actually proud of being a soldier; and, later, it was a great disappointment to be dropped at the last minute from the AAS team selected to perform a physical training routine at the Edinburgh Tattoo.

There was a little cafe on the camp known as the Red Shield Club, run by an elderly Salvation Army lady, and, every Saturday for a short spell, me and another HQ boy called Gray earned half-a-crown (12½p) and as many cakes as we could carry for scrubbing out the premises. As our army pay was five shillings (25p) a week, the money was a welcome bonus.

Incidentally, on the wall of the Red Shield hut, there was a board which bore the following words:

As a rule
Man's a fool,
When it's hot,
He wants it cool,
When it's cool,
He wants it hot,
Always wanting
What it's not.

I was well organised in supplementing my income in various ways, one of which was to get dressed after lights out and visit a chip-van that parked just outside the main gates of the camp on Saturday nights. Handling fish and chip orders from my barrack-room colleagues not only meant a free meal, but the bonus of a couple of shillings.

There was, of course, a lot of spit and polish involved in being a soldier, but I proved myself something of an expert at using a spoon and a tin of Cherry Blossom to get a glass-like gloss on the toe-caps of my best boots, and, for a few pence, I provided a polishing service much appreciated by those of my mates who preferred to avoid the chore. Sadly, I wasn't nearly as good as most of the others at making a bed-pack with my blankets, and was all fingers and thumbs when blancoing my belt and gaiters. Moreover, I made a right mess of 'slashing' the peak of my cap to make it point downwards instead of forwards – a style then very popular with boy soldiers.

Naturally, I preferred those evenings when one could simply stretch out on one's bed and dip into a good book, but, unfortunately, my bed was rather too near the barrack room door, and, when a corporal came looking for someone to undertake extra duties, I got roped in more often than most. Indeed, there was one boy corporal from an adjoining barrack room, an obnoxious lad called Melia, who seemed to delight in recruiting my reluctant services, and, unfortunately, I discovered the hard way that it didn't pay to give him lip or show any signs of disobedience.

Of course, once the senior staff recognised my resistance to a career in khaki, some questioned my character and courage, and one of my biggest critics was a man called Major Walker, who became my commanding officer after I was transferred to 'B' Company. Walker was always lecturing me on my lack of guts.

Then one day we were ordered to participate in the company's boxing tournament, and I ended up being paired with a lad who, though in my weight bracket, was much more solidly built. I believe this boy, whose name I have long forgotten, had been brought up in Malta, and I remember he was dark and swarthy – and looked as if he was a physical culture enthusiast!

The look Walker gave me as I climbed into the ring told me he didn't expect this bout to last the full three two-minute rounds, and, within seconds, I was inclined to agree with him when I walked straight into a full-blooded punch on my nose and slumped to the canvas. Yet, somehow, despite being knocked down twice and suffering a terrible beating, I survived to the final bell. For perhaps the only time in my life when I have been in that situation, I refused to give in – and my pluck was rewarded with a pat on the back and the comment from Walker: 'I didn't know you had it in you.' I hope the look I gave him said: 'Sir, you obviously don't know me.'

Reference to boxing reminds me of an amusing episode which occurred after my transfer to a REME attachment at the RAOC Boys School at Blackdown, near Aldershot, in October 1955. Anyone who knows me well will be intrigued and surprised to learn that I had only been at Blackdown a few days when I was recruited to the boxing team – and, initially, on merit!

What happened was that the four boys who had been moved from Harrogate were paired off and put into a boxing ring, and I had the good fortune to be facing a lad who was even more of a weakling than me. I wish I could recall my opponent's name, for he was a likeable boy, but he hadn't a clue how to fight. I wasn't much better, but, at the time, a famous American boxer called Sugar Ray Robinson was the great sporting hero, and I tried to imitate his style by dancing all over the ring. As the other lad had no idea how to defend himself, I landed punches at will. Indeed, I looked so good, the officer in charge invited me to join the boxing team.

Of course, it couldn't last, and, as I feared, I was found out the first time they paired me with someone who could really box – but not before I had taken another thrashing. In the meantime, however, I savoured the daily training sessions, which involved a long run before breakfast and half-an-hour on the punch-bag in the gymnasium. The real attraction was not just an extra-large late breakfast, but being excused morning parades.

* * * *

If I had put my heart into being a soldier, I don't doubt I would have made the grade, but I stopped trying. It might have been different if I could have erased Sheffield from my mind, but every time I went home on leave the desire to stay grew stronger, and my frustration was compounded when my Easter leave coincided with the delayed reunion of my parents.

The Danville Street house in which my father and Grandfather Johnstone lived had been earmarked for demolition, and, rejecting the chance to move into a modern home on the Shiregreen estate, they negotiated an exchange and ended up staying in the Pitsmoor area in a back-to-back house in Bramber Street. Mother chose this moment to agree to return to my father.

At the time, it did appear there was a genuine desire on both sides to make a fresh start. This may have really been the case, though, frankly, it seems doubtful. What was not evident until much later was that, on my mother's part, it was a reunion of convenience. She and Ernest Thornhill had been asked to leave their lodgings in Swallownest, and, though it meant a temporary separation, Bramber Street offered a ready-made solution to at least half the problem. It was to be several months before my father discovered that my mother's frequent trips to see her sister Charlotte were, in fact, cover for nights out with Ernest.

However, all was peace and harmony on my visits on leave, and, though the house was rather overcrowded with six residents and I had to sleep on the living-room sofa, I felt it was home – somewhere I would much rather be than in the army.

Despite my determination to leave the army, I don't think I contemplated doing anything dramatic or silly because I felt that if I continued to beg for my release, eventually my wish would be granted. I kept reminding them I wasn't a good bet, but had a fear of acting in any way that might land me in serious trouble.

The first time I went absent without leave was not something I planned. Indeed, I was packed and at Sheffield station ready to catch the train back to camp on schedule when the urge to miss it occurred. I admit it only took a nudge to persuade me, but if my fellow apprentice hadn't put the thought in my mind I wouldn't have had the courage to act as I did.

The boy was called Joe M. His family came from just outside Sheffield, and I think his father was a soldier who had served with distinction. Joe, however, was not really cut out for the army, but, unlike me, he wasn't particularly set on leaving. He was simply an easy-going lad who was full of devilment, and he seemed to fancy the idea of going AWOL. 'What's tha say, shall we not go back, eh?' he asked. 'Come on, let's bugger off somewhere.' Before I knew it, we were on a bus to the outskirts of Sheffield, and thumbing a lift to I don't know where.

I think we travelled via London and ended up in Bristol, settling into digs in a lodging house which faced on to the river. We both got fixed up with jobs, and, ironically, mine was in a newspaper office. As I recall, I was put in the circulation department, and, as one of my duties was making plates for new subscribers, I couldn't resist using one quiet period to add the names and addresses of a few Sheffield friends to the list. They must have spent the next few weeks wondering why they were getting a Bristol newspaper through the post!

However, I was uncomfortable in the lodgings. The accommodation was very basic, and I couldn't stomach the food. So, after collecting my first wage at the end of the first week, I told Joe I was moving on. Joe, who had landed himself a decent job in an office, said he preferred to stay. He was destined to remain there for about three months before the army tracked him down.

I hadn't a clue what to do next, but found myself in Torquay with just enough money to get lodgings for a week. When that was over, I simply thumbed my way back to Sheffield – and, as you might expect, I hadn't been home long when there was a knock on the door. The police had come looking for me, and promptly arranged my collection by two burly Military Police 'redcaps'. After being AWOL for about fourteen days, I returned to Harrogate in disgrace.

I was hauled before the camp commandant, a distinguished military figure called Colonel J.P. Carne (he had won the VC while serving with the Gloucestershire Regiment), and, while listening patiently to my tearful plea for an early release from the army, he still sentenced me to seven days detention in the guardroom. I had my first taste of life under lock and key, and it was certainly an experience – though, apart from having my hair cropped very short and being marched everywhere at the double, it was not half as bad as I had feared.

I didn't run away again during my time at Harrogate, though I was tempted to do so on one occasion. Indeed, I actually walked out late at night and had got halfway down Penny Pot Lane when heavy rain started to fall. I went into the camp church for shelter, ended up sleeping there, and, just before dawn, crept back into the barracks and pretended I had never been away.

After moving to Blackdown, I spent exactly 56 days in the small REME attachment before the army finally decided I could leave, and, in that time, I had a few weeks in the boxing team, produced a camp magazine, and made a fairly good impression as a pupil if not as a soldier. It was a short but eventful phase.

The officer in the Education Corps who took us for English was a likeable Yorkshireman, and he and I got along famously from the start. The first time I met him, he was running the camp library, and was impressed when I chose to borrow a novel called *Sorrel and Son* by Warwick Deeping. 'Not the sort of book you expect a boy soldier to choose,' he said.

We ended up discussing writing and journalism, and I remember the conversation because he was the first person who ever mentioned J. B. Priestley to me. Priestley, he said, was a good model for a would-be author. I didn't know then that, within ten years, I would have the experience of interviewing Priestley then write a piece which earned the praise of a man who was one of the greatest literary all-rounders of his generation.

The officer took an interest in the essays I produced in class, and, keen to make an impression, I deliberately produced pieces which were certainly different from anything he can have expected. Unfortunately, I rather shocked him one day when I wrote a 'mock' letter to the editor of the *Daily Mirror* purporting to be from a boy who was being kept in the army against his will. Nobody believed I didn't intend to post it – and I was hauled up on a misconduct charge!

It just so happened that, a week or two later, I got a message to say my mother had broken her arm. I made an application for compassionate leave, and, when this was refused, I decided the time had come to go AWOL again. Thumbing a succession of lifts, I had got as far as just north of London on the A1 when a quick-eyed policeman stopped me. By the next morning, I was back at Blackdown.

I must have spoken with great eloquence when I faced the Commanding Officer, for he decided to give me only nominal punishment. In fact, he listened with great patience as I poured out my heart and told him how desperately I wanted to leave the army – and he promised to look into the matter. 'After all,' he said with a faint smile, 'we don't want you writing to the newspapers again, do we?'

The upshot was that within a week I had been sent for a medical examination and a long discussion with a doctor, and, soon afterwards, the news came through that I had been granted a discharge. In the circumstances, the Commanding Officer said, I wouldn't qualify for a free civilian suit, but I didn't care, and I used up what little money I had to buy a jacket and flannels from a barrack-room colleague.

I owned only the clothes I stood up in when I left Blackdown, and shabby and inadequate they were; but, with a rail voucher in my pocket and just enough cash to pay for a meal on the journey, I savoured the moment when a bus-ride into Aldershot signalled the first step to freedom.

I was warned that, within six months, I would almost certainly be called up for National Service and find myself in khaki once again, and that knowledge may explain why I was subsequently haunted for years by regular dreams of being forced back in the army. In the event, and thankfully, they chose to write me off as a permanent loss.

Sheffield, when I returned, hardly proved the panacea I probably hoped for but was wise enough not to expect. However, what mattered then was being where I felt I belonged, because I knew I would adapt to whatever problems there were at home with a resilience and determination I had been unable to muster in the army. For better or worse, this was where my heart was – and where I wanted to be.

Home Again

I CAME out of the army in late November 1955 with a testimonial which described me as 'a pleasant lad who is inclined to be too quiet and reserved, but he has a natural flair for writing, and, with good tuition, should eventually do well as a reporter.' Unfortunately, as this wasn't backed up with any qualifications in English, the encouraging and perceptive remarks of my last commanding officer were not enough to gain me a foothold in journalism. So, after a tour of the editorial rooms of several local newspapers failed to prompt any positive reaction, I settled for a job as a clerk in a coal merchant's office.

I spent about a year working for a firm called W. H. Hewitt & Co, a family business run by Ted Noon and his son Len, and based at the far end of a row of single-storey buildings which have long since disappeared but for many years stood just inside the entrance to the old Queen's Road railway coal depot. There were probably six or seven firms on the site, which was similar to one which then existed in the Canal Wharf area opposite Victoria Station, and, throughout the day, a succession of lorries were loaded in the sidings from waggons fresh from several local collieries.

My work was fairly simple and involved writing out delivery slips, helping to keep the books, and generally making myself useful. I learned about the different grades of coal, pricing, how to transfer details of deliveries and payments due into a range of registers which related to different areas, etc. Later, I helped with collecting payments, and calling on housewives in the St Mary's area was an intriguing experience because I felt sure I would gather rich material for future novels!

Ted reminded me of Clem Ambler, my boss at CWS (Scales), in that he, too, was a veteran in his trade, rather serious, and a chain smoker. White-haired and somewhat severe-looking at first glance, he was, in fact, a kindly chap, and, as I was suited to the work and made a better impression on Ted than I had on old Clem, he quickly warmed to me.

Ted's great enthusiasm every lunchtime was the card game he played with a man called Constantine, who was boss of an adjoining office. Ted's pal, incidentally, always seemed to me rather posh for a coal merchant, as did another neighbour called Styring. Anyway, to listen to Ted and his pal reminiscing and discussing trade and other matters while coughing and spluttering over their cigarettes and studying the cards provided an amusing and instructive interlude.

It was a tiny office divided into two sections, and the desk at which Ted worked and played cards was in the front part, where it faced a grate in which a welcome coal-fire invariably blazed. It was a cosy place, pleasant and easy-going. Indeed, the only moments of drama I recall were on occasions when news arrived that a neighbouring firm's driver had been caught 'on the fiddle' by the Weights and Measures man.

Converting a load of forty one-hundredweight bags into 42 or 43 was not difficult, and selling the extra bags meant the bonus of a few quid for the driver and his mate. Unfortunately, to be found 'fiddling', and especially giving short measure to 'proper' customers in the process, inevitably led to instant dismissal. The implications were brought home to me one day when one of Hewitt's men returned shamefaced to admit he'd been 'nabbed' by the man from the Town Hall.

Ted and his son were both keen on football and cricket, and, in the summer, by when he felt able to leave me in charge, Ted would occasionally take time off to watch Yorkshire when they played at Bramall Lane. If things were rather quiet in the office (and I never remember it being hectic), he would sometimes return at about four o'clock, give me his member's ticket and tell me to push off and watch the last couple of hours of the day's play at the Lane. It was quite a novelty being able to view games from the pavilion for the first time.

I imagine Ted had once been an employee of the firm, and then acquired the business when his boss retired; and, by 1956, he and Len had diversified into a drapery and check operation. It made sense, for they had a ready-made clientele with so many coal customers, and Len, who was a jolly and affable man then in his thirties, had exactly the right blend of enthusiasm and personality to ensure the new venture succeeded.

Len, incidentally, was just starting to use his spare time to develop a solo comedy act with which, under the name of Len Norton, he went on to establish a big reputation on the local club and entertainment circuit. He was a large man, but his was a gentle humour based on human frailty and tending towards slapstick, and it was hilarious to watch him try out a new routine as a vicar delivering a sermon in which he got his words and phrases in a tangle.

Indeed, the way he loved to put a smile on faces in an audience said a lot about the type of man he was, for he was never happier than when making others laugh in everyday life. He didn't go around cracking jokes, for that was not his style, but he had a sense of humour which grew out of situations and somehow expressed his instinctive kindness and consideration for others.

When, late in life, he suffered an illness which caused him to lose his legs, it was a fate he did not deserve; but, typically, he faced the misfortune with courage, humour and a total lack of self-pity. Remembering him from the old days, it was a moving experience for me one day in the 1990s to watch unobserved as he battled his way up the stand at Bramall Lane, showing a determination to continue to watch his beloved

Sheffield United when many in similar circumstances would have given in and stayed at home.

As you might expect, Len took a keen interest in my welfare, and, when it emerged that my situation at Bramber Street was far from ideal, he arranged a move into lodgings not far from the office. It remains a source of regret that, for a variety of reasons, I did not stay in those digs for long, and Len's disappointment was compounded when my career at Hewitt's was curtailed just as I was becoming really useful.

* * * *

When I left the army and moved in at 39 Bramber Street, it was soon evident that things were not working out for my parents. Mother spent as little time as possible at home, and, when my father discovered that her regular visits to 'Our Charlotte's' were pure fiction because in reality she was continuing to see Ernest Thornhill, the atmosphere at home took a dramatic turn for the worse. The pair didn't simply argue, they seemed to be always shouting at each other, and, on Saturday and Sunday nights, when my father had been in the pub, their fall-outs invariably erupted into rather more than verbal violence.

It was a sickening experience to see them tangle, try to separate them, and watch my mother run out into the street in search of a policeman. Pots and pans would often fly across the living room, and to say the situation was crazy would be an understatement. On one unforgettable occasion, taking my mother's side in one dispute and trying to prevent my father reaching her, I picked up a bottle of Henderson's Relish from the table and hit him over the head. The bottle smashed, and he ended up covered in relish. Astonishingly, he didn't bat an eyelid (perhaps because too much beer had dulled his reactions) and even had the wit to suggest his blood had turned a funny colour!

Only later did I realise I could have done him a serious injury, and, not for the first time in that spell, I wept in sheer frustration at the hopelessness of the way things were.

The problem I found with my father at this time, and for some years to come, was an inability to engage in a discussion which made any sense. Somehow, he turned everything into a joke, and, when I look back, I feel perhaps it was the only way he could cope with the reality of a situation he knew we children could not understand.

Just to add to the misery, my parents' most furious domestic battles always seemed to coincide with occasions when Grandfather Johnstone had returned from the pub too drunk to assist in restoring order. After my grandmother's death, old Billy simply went to pieces and it was almost as if he couldn't drink himself to death quickly enough. He would sit for hours, still in his street coat and white muffler, staring at the living room wall with glazed eyes and the demeanour of a man in deep despair.

You were never quite sure what disaster might befall him next, for he was always dropping cups and plates. One night he interrupted a typically fierce row by falling down the stairs and bouncing straight into the room, collapsing in a heap at my father's feet. It didn't help that he had been carrying a full slop bucket from his bedroom at the time! The tragi-comedy that moment represented prompted me to decide I risked going insane if I remained in the house for much longer.

Mother had already said she would leave as soon as she could find some place that could accommodate me and my sisters as well as herself, and it made sense if I eased her search by finding my own digs. I didn't tell Len Noon all the gory details, but, when I explained my situation, he made some inquiries and soon alerted me to lodgings that were available at 185 Clough Road, the home of an elderly widow called Mrs Headford.

It was another development which might have been a major turning point, and the experience of moving into lodgings and, in a sense, becoming my own master even though not yet eighteen years old, was something I savoured. I took to it very well, but, in the long term, it didn't work out because I was soon living beyond my very modest means.

I cannot honestly remember what I was then earning, but it was certainly less than £3 a week. When I was first taken in by Mrs Headford, she charged me 30s (£1.50) for board and lodgings, but this was subsequently reduced after she switched me into the smaller of her downstairs rooms so she could accommodate a young couple, and we mutually agreed it would be preferable if I just paid rent and provided my own food.

I was still very young and immature, but being independent induced me to believe that, overnight, I had grown up and could live as if I were a man of means. At the time, I was just into the works of Somerset Maugham, and, influenced by novels like *Of Human Bondage, Cakes and Ale* and *A Writer's Notebook*, I imagined that, as Maugham had started out in a rented room, my destiny, too, was that of the literary man.

As a symbol of my new status, I remember buying a trilby because I wanted to look older, and, for the same reason, I also tried smoking a pipe. In truth, I always looked much younger than my years, and, rather than ageing me, wearing a hat merely emphasised my youthfulness. As for the pipe, hard as I tried, I couldn't take to something that made me feel poorly, and was soon back on cigarettes.

I wanted to wear good clothes, eat well, and get out and see life, acquiring knowledge, experience and a few social accomplishments in the process. Len Noon arranged for me to buy a new suit and some quality shoes on hire purchase, and much of my spare cash went on weekly visits to a dancing class, the theatre and at least one football match. Being a Saturday night regular at the Empire Theatre in Charles Street seemed then the height of sophistication, and to pop into Marsden's Milk Bar before the show, and, later, to round off the evening with a coffee and a read from *Books and Bookmen* led me to believe I was a J. B. Priestley in the making!

I wasn't really a gadabout, and most of my evenings were spent in my room, where, having invested in an ICS correspondence course in journalism, I attempted to study. The influence of Arnold Bennett's *How to Live on 24 Hours a Day* and similar self-improvement manuals was evident in my dedication to keeping a diary and plotting a course of study which I was sure would turn me into a brilliant author within a few months. My trouble, perhaps, was in believing I had already arrived when I had barely started; and, if I am honest, there was probably a sense in which, because there was nobody to point me in the right direction, I was unable to face up to the reality of what effort was necessary to get where I wanted to be.

However, at the time, the correspondence course was probably the best thing I could have invested in, for it gave me a focus and ensured I wrote something most days, even though much of what I produced reflected my immaturity and lack of awareness. I knocked off everything from letters to editors and small items intended to earn me half-a-guinea (52½p), to full-blown short stories that might bring in several pounds. I spent a fortune in postage sending them to magazines and periodicals – convinced the 'big' breakthrough and the first step to fame lay just around the corner, when a regular spate of rejection slips said the opposite.

I got into hot water with Ted Noon when my anxiety to impress editors prompted me to put the firm's telephone number on my notepaper. When Ted Hart, sports editor of a national weekly called the *Weekend Mail*, unexpectedly responded to some pieces I had sent by ringing for some urgent material on a Wednesday idol called Albert Quixall, my excitement at gaining recognition was tempered by my boss's inquiry about how the paper knew where to reach me at work. Ted asked if I was contemplating taking up journalism full time, and he wasn't impressed by my cheek in using the firm's facilities!

When I earned £12, a sum equal to four weeks' wages, from the *Weekend Mail* for providing just a few facts and figures, I felt as if I had won the pools; but, in fact, that was just about the only money my efforts brought in. The idea of buying lots of magazines for market study didn't really prove a good one, for the outlay ultimately added to my financial embarrassment.

My inability to manage my small income led me into a number of difficulties. I hadn't the sense to recognise the need to avoid buying things that were not absolutely essential, and when, halfway through a week, I started finding myself without the funds to buy food – and getting a sub in advance of pay-day became a habit which only worsened the situation – I knew something would have to be done.

I knew that, even with restraint, it would continue to be difficult to live on my own until I was able to earn a man's wage, and, when I learned that my mother and Ernest Thornhill had found lodgings where I could be accommodated, I saw it as at least a temporary solution. It seemed to make sense to put my venture into independence in abeyance.

As it happened, the reversal of my domestic circumstances coincided with a decision to seek a job which I felt might aid my attempts to improve my writing, and, though I quit Hewitt's with reluctance, I felt I had taken a step in the right direction by obtaining a position as a correspondence clerk at Hadfield's East Hecla steelworks.

Teenager About Town

THE second half of the 1950s, or, to be more precise, the period between my departure from the army in late 1955 and just after my 21st birthday in May 1959, was an eventful, up-and-down phase during which I suppose I was searching for a kind of self-discovery and seeking, not without impatience, to graduate from late adolescence into full maturity.

The irony was that while I desperately wanted to grow up quickly I looked and in many ways acted much younger than my years, and being somewhat over-serious with a tendency towards introspection no doubt emphasised my immaturity. Yet, if there was a sense in which I wished to by-pass the last of my teenage years, it didn't prevent me from embracing them with enthusiasm, and, looking back, there is much about the period that I recall with affectionate nostalgia. They were years during which I made many mistakes but enjoyed myself nevertheless.

It is a wonderful stage in one's life, for the world suddenly opens up and you feel a sense of freedom and become conscious of what seem unlimited possibilities. It doesn't matter that the majority of your dreams will always remain beyond your reach, for somehow you believe that, whatever your present circumstances, something good and exciting beckons from just beyond the horizon.

If, when I was eighteen, anyone had asked me what I hoped to get from life, I would have said all I wanted was a career that had some connection with writing and, ultimately, a settled marriage which promised comfort and contentment. Of course, fame would be welcome because one imagined then that it would guarantee wealth, but the things I craved more than anything were not unlimited financial resources, but simply professional and personal security and stability.

Around the time when I was living at Clough Road and getting my first taste of independence, I felt an essential part of the process of equipping myself to become a writer or author was to get out and about – to 'see a bit of life' and meet people. I had no great desire to go off and travel the world, for I believed it was just as easy to embrace the university of life in familiar surroundings – and far more convenient. Perhaps the fact that a weekly visit to the theatre seemed a peak of sophistication speaks volumes about the limits of my knowledge and experience, but, if I was unaware of restrictions resulting from an inadequate education and a lack of understanding of what might be possible with greater ambition, the route I was taking was harmless – and at least it pointed in the right direction.

In fact, the theatre then meant little more to me than regular trips to enjoy variety shows at the Empire in Charles Street. It was not until two or three years later that I discovered the pleasures of playgoing when, quite by chance, I dropped in on a Sheffield Repertory production of an Arthur Miller play at the Playhouse in Townhead Street – and found myself wanting to keep going back for more. Yet even then, when it came to drama I still felt a good film took some beating.

It may have been J. B. Priestley, one of my great literary heroes, who influenced me to look to the variety theatre, for he wrote several essays about some of the great comedians and other entertainers of his own youth. Priestley, of course, was the author of some outstanding plays, but, at this particular point in my life, I was bowled over by the wonder he conveyed in his pieces about the magic of the old music halls – and wanted to experience my own version of that magic. I was, after all, still the essential romantic.

If my viewpoint seems somewhat naive in hindsight, you have to remember that my attempts at self-education were based solely on reading, most of which was haphazard. It was by accident rather than design that I found some good models among my favourite authors, but I lacked the instruction, guidance and intellectual company to develop a critical approach which might have enhanced my progress. It is as if I was looking in the right direction without really seeing or understanding, but didn't know this was so because I wasn't conscious of the need for interpretation. There is a difference between knowledge and understanding.

It was not long after the Clough Road phase that my sister Pat persuaded me to do something you might have thought I would not have needed telling. She urged me to attend evening classes with a view to gaining a GCE (General Certificate of Education) in one or two subjects. I did so, soon obtained an 'O' level in English which remains my only formal qualification, but, ironically, failed in English Literature through a lack of concentration – although one benefit of the class I attended was discovering Shakespeare and consciously starting to work my way through the plays. Being able to quote from memory large chunks of *Macbeth* and *Julius Caesar* did not make me more mature, but it gave me a lot of pleasure.

There was a sense in which my self-education was too casual, without direction or design, and I have never ceased to regret not making greater effort and allowing myself to be distracted. It was as if I stumbled along and, every now and then, fell upon something which added to the sum total of my knowledge – and, by some miracle, I was eventually equipped to pursue the career I wanted, though not with the ability and confidence that I might have enjoyed in other circumstances.

An old second-hand bookstall in the Norfolk Market, which then stood at the corner of Exchange Street and the Haymarket, was one of my favourite haunts, and the sort of book which I occasionally discovered and devoured with profit was a slim volume called *Cobbett's English Grammar*, which cost me sixpence. I was aware of the merits of this book simply because Howard Spring, in his autobiography, had revealed how he had used Cobbett's letters to his son to teach himself the elements of grammar. I gladly followed Spring's example.

I wasn't as successful in following Spring's lead and mastering shorthand, and can now admit that, when I did eventually get into journalism, I somehow managed to get by with only a modest grasp of the subject – though I shall always feel not being able to write shorthand was one of the two major handicaps which limited my later progress. The other was an inability to drive – a talent which, perhaps as a consequence of my background, I never showed the slightest desire to acquire. At least I took on board Spring's practice of keeping a notebook as an essential habit of the would-be writer, recording all manner of reflections at random.

Unfortunately, the notebooks I kept so religiously in the Clough Road days have long since disappeared, but I imagine I sketched a few lines about seeing the likes of singers Jimmy Young, Lita Rosa, Gary Miller and Ruby Murray at the Empire, and probably made a point of writing something about the thrill of watching G. H. Elliott, the veteran Chocolate Coloured Coon, 'in the flesh' on what was his final tour of the Moss Empire circuit. Maybe I also noted my only experience of seeing a Scottish comedian called Chic Murray, who captured my imagination with what I felt was a simple but hilarious style of humour. Murray's wit was typified in the tale he told of arriving at a night club to find a notice reading 'Dogs must be carried', and turning to his colleague to ask: 'Where the devil can I find a dog at this time of night?'

* * * *

I didn't have much money then, and, as is recorded elsewhere, found it difficult not to live beyond my means. In this context, it didn't take much for me to be persuaded that, even though I couldn't afford it, a record player (they were then all the rage) was an essential addition to the comfort of my lodgings – and, of course, once that had been acquired on hire purchase, it was necessary to start building a record collection.

Long-playing 33rpm 'unbreakable' records with ten and twelve tracks were then starting to enjoy popularity, but my limited resources prompted me to settle for buying 78rpm discs on my calls at Cann's in Dixon Lane. Like scores of other teenagers who visited 'Cann the Music Man' on Saturday mornings in those days, I could never wait until I got home for my first listen to a new purchase, and always insisted on hearing it in one of the shop cubicles before leaving.

In my short Clough Road spell, I doubt if I owned more than a dozen records, but every one was precious and special in a way only the youngster I then was could appreciate. At the time, I was crackers about Al Jolson, so the majority in my initial collection were his, and I especially revelled in discovering and learning by heart the lesser-known songs on the 'flip' sides of the records. Ah, the joys of such innocent pleasures!

However, like most of my contemporaries, I was also attracted to songs that were in the current hit parade. Much to my landlady's dismay, I played over and over again, and long into the night, such 'noisy' records as Bill Haley's *Rock Around the Clock*, Tommy Steele's *Singing the Blues* and Elvis Presley's *Heartbreak Hotel* – a memory which reminds me that, while I had a personal preference for Frank Sinatra, Nat King Cole and other 'vintage' performers, this was a phase in which trends in popular music reflected changes that were occurring in life at large.

Yet, if things were happening which marked the beginning of a new era that would influence all areas of society, this was still a time when pubs, theatres and cinemas were the main areas in which the majority sought entertainment – and, in terms of meeting girls, the best place for lads of my generation remained the dance halls.

I had this notion that, if I once met the 'right' lass, my world would be transformed, and I could begin to move towards my ideal of a settled domestic situation and an environment in which my career would 'take off'. I'm not saying that, at eighteen, I was aspiring to an early marriage, for my financial status put that prospect well beyond my reach; but I did rather feel that some regular female companionship might be more than welcome, not least in terms of boosting my confidence and self-esteem.

The first challenge, of course, was to learn to dance, or, at least, to acquire sufficient mastery of the intricacies of the waltz, the quickstep and the foxtrot to be able to shuffle round a ballroom. It was a quest which led me to a place where I passed many happy hours over the next couple of years – Alfred Gold's dancing studio.

Alfred's place was a fairly small, low-ceilinged room on the top floor of premises in St Paul's Parade, overlooking the old Peace Gardens and the Town Hall. We danced to nothing more than a succession of 78rpm records, mostly current hits, but, in that spell, it was a haven of happiness for me every Friday evening. The night when I climbed what seemed a hundred steps to reach Alfred's place could never come round quickly enough.

More than forty years later, I never hear those long-forgotten hits of 1956, *It's Almost Tomorrow* by The Dreamweavers and *Rock and Roll Waltz* by Kay Starr, without being reminded of Alfred Gold's, for they were always Alfred's choices for the final waltzes of the evening, when there was always a rush to have one last dance with the girl you liked best.

Frankly, I didn't have much luck with the girls I met at those Friday sessions, largely because I tended to be too serious and probably scared them off. I lacked the knack of being relaxed about the business of making a good impression, and envied those lads for whom it all looked so easy to say exactly the right thing.

There was one dark-haired girl for whom I carried a torch for months. Her name was Jean, and she seemed ideal because she was very attractive and intelligent, and we got along very well. When I learned she was attending college and training to be a teacher, I couldn't believe my luck, because that suggested she might appreciate my literary aspirations. Alas, she always declined my requests for a date, and while I tried to win her over with a succession of letters to which she always replied at length, it was soon obvious that I was wasting my time.

She raised my hopes just once when, out of the blue, she wrote to invite me to partner her in a foursome on a cinema trip, then dashed my dreams by insisting I was only making up the number to ensure she wasn't a wallflower in the company of a college pal and her boyfriend. Such were codes of conduct then, I didn't even get a 'thank you' kiss!

It was during this phase that I met up with two lads I had known, albeit only slightly, at Burngreave. Ken Chambers and Keith Armitage had been a year behind me in school, and we now formed a trio and spent the next few months making a regular weekend tour of every dance hall in the region. Those were the days when Saturday evening offered the choice of the City Hall or the Cutlers Hall in Sheffield, such places as the Embassy Ballroom in the suburbs, and the Clifton Hall in Rotherham. We became familiar with them all.

This was also a time when most of the leading firms in Sheffield invariably held annual dances, and the three of us welcomed the change in routine offered by these occasions. Somehow, they always seemed rather more up-market than the usual gig, and it helped when there were so many people around whom you knew. I had Ken and Keith as my guests at Hadfields' dance in the Cutlers' Hall – where, incidentally, they used to have modern dancing in the large upper hall, and Old Time in the Hadfield Room downstairs.

It all seemed so 'classy'…and, if you chose your moment, you could even get yourself on the group photograph which invariably appeared in the local evening paper on the following day!

Ken and Keith, who both then lived just off Grimesthorpe Road, were the only regular mates I had in my teenage years, and the phase in which we went about calling ourselves 'the Three K's' didn't really last all that long, for Ken soon met a girl and started courting seriously. My pals were both engineering apprentices, bright, intelligent and steady young men. We were all different in personality, but still had much in common, and I appreciated their friendship because it came at just the right time to encourage me to extend my social life. I doubt if I would have visited those dance halls alone.

We were all sober lads with simple, innocent tastes, and it didn't take much to make us feel we had had a good night out. If we drank, our intake was modest, and, if the bands, the venues and the girls seldom proved anything to get excited about, we enjoyed ourselves – and even got some fun out of missing the last bus (trams disappeared from Sheffield streets in 1960 and did not reappear until the coming of the Supertram in the 1990s) and facing a long walk to get home on a frosty night. It was better than spending every night in a pub, which was something I had tried and, unlike my parents, found less than satisfying.

My friendship with Ken and Keith coincided with an eventful spell at home, for, after leaving Clough Road, I lived for a time with my mother in lodgings at Fox Street, then, briefly, following the death of Grandfather Johnstone, we moved back to join my father at Bramber Street before the impending demolition of the house saw us end up in another part of Pitsmoor at Rising Street. Moreover, in a period which spanned barely three years, I also managed to work my way through a string of different jobs and occupations!

A Clerk's Progress

OCCUPATIONAL variety was certainly the name of the game for me between the late summer of 1956 and the early autumn of 1959. In three years I had four different clerical jobs, and, as well as making two unsuccessful attempts to settle into the role of hotel porter, I had a brief spell working in a city-centre tailor's shop – and even spent occasional weekends selling ice-cream on one of Walls' three-wheel stop-me-and-buy-one bikes!

Those were the days when there was no shortage of work, and all areas of local industry were booming. Every day the local evening paper carried page after page of situations vacant, and a man could walk out of a job one day and step straight into another the following morning.

I was a good clerk, and, whether dealing with correspondence or some form of accounts, it never seemed difficult to pick up the routine and master whatever task I was given. In truth, some were dead-end jobs without prospects, for I could not believe promotion to chief clerk or something similar after waiting one's turn for ten or fifteen years ranked as a major achievement. One or two jobs might have led to something more rewarding, but, while the majority promised security, a 'job for life' seemed to add up to a lifetime without real incentive and variety. Whenever I paid a return visit to an old office after twenty years or so, it was invariably good to see familiar faces again, but the places always appeared so much duller than I remembered, and I marvelled how anyone could endure the same environment and exactly the same job for so long.

Moreover, when I look back, I often ponder on what might have happened had I remained in that type of work for the next twenty years or so. As most of the firms in which I was employed either no longer exist or have since changed beyond recognition, it is difficult to believe I could have made a decent living at that level in the longer term, and it would have required a huge slice of luck to have survived the effects of a succession of dips in trade and the many takeovers and closures that subsequently occurred in every area of local industry. So much for job security! The problem for many of those who stayed loyal to one firm was their working world collapsed just when the passage of time had stranded them beyond a point when they could change direction.

So far as I recall, there were no schemes then by which clerks could be trained to progress into genuinely senior management positions. Most clerks wouldn't have been in the role anyway if they had the qualifications to start higher up the ladder or in a position offering greater opportunity, and the majority were expected to remain in the same job indefinitely. There was a sense in which blind loyalty and a lack of ambition were hailed as sterling qualities, and it always seemed the route to something better was largely a matter of luck.

At some small or medium-sized firms, of course, there was always the possibility of being spotted by the owner or boss and being plucked from obscurity and groomed for a key role. No doubt many a youngster's career enjoyed a sudden upturn because the chairman took a shine to him, but, even then, progress invariably demanded commitment which meant 'living for the job'. Such an opportunity never came my way, but this may have been because I was only prepared to give a company my heart and not my soul. I lacked the patience and inclination to want to impress the boss by hanging around a factory after hours.

At a couple of firms, there was some talk of my being switched to a sales representative's role in the longer term, and, with this in view, plans to teach me to drive were mooted. Nothing developed from these suggestions largely because I lost patience when they kept deferring a final decision – though, if I'm honest, I knew I wasn't cut out to be a salesman.

However, the chance to learn to drive would surely have had long-term benefits. I didn't realise then what an asset the ability would be. Frankly, owning a car was not an ambition, and, anyway, in those days I used to think I could never afford it. Like a lot of people of my generation and background, I didn't have the slightest inclination to want to drive, and, perhaps because nobody in our immediate family had a car or showed any interest in them, you might even say my mind was closed to the possibilities of ever having my own transport. Not until many years later (by which time almost everyone considered a car essential) did I regret an attitude that left me with a self-inflicted handicap which hindered my hopes of journalistic progress.

* * * *

The thing I remember most about the clerical jobs I held in the late 1950s was the contrasting conditions and circumstances at the different firms. One day I would be working in a comfortable, well-furnished office at a company which provided a range of facilities for its employees, and the next I might find myself in some pokey backroom or makeshift place at a firm where there was nothing for the staff but somewhere to sit and fulfil their duties – nowhere away from the job to eat one's sandwiches, and not even a decent toilet.

After the cramped, one-room premises at Hewitt's, going to Hadfields was like stepping into another world. This was one of the biggest and most famous steel firms in Sheffield, and when I walked into their East Hecla offices in the autumn of 1956 they seemed so imposing and palatial – what luxurious working conditions! I had never previously been inside a firm which boasted so many different offices and such extensive workshops, and the sheer size of the operation was overwhelming.

I was even more impressed when I saw the works' catering facilities. It was not so much that the dining rooms were more 'restaurant' than 'canteen', but, with different areas for various grades of staff as well as workmen, this place alone was ten times larger than any office in which I had ever worked. If I am not mistaken, the meal prices were subsidised, and this was another example of the sort of supplementary benefits employees enjoyed at big firms like Hadfields.

Incidentally, one reached the dining rooms up some outside steps, and I have a painful memory of those steps because, in my first week, I made the mistake of running up them with my hands in my pockets. Unfortunately, it had been raining, I slipped on a wet patch, and ended up breaking three of my front teeth. It was three years before I plucked up the courage to have them removed and false teeth fitted so I could smile properly again!

An abiding memory of my time at Hadfields is of the long queue of tramcars that awaited the departure of the staff from the premises every day at around five o'clock. In the previous hour, a similar battalion of trams had shipped hundreds of workmen home at the end of their shift, and, no matter what the time of day or night, there always seemed to be abundant public transport on hand. I have not forgotten, either, that, when I arrived in the mornings, there were so many people dropping off trams and heading for the main gate, it was just like going to a football match!

I didn't recognise the fact then, but in 1956 I was witnessing the final stages of an era in local public transport in that the trams were soon to disappear from Sheffield's streets. Not for much longer would those 'stately galleons of the road' surge and sway through the morning and evening gloom, carrying us to and from work. It was always intriguing to see a tram turn into Vulcan Road, and watch the driver move from the front to the back platform, then switch his vehicle into the city-bound tracks. In the meantime, the conductor reversed all the seats in the upper and lower decks.

A group of us who caught the same tram always preferred to sit in the front bay of the upper deck, first because it was a place where we could stay together and converse during the journey, but also because there was something satisfying about savouring the full 'roll' of the tram and enjoying such a vantage point as we sailed along the Lower Don Valley.

Today, at the end of the 1990s, the site once occupied by Hadfields forms part of the famous Meadowhall Shopping Complex alongside the M1 Tinsley Viaduct, but forty years ago it was impossible to imagine such a transformation. The firm's workshops and offices seemed to stretch for miles, and the place was so important and had been such an integral part of so many people's lives for so long that nobody could believe it might one day cease to exist.

Everything about the place appeared so august, so solid, so steeped in tradition and respect, and I'm sure the majority of those who worked at East Hecla believed they had a job for life – and took great pride in belonging to such a famous organisation. People didn't just work there, for many employees belonged to at least one of the sports or social sections, and events like the annual dance at the Cutlers' Hall, hailed as one of the great social occasions of the year, enjoyed massive support. The firm was a community.

People seemed to enjoy working at Hadfields, and certainly I remember the Sales 'R' department in which I was employed as a happy, easy-going office in which there never appeared to be any pressure. No doubt it was very efficient and well-organised section, and the place had an atmosphere that might be described as conservative and dignified, but there always seemed time for a chat, and there was a lot of laughter.

I imagine that as there were so many different sales departments, each one handled a specialised range of products, but I have no memory of what we dealt with in Sales 'R'. I only recall that we had regular contact with one of the rolling mill offices, and sometimes I would wander down into the works with an inquiry – an absorbing experience which I invariably prolonged because the sight of red-hot metal being rolled was never less than fascinating.

My job was something to do with answering queries from customers about the delivery of their orders, but all I remember now is the novelty of dictating letters to a shorthand typist. The typing pool, which served all the sales offices, was just down the corridor, and I have never forgotten my first sight of that large room filled with so many attractive young women. Using the internal phone to request a typist made me feel very important, but I lacked the poise to impress the girls when dictating to them!

I was placed under the wing of an older clerk called Mike Williams, and as either he or Jack Bowles, the chief clerk, usually told me what to say in my letters, then checked the finished article, I doubt if I reached a stage when I could do the job without supervision. It wasn't really cost-effective for the firm, but I enjoyed the experience.

I suppose the office I worked in was what we would call open-plan in that it was a huge room which housed two sales departments and perhaps a couple of dozen desks plus all the related paraphernalia of administration such as filing cabinets, bookcases, telephones, wall charts, etc. This, of course, was an era in which all records and statistics were compiled by hand in ledgers and on card indexes, and most offices were cluttered with boxes of documents and files. To an outsider, it might suggest chaos and inefficiency, but somebody always knew where everything could be found.

The clerks each had specialised tasks ranging from documenting simple stock control to estimating complicated prices, and if the majority were essentially laymen with limited technical knowledge of the products, the range of expertise and experience in every office was remarkable. There were many veterans around who might never figure in any formal history of Hadfields, yet the contribution they made, and the wisdom and knowledge these forgotten men brought to their daily tasks, was unique.

As always, I was fascinated by the variety of personalities: from the elderly spinster who sat opposite me and seemed to spend every day patiently ploughing through what seemed a mountain of dispatch sheets, to the portly young clerk, already a confirmed bachelor, whose enthusiasm for the stage was such that he frequently broke off from his work to quote nuggets from the latest Shakespeare or Noel Coward play which he was currently rehearsing with some local amateur dramatic society.

It is invariably the humorous and tragic moments that stick in the memory – like the day I won a small dividend on the pools and lost the friendship of a colleague, and the morning when we were shocked by the sudden death of a fellow clerk.

I cannot now recall the name of the spinster mentioned earlier, but she was a kindly woman whose greying hair and rather reserved, quiet manner disguised a lively and liberal personality. No doubt she had to work to make ends meet, and the job she did was probably boring, but she was the epitome of contentment and seemed prepared to endure the drudgery because she enjoyed the company.

There was one occasion when she prompted me to form a pools syndicate with her and her friend in the department, Mrs Collins. She felt that if I wasn't legally old enough to do the pools, I was obviously familiar with football, understood the mysteries of permutations, and knew how to fill in a coupon. Mrs Collins, a pleasant little woman with blue-rinsed hair, agreed to submit our entry using her name and address.

All went well for a few weeks, with the three of us sharing the cost of a five-shilling entry on the Treble Chance, but then things got complicated when I elected to use the same coupon to have a go on the Three Draws. Neither of the ladies had the slightest clue about what a pools coupon contained or how it worked, but, when I made it plain that my entry was completely separate from our formal arrangement, they seemed to understand.

Alas, when I came up on the Three Draws and a postal order for sixteen shillings arrived on Mrs Collins' doorstep, she couldn't believe she didn't qualify for a share. Happily, our spinster friend understood, but not even her powers of persuasion could prevent Mrs Collins from feeling she'd been cheated and breaking up our syndicate.

One of the most popular and respected clerks in the department was a young man I only remember now as Ken. Then in his early twenties, Ken was a cripple, a victim of polio I believe, but that didn't prevent him from living life to the full. Everyone admired his courage and independence, and especially the way he accepted his handicap with a smile.

It somehow summed up Ken's spirit that, when Lambretta bikes became fashionable as a new form of transport, he acquired one and revelled in the freedom it gave him. When we arrived at the office one morning to learn he had been killed in a road accident on his way to work, it was like a hammer blow, all the more painful because we couldn't understand why it had happened to someone so young, so joyful and so undeserving of such a cruel fate.

Hadfields was a firm at which I might have stayed much longer than was the case, and, while I have forgotten the circumstances in which I left, I suspect my decision was prompted by the opportunity of another job which offered a dramatic increase in my earnings.

Gregory & Taylor, a firm then based in Howard Street and dealing in supplying pumps and similar generating and other equipment to local industry, attracted me because the wage they offered was almost double what Hadfields were paying. The prospect of earning £7 a week was too good to reject, but, in the event, I lasted only a few weeks because the job didn't suit me – and I didn't suit the boss.

The tight little office, squeezed between the shop part of the building and the rows of shelves housing the stock, was uncomfortable and inhibiting, and I knew within hours of starting in the job that it wasn't for me. It didn't help when the boss, a rather self-important, aggressive and decidedly unpleasant little man called Mr Taylor, appeared to take an instant dislike to me.

Every time he arrived on the premises seemed to coincide with a moment when I was temporarily unoccupied and just about to light a cigarette – and, as I didn't take kindly to his Victorian attitude and what I considered unfair verbal abuse, I couldn't resist answering back. I felt he never gave me a chance, and, as in those days you were not expected to argue with the gaffer, we didn't part the best of friends.

* * * *

When I turned my back on Gregory & Taylor, I came up with the notion that my prospects might improve if I looked for something different from office work, and so, before recognising the wisdom of resuming my clerical career, I had a three months spell during which I worked in a tailor's shop and attempted without success to become a porter at a Matlock hotel.

I was still preoccupied with dreams of turning myself into a 'great writer', and one of the reasons I tried these unlikely and unsuitable jobs was because someone suggested an author needed a wide variety of experience of different walks of life –

and it seemed that dealing directly with the public would enable me to meet a lot of 'characters'. One of my favourite authors, Somerset Maugham, said his time as a medical student at a famous London hospital had given him a great insight into human nature, and, while I was not equipped to follow that course, it did seem that shop work might provide some good 'raw material'.

I ended up at the now-forgotten Haymarket branch of Weaver to Wearer, where, for a while, I found the work novel and interesting. The wages were a good deal less than in my previous job, and the position meant having to work every Saturday, but there was the compensation of sharing in the commission paid on weekly sales. Some weeks, thanks largely to the efforts of my workmates, that 'bonus' increased my modest salary by fifty per-cent.

Sadly, I cannot recall the name of a single colleague, but I have not forgotten that the manager, a thin, enthusiastic little chap with small eyes and features, was certainly a 'character'. Immaculately dressed, with a tape measure permanently hanging like a scarf round his neck, he bounced about the shop, fussing over every customer and ending every sentence with the word 'sir'. You felt his eyes were like a cash register because they would shine with excitement after every sale as he calculated how much commission he had just made. That he was more interested in how much a customer would spend than whether the man got what he really wanted left me with a permanent dislike of being called 'sir' by shop assistants.

In quiet periods, the manager kept us busy brushing ready-to-wear jackets and suits, or straightening rolls of cloth, all the time regaling us with stories of his many successes in a long career during which he had started as a junior salesman and gone on to manage several tailoring establishments in the city. Nobody in the firm's history, he contended, had broken more weekly sales records – and you sensed he could prove it with statistics meticulously kept with great pride ever since he started in the business. His achievement meant little to anyone else, but he was a happy man who found fulfilment in his work.

His senior assistant was a younger and larger man whose manner was rather more reserved, but he, too, was a 'natural' salesman, and, as we sat in the stockroom having our morning cup of tea, he was just as boastful as his boss on the subject of his flair for selling. No doubt he soon graduated to managing his own branch.

I was one of three junior salesmen, and both my colleagues were lads who saw their work as a career in which they expected to progress to better things. Working at Weaver to Wearer, it does not seem quite right to say they dressed like dummies out of Burton's window, but the point is they always looked so smart and immaculate in their 'working clothes', while I had to wear my Sunday suit to ensure I looked the part! Except when discussing their social activities and sexual exploits, which, admittedly, was often, my colleagues seemed preoccupied with aspects of the shop and the trade in general. In later years, I often wondered what became of them, and how they were affected by changes and trends which transformed the industry.

I never reached the stage where I was allowed to measure anyone for a suit, but, of course, I assisted the manager when he was measuring up by writing the length of a customer's inside-leg and such statistics in a book as the boss called them out; and I did have the satisfaction of completing some ready-to-wear sales off my own bat.

However, while I enjoyed the challenge, I soon grew bored, and, being on my feet all day, found the job more tiring than expected. Having too much time to think, I soon decided I was ready to move on.

I was then back living with my mother and sisters in lodgings at a large house in Fox Street – just across the road from the top of Macro Street. The house was owned by old Ma Easy from number 78, and while she had originally bought it on instalments as a home for her younger daughter, by now it was occupied by ourselves plus the Uptons, Johnny, Sarah and Jackie, while a young couple rented one of the ground-floor rooms.

In fact, the Uptons only used the place as sleeping quarters, for they spent most of their time at 78, but, unfortunately, they had a habit of arriving in mid-evening and shattering our peace and independence by 'taking over' the living room. Still in his working clothes and unwashed, Johnny would suddenly appear, claim 'his' easy chair by the fire, and, with great deliberation, walk across to the television set and switch it to the opposite channel from the one we were watching.

In this and other small ways, we were made to recognise that we were merely guests in 'their' house, and, while the irritation might seem trivial, our situation was never quite comfortable. Certainly it was better than living at number 78, but the circumstances were nevertheless far from satisfactory, and, having once escaped the Macro Street syndrome, it pained me to be reminded by the Uptons that we were, in a sense, back in a similar trap in which our lives weren't entirely our own. It only added insult to injury that old Johnny's stockinged feet were as smelly as ever!

The situation prompted me to come up with the idea of going off to work as an hotel porter. I had probably been re-reading the now-forgotten Warwick Deeping novel, *Sorrell & Son*, or maybe I had borrowed Arnold Bennett's *Imperial Palace* from the Central Library; but, anyway, when I obtained a job at the New Bath Hotel in Matlock, I packed my case and felt convinced I was off on a great adventure which would finally free me from the frustrations of home.

I lasted exactly two days at Matlock. There was nothing wrong with the hotel or the people. On the second morning, I couldn't resist responding to an overwhelming desire to return to Sheffield, and simply re-packed my case, told the manager I wasn't staying, and made the long walk to the bus station.

In fact, the return to Fox Street was not for long because, within a few months, we were all back with my father at Bramber Street as a consequence of circumstances which included the death of Grandfather Johnstone, an urgent need on my mother's part to find us fresh lodgings, and the fact that my father's wish to negotiate another house switch so he could stay in Pitsmoor required him to be in a 'family' situation rather than living alone.

In the meantime, I returned to clerical work, and the two years I spent at International Twist Drill's Watery Street branch, off Infirmary Road, proved the longest period I had stayed in one job up to that point. My duties were those of an order clerk, dealing mainly with the firm's branches in London, Birmingham and Manchester, and, while the work, which involved taking down orders for a wide range of drills and reamers over the telephone, was dull and unchallenging, I was comfortable and content. Moreover, there were plenty of 'characters' to amuse me.

The manufacturing part of the firm was based two or three miles further up the valley at Claywheels Lane, and Watery Street was essentially a sales and warehouse operation. The entrance, which included a reception and switchboard area run by Madge Gill, plus the offices occupied by sales manager Tony Neill and a sales director called Schindler, were in what had once been a large domestic residence; and at some stage a sales office and an extensive warehouse had been added to the side and back of the original house. The premises no longer exist, and today a modern property in which the Coroner's Court is the centrepiece stands on the site.

The first office in which I was placed was situated in the corner of the lower warehouse. After the luxury of Hadfields, it seemed rather basic, lacking decoration and boasting just two desks and a single telephone, but it was not unpleasant and had the advantage of being off the beaten track, away from the bosses. At least Intal boasted a small staff canteen where the mother of one of the typists cooked a mid-day meal.

The only disadvantage I found in the early weeks was that, to reach my office, one had to walk through the heart of the inspection and packing department, and it took me some time to get used to being stared at by a long line of female packers who seldom allowed anyone to pass without some ribald comment guaranteed to embarrass a self-conscious young man.

In fact, they were a friendly bunch of women, and, once you accepted their humour and constant banter in the spirit intended, it wasn't difficult to gain their respect. 'Sandy', a large, red-haired woman who was the key character in the group and seemed so daunting at the outset, proved to be as soft as a brush once you got to know her.

However, they must have been a handful for Percy Bowers and Lol Dyson, the foremen, to cope with, although, in their different ways, Percy and Lol seemed to take the challenge in their stride. Percy, a dapper little balding man who might have stepped out of an Al Capone film, was often described as 'crafty' by colleagues, but his guile and no-nonsense manner were tools in his psychological armoury. He may have looked tough, but he was an efficient foreman and a friendly colleague, although he never seemed quite as readily receptive or as popular as Lol, who was able to combine an ability to get the job done with a natural friendliness.

There must have been hundreds of Lol Dysons in the industrial warehouses of Sheffield in those days: the sort of man whose enthusiasm was matched by an encyclopaedic knowledge of a company's products and a dedication which was invariably taken for granted. Lol worked for Intal for nearly fifty years until being made redundant at the age of 62. In retirement he suffered three strokes, but, at eighty and despite a memory impaired by ill-health, he was still recalling his Intal days with pride and pleasure.

When I started, my immediate boss was a thick-set, bespectacled clerk called Harry Levitt, who was like no other colleague I had worked with before. Then just turned thirty, he was an aggressive, domineering sort of chap who tended to rule not so much by fear as with impatience and intolerance which sparked occasional bouts of ill-temper. I don't mind admitting he had me in tears more than once, and I wasn't his only victim.

Yet, if he was never a colleague with whom I could feel an affinity, and not someone whose company I would seek away from work, I always felt there was something very human about Harry – if you accepted him for what he was. Harry was perhaps the first man to make me aware of the complexity of human nature.

He was rather boastful, gave the impression of being a bit of a know-all, and tended to be rather ruthless in exploiting weaknesses he found in other people. He was a bit of a bully. Yet he had a soft streak. He could shout at you one minute and tell you a joke the next, and, if you were never quite sure what to expect, I found the best way of winning his respect was to stand up to him.

At the outset, he regaled me with tales of his National Service in the Far East, and, if you took what he said at face value, you would think he had won the war on his own. He did not rise above the rank of corporal, and there was a sense in which I came to feel that two stripes somehow represented the measure of his talents.

Harry was a very able clerk, and a good man to have around in a crisis because he had an instinct for taking control of a situation when others hesitated, but some flaw in his make-up seemed to limit his progress. He probably knew he was not cut out to become a commissioned officer.

It transpired that when I joined Intal, it was thought to be because Harry was in line to become manager of the firm's Birmingham office. In the event, he was passed over for the job, and, typically, Harry was shocked at what he considered the firm's lack of foresight. Later, when a vacancy arose after the chief sales clerk left Watery Street, Harry was again pipped to the post, this time by a junior colleague, and he only got the job some months later when the same colleague left to get married and help run a boarding house in Bridlington.

Harry was also somewhat smutty in that his talk was frequently peppered with sexual references. Most of what he said could be taken with a pinch of salt, but, sadly, he could seldom refrain from getting over-personal, such as when he told a junior colleague who was getting married that his bride would benefit from a pre-wedding night session of 'the Levitt treatment'. One lad who admitted to being upset at learning his wife couldn't have children didn't take kindly to being told by Harry: 'You're not doing it right, lad. Let me come up and service your missus.'

When Levitt was switched to a different office, it was much more enjoyable working alongside another Harry, a younger man called Truelove. The contrast between the two men could not have been greater. Young Harry was, in fact, the man who later pipped his older colleague to the position of chief clerk, and his promotion over Levitt was not surprising, for he was not only capable and less 'pushy', but had the ability to get things done without reducing his staff to tears.

The younger Harry, incidentally, was troubled with ill-health, and this was one reason why he later moved to live at the seaside. There was one occasion when he suddenly collapsed midway through a telephone conversation with the manager of our Manchester branch. The lad was out cold, and I was never more grateful for Harry Levitt's arrival on the scene, and his ability to respond to a crisis.

The place abounded with people whom I looked upon as 'characters' – from a little balding warehouseman called John Coddington who had a spare-time job as a cobbler (he later left to open a shop, departing with the words 'I'm off to start mending broken soles!'), to a distinguished-looking elderly director called Schindler, whose young girl friend was a typist at the firm. The illicit romance between another typist and the office manager, a married man; the mystery of the background of a newly-arrived elderly clerk called Duggie, whose history was plainly less adventurous than the lurid tales of sexual exploits with which he amused us in the works canteen; and the colleague who insisted on signing his correspondence 'George the Second' as if he were a king: it all added up to what I then considered ideal material for the great Sheffield novel I was destined never to write.

Schindler, incidentally, was a kindly fellow who listened with amusement to my talk of becoming a writer, and he was the first person to point me in the direction of the stories of Damon Runyon, who proved an illuminating discovery – all the more so as I discovered he had first made his name as a sports writer.

At the time, however, I was rather taken up with another American short-story writer of an earlier vintage called O.Henry. The tales of O.Henry, which always featured an unexpected twist in the climax, were then being shown on television, with Thomas Mitchell playing the author; and, while the black-and-white films were not really up to much, they captured my imagination.

They inspired a brief phase in which I attempted a few O.Henry-style stories, and even had the cheek to bore some colleagues in an adjoining office with lunchtime renditions of tales I made up as I went along – all the while kidding myself that I was Sheffield's own William Sidney Porter. No wonder some colleagues thought I was plain daft!

Dale Carnegie

ONE evening in the late autumn of 1958 I spotted an advertisement in the local evening paper about a meeting being held at the Grand Hotel to promote a Dale Carnegie course in Sheffield. Being interested in anything that remotely touched upon the subject of self-improvement, I went along out of sheer curiosity – and ended up a star of the show!

At the time the only thing I knew about Dale Carnegie was he was an American and famous as the author of a best-selling book called *How To Win Friends and Influence People*. It was intriguing to think that a course associated with him, promising 'to develop courage and confidence, effective speaking, leadership training, improving the memory and human relationships', was available on my doorstep, and while I didn't expect to get involved, just dropping in to see what it was all about seemed sure to provide an amusing diversion for a couple of hours.

In the event, while the Carnegie experience was hardly a major episode in my life, the link lasted for about two years and contributed to my education. A number of the people with whom I came in contact proved helpful and encouraging, and, modest though my development was during this phase, my horizons were broadened.

The old Grand Hotel, with its main entrance opposite the bottom side of the City Hall, has long since disappeared and been replaced by the Fountain Precinct office complex, but in those days it was a focal point in the social and industrial life of Sheffield. The Grand's only serious local rival then was the Royal Victoria Hotel, and, with the Grosvenor and the Hallam Tower hotels not yet built, it hosted the bulk of the top company and trades association annual dinners in the city – and was a major venue for promotions like the Dale Carnegie event.

To me at the time the Grand was just a posh place which I had only seen from the outside. It didn't figure on my social map, and it was something of a novelty to have an excuse to enter and explore the building. Within a few years, of course, I became familiar with staying in and attending functions at top hotels, and soon took it for granted; but at the age of twenty, it seemed like another world. Just using one of the hotel's cut-glass ash trays made you feel you were mixing in exclusive circles!

The organiser of the Carnegie courses in the north was an energetic and likeable man, then in his late thirties, called Ronnie Grierson. He boasted an experienced background in selling, and had a capacity to perform in public which many an established actor or professional entertainer might have envied. You might say he was an Englishman selling an American culture, and this was my first experience of the 'super-salesman' type, the sort who captured your imagination with his unbounding enthusiasm and a well-rehearsed line of patter which had you absorbing every word – leaving you so convinced about the merits of his product that you knew you would be a fool not to buy.

Don't get me wrong. Ronnie was a genuine guy with a sincere passion for the merits of the course he was selling. But the secret of his success was an ability to produce 'a performance', and I was conscious of the links between what he was doing and the stage when, following a demonstration and after most of the others had left, we had a short conversation during which I felt I was looking at a tired actor minus his make-up. There was an ordinary guy behind the mask. I sensed that working himself up to deliver his 'act' had taken its toll on a man who was remarkably different when he 'switched off' and the adrenalin stopped flowing.

There were about forty men and women in the Leopold room that first evening. Many were experienced businessmen, although the majority were people in promising careers who wanted to enhance their progress. Indeed, some had been sent by their employers. Two or three ran their own successful firms in steel, engineering and building, but others included a schoolteacher, an optician, a Customs and Excise official, a couple of personnel officers from leading local companies, and several salesmen and sales executives. It was the kind of audience you imagined would not be easily persuaded, yet, throughout the two-hour session, Ronnie had them enraptured.

Before the evening was through, Ronnie had us all standing and enthusiastically repeating such axioms as 'ACT enthusiastic and you'll BE enthusiastic!' and 'I know men in the ranks who will stay in the ranks. Why? Simply because they haven't the ability to GET THINGS DONE!' Everyone was punching their right fist into the palm of their left hand as they emphasised each word – and a neutral observer might have thought he was witnessing some religious ceremony!

There were probably few in the audience who were really shy, but all semblance of reserve disappeared when Ronnie had everyone taking turns to entertain with an attempt to play the role of an old man limping across the room crying 'Ah'm a-coming as fast as I can...why Ah is almost a-running now!' If the aim was to ensure everyone was relaxed, it worked a treat.

We were 'hooked' at the outset by Ronnie's short talk on memory training, which he cleverly previewed by inviting everyone in the room to stand up and repeat his or her name. He promptly proved he had memorised every name by identifying us all individually, even though he had not met any of us before. Then he explained the simple technique by which he had remembered forty names. To say it was better than being at the Empire was an understatement. Certainly by the time half-a-dozen members of the audience had tried with varying degrees of success to match Ronnie's record, the room was buzzing with anticipation of good things still to come.

We were then invited to test our ability to speak in public. In relays of four, people stood at the front and each person spoke for one minute about himself. The idea was to explain your work and ambitions, and say what you felt you might gain from taking the course. It lent a novel touch to the event that the audience voted for the best performer in each 'heat', then the winners were invited to deliver a second speech, with the over-all winner getting a Dale Carnegie 'special award for achievement', a propelling pencil.

Remarkably, I was the one who landed the prize, and it probably happened because I spoke with passion about wanting to write for a living. It wasn't an act, I was speaking from the heart, but, if much of what I said was more about romance than reality, my youthful enthusiasm won the hearts of my audience. It was my first experience of public speaking, and, had I gone along expecting to talk to a group of strangers, I might have been too inhibited to make a decent job of it. However, it was one of those occasions when, perhaps because I had nothing to lose and got carried along by the mood of the meeting, facing an audience and expressing my feelings was a challenge I savoured – and it helped not to have had much time to think about what I was doing before I did it.

At the end, I was ready to slip away with my pencil and leave Dale Carnegie to those who could afford the 35 guineas for the fourteen-week course, but Ronnie Grierson, perhaps reacting to the impact I had made, was keen to turn the situation to advantage. When I explained there was no way I could raise £36.15s (£36.75), he announced to the group that I was being offered a unique five-guinea (£5.25p) scholarship – and could pay in ten shilling (50p) instalments. When everyone applauded, I knew they would expect to see me at the first session on the following Tuesday.

It was a change of environment which, in the context of my circumstances and background, proved beneficial, for, apart from trying to absorb the lessons and doing some speaking in public, the experience stretched me as a person at a time when that was just what I needed. I was mixing with people whom I would not normally have met, and, in doing so in a social context, my awareness and confidence improved. At least there was a sense in which I progressed – albeit very slowly.

At that age, one is never fully conscious of what one is picking up and absorbing which might prove essential to one's long-term development. Over the following months, simply joining in some of the social events connected with the course helped 'bring me out'. Then, at the end of the fourteen weeks, when the group decided to form a Dale Carnegie Club and I was asked to serve as its secretary, the duties, though not difficult, got me involved in situations which were a whole new experience. That I was doing something to exercise my brain and test my initiative was better than sitting at home doing nothing but idly dream of 'making the grade'.

Grierson, who soon had me volunteering to assist at subsequent courses in the Grand Hotel, was essentially a realist, and, having listened with patience and amusement to my constant talk of all the great things I was destined to write, he shook me one day with an unexpected question which stopped me in my tracks. 'How much serious writing are you actually doing right now?' he asked. When I admitted the answer was none, he said: 'It's time you stopped talking and started producing – talk is easy, turning what you say you are going to do into reality is rather more difficult. Do you want to end up being someone who always talked about being a writer and never got there?'

I must admit I didn't go straight off and start writing a novel, or even a short-story, and, in truth, I was a bit upset by Ronnie's tone. It hurt to think he had deliberately put me down and was suggesting I was simply a dreamer. However, I recognised the wisdom in his words, took them to heart, and began to make a more conscious effort to produce some 'proper' writing. Doing so was harder than you might imagine, for, while I was reading widely and studying all sort of books on authorship and suchlike, I was still drifting along without much idea of how to hasten my progress.

The situation at home was hardly ideal in terms of providing somewhere to work, and, of course, I didn't possess a typewriter, but environment and circumstances are poor excuses for lack of meaningful endeavour. In fact, I was doing rather a lot of writing, but much of it lacked purpose and self-criticism, and constituted little more than extended notes. Some of that material still survives, but, while it remains useful in reminding me of personal events and episodes I had forgotten, it confirms just how immature I was as a person and shows how desperately I needed guidance in my attempts find a formula to develop my writing.

What progress I did make in the next few years was as much by accident as design, more about luck than planning, but I suppose the important thing was I held on to a dream and blindly inched towards my goal. If my ultimate achievement was comparatively modest, it proved a good deal more than even dear old Ronnie might have predicted, and it's amusing now to recall that much of my motivation then was generated by simple axioms picked up from the Carnegie course. A piece of verse I recall from this spell, for instance, included the lines:

So you've had a raw deal?
I know, but don't squeal,
Don't be a piker, old pard,
Just pull on your grit,

It's easy to quit,

It's the keeping on going that's hard.

You can only take one step at a time, and each step is governed by what stage you have reached at a particular moment. People around you can have an incidental or accidental influence which proves important. For instance, one of my best friends in the Dale Carnegie years, a confectionery salesman called Ken Swindells, said one day he had seen an advertisement for the Sheffield Authors' Club and urged me to join.

The club met every Tuesday in the YWCA library in Division Street, and while the period of my membership, which lasted a couple of years or so, hardly constituted a major turning point, it was, like the Carnegie experience, another small step in the right direction. At least I was persuaded to attempt more short stories and absorbed much useful knowledge from some of my new friends.

Most of the members were women, and while I did soon begin to suspect that one or two were playing at writing rather than being serious about the task, several were regularly getting stories and serials published in leading women's magazines. Unfortunately, the most successful ones were the people who had the least to say, probably because they knew that action speaks louder than words. Yet, when a beginner's story was read to the group, it was illuminating to listen to the criticisms and comments of the professionals.

I suppose the kind of stories most of the women discussed was what might be called formula fiction, when I was hoping to meet people who were attempting the great Sheffield novel and who wanted to talk about books and literature. Yet the atmosphere was pleasant and positive. For instance, a lovely lady called Kathleen Day, who worked in A.B. Ward's Bookshop in Chapel Walk, was modest about her achievements but clearly had a great talent and enthusiasm for the type of stories she was writing and selling; and Brenda Lowery, who worked as a secretary at a local college, was similarly successful but generous with her knowledge.

The club secretary, dear old Nella Leach, was a remarkable character. I never knew what she had produced in the way of published stories, but, living alone in a quaint old property behind Firshill School, she played the role of friend and confidante of the would-be writer to perfection. If you left a story with her for a personal criticism, she would send you a note asking you to call at her home, where, over a cup of tea, she would deliver a concise analysis which was invariably laced with words of encouragement to balance her sterner comments. You felt that the Author's Club, at whose meetings she took centre stage and was always the dominant figure, was her life, and while she never seemed really interested in discussing such masters of the short story as Pritchett, Bates, Coppard and the many Americans I was then reading, she knew what qualities were required in a story for magazines like *Woman* and *Women's Own*.

Nella would probably have been a lonely old lady without the Authors' Club, and I recall that, around the time I was seeking her guidance, my quest for self-improvement led to a brief contact with another elderly woman whose situation was not dissimilar to Mrs Leach's. Miss Jones, from whom my sister Pat had persuaded me to have some private lessons in English, also lived alone, and her role, mainly concerned with helping children through their eleven-plus and GCE exams, was probably fulfilling not for the financial rewards but because it provided her with regular company.

An abiding memory of the six or seven calls I made at the home of Miss Jones in Ellesmere Road is of the huge fire that always burned in her living room grate. Frankly, I don't think I got much benefit from her lessons, which was one reason I stopped going, but she was a kindly old dear, and I have not forgotten her because, a few months later, we learned with horror that she had been murdered by an intruder who had apparently robbed her of a few shillings.

I did find one good pal at the Authors' Club in a lad from Rawmarsh called David Depledge. Then working as a clerk in a steelworks, David's aspirations were not unlike mine in that he wanted to write serious fiction. We were of a similar age and background. However, at the time David, a well-built young man who wore rimless spectacles and smoked a pipe, was a bit further down the road than me. I was impressed when I read some of his stories, all unpublished, and, when I visited his home, envied the quiet study he had created for himself in what had been a spare bedroom.

We talked for hours about books and writing. He was particularly keen on the stories of H.E. Bates, and it wasn't long before I was sharing his enthusiasm. David's loan of *The Modern Short Story* by Bates was a gesture I especially appreciated, not least because it prompted a renewed interest in writers like Chekhov, Maupassant, O'Connor and Coppard. David and I used to joke about which one of us would emerge the first published author, and vowed we would always keep track of each other's progress. He eventually moved to London and obtained a position as editor of *Smith's Trade News*, a magazine about books, around the same time as I became a sports writer in the mid-1960s. The last time I saw him was when we met up on the day I covered a Wednesday match at Highbury in 1968. We remained in touch until around 1976, when he was living in Hereford, but then lost contact, and when I finally got a book published in 1982, my attempts to locate him proved unsuccessful.

Birthday Blues at Twenty-one

I WAS flat broke, jobless and without two farthings to rub together when I celebrated my 21st birthday in late May 1959. Having returned to Sheffield following another very brief and unsuccessful spell as a porter, this time in a seasonal situation at a Bournemouth hotel, I was out of work for four weeks; and, though I eventually received £5.16s.4d (£5.81) in dole money from the Unemployment Assistance Board (UAB), the only way I could raise a few shillings to toast my coming of age with a drink was by selling some old clothes to a local rag merchant.

Happily, I never found myself in such a prolonged state of embarrassing personal poverty again, and within six months I had taken a step which, while not obvious as such at the time, ultimately marked a turning point for the better in my life.

However, overall 1959 was a troubled year during which I invoked a series of disasters that were entirely of my own making. No doubt they confirmed a naivete and immaturity I blush to recall, but perhaps the pattern reflected an impatience with things as they stood and a desperate if often misguided quest for order and stability.

I have made more than a few daft decisions in my life, and, looking back, it seems remarkable that the majority didn't prove costly. It would have been so easy to have taken a step from which I might not have readily recovered, but, in the event, I can recall even the most unfortunate episodes with a smile knowing they didn't do me any harm. At least when I did finally settle down and start to savour a sensible and contented way of life, I could appreciate it all the more.

When my parents got back together and we returned to the back-to-back house in Bramber Street, yet again things didn't work out for them. Even after moving to a larger, more comfortable property at 28 Rising Street, their relationship continued to deteriorate. It was some consolation to be under our own roof again and no longer beholden to outsiders, but the odds were always against us enjoying harmony for long.

With hindsight, I can see it was never going to work because their marriage was as good as over. There was no mutual respect, no common bond, and, had circumstances permitted, they would have called it a day and gone their separate ways for the last time long before they did. That they didn't was down to a number of factors over which, for the most part, they had little control.

As had happened before, this was a reunion entirely down to convenience. When we left Fox Street, it was because old Ma Easy had given us notice, I think because she wanted to sell the place, and, as my father was now living alone following Grandfather Johnstone's death, returning to Bramber Street seemed an obvious short-term solution to Mother's problem of alternative accommodation. My father encouraged the step partly because, with the house due for demolition and him hoping to stay in Pitsmoor, he needed to be in a family situation to negotiate an exchange; but it is not difficult to believe that he hoped this might at last be a successful reconciliation.

Ironically, I was inadvertently responsible for the development which brought my parents back into contact. During our time at Fox Street, I had maintained occasional links with my father, and there was a spell when he wasn't aware that I was living with my mother. Shortly after 'Billy' Johnstone's funeral, Dad won a few bob on the pools, and, typically, marked his success by buying me a second-hand overcoat. When I returned to Fox Street wearing it, Mother promptly dispatched my sisters Pat and Jean to claim their share of Dad's winnings.

The upshot was a phase during which Dad saw more of his three children than for some years, and, of course, Mother was aware of this. That it happened around the time when our departure from Fox Street was imminent was the coincidence which made a family return to Bramber Street suddenly seem a reasonable solution.

I have never forgotten that I was naive enough to interpret Mother's decision as a turning point signalling a bright new beginning for my parents, and it is embarrassing now to recall how, feeling very grown up and playing the responsible son, on the day we moved back I begged Ernest Thornhill to stay out of my mother's life and give her and my father the chance to rebuild their marriage.

How was I to know Mother had arranged to meet Ernest the same evening – and that there was no question of them ending their relationship? I hadn't the nous to appreciate the reality of a development which was nothing more than a temporary compromise.

However, as a family we were destined to remain together for five years until my own marriage in 1963 marked the start of the final break-up which saw my mother and sisters walk out on my father for the last time. Sadly, but perhaps inevitably, there were seldom more than brief spells when my parents enjoyed an atmosphere of mutual peace and goodwill.

Within weeks they were at war, and some of the scenes we witnessed in the next few years were as verbally and physically violent as anything I had seen before. There soon came a time when Mother, my sisters and myself occupied the front part of the house while Dad lived in the kitchen and slept alone in the back bedroom; but, of course, as we had to pass through the kitchen to reach 'our' room, and as Mother used the kitchen for cooking, there was abundant opportunity for my parents to clash and argue.

A peaceful evening would suddenly erupt into domestic chaos. They seldom met without exchanging a flurry of verbal abuse, and pots and pans would often fly across the room. As the television, which my sisters and I liked to watch, was situated in Dad's part of the house, we invariably had a front-row view of the latest episode in our own domestic drama.

This was the phase during which I despaired of my father, and, at the time, I think my sisters and I all blamed him for the hopelessness of the situation. I can see now it was six of one and half-a-dozen of the other, each parent the victim not only of conditions they had themselves created and couldn't or wouldn't change, but of the circumstances that had made them the kind of people they were. It was all the more heartbreaking to witness because, as their oldest child, I could remember a time when they had been happy together, and, indeed, I still treasure the memory of those precious moments.

Both deserved sympathy for what had happened to them, but it was Mother to whom my sisters and myself leaned, probably largely because at least she made some effort to hold the family together, while Dad didn't seem to feel any responsibility on that score.

We accepted with little criticism the fact that Ernest remained central to Mother's life, and, if there were times when one wondered whether things might have improved at home had Ernest not been in the background, we knew the question would always remain hypothetical. We didn't feel we had the right to question her decision to stick with Ernest. Indeed, we felt that without him she might have lost the will to endure her situation, although what we did find difficult to understand and tended to question was why Ernest never seemed to make any effort to create a home to which she could escape.

One way or another, she didn't have much of a life in those years, but, if most of my memories of this phase are of her tears, I remember she also remained remarkably positive and cheerful. At her best she was a bundle of energy, tenacity and high spirits, but one ill-chosen word that might be interpreted as criticism could shatter her confidence in an instant. As children we were always supportive in her clashes with Dad, but, like most kids, we were sometimes selfish and thoughtless, and, occasionally, our words or actions would induce anger and tears.

Many years later, she could smile at our recollections of those instances when our lack of gratitude or understanding would prompt her to threaten to 'throw myself under a bus' or 'take my bloody hook', but it wasn't funny at the time. She often acted on the spur of the moment, but we knew those particular threats were merely words spoken in sheer frustration.

She worked full time as a domestic help and her duties at the Bramall house at Middlewood meant it was often after seven in the evening before she got home – and, as neither of my sisters had been brought up in circumstances which made them domesticated, her first task was invariably to prepare a meal. At least we spared her the job of making the fire on most evenings, and one of us would help with washing the pots; but, overall, we tended to take her for granted.

On one evening each week, she had to trail to a wash house at Upperthorpe on the Inner Circle bus. I would often carry her cases to the bus stop, and meet her when she got back a couple of hours later, but there were many occasions when she struggled alone. There was one painful evening when a sudden snowfall put the buses off the road and Mother eventually stumbled home at after ten o'clock. Having pushed two cases in a small pram for three or four miles she was in a state of near-collapse. As I remember, it just happened to be a day when we had all been delayed by the weather, and we had to set about lighting the coal fire in the front room grate before Mother could start to get warm.

After the separation of the house into two parts, she survived without any financial help from Dad other than that he paid the rent. She managed on her own earnings and the board that Pat (who had left school and started work at the Charles Clifford Dental Hospital before going into private practice as a receptionist) and myself contributed. We hardly lived in style, but, if the food was often basic and came mostly out of tins, at least we didn't starve. In fact, the biggest problem was ensuring that Dad didn't nick our food (and the coal we kept in our room) when he was too skint to buy his own!

I despaired because I felt Dad had lost so much self-respect and seemed so defeated. Of course, I can see now that he knew their relationship had long passed beyond the point of reconciliation, which may explain why he simply gave up all pretence, but from time to time he would compound the misery of the situation when his frustration erupted into a blind rage.

The most unforgettably painful incident among the many I recall from this period, the one which summed up just how bad things had become between them, occurred at after eleven o'clock one Sunday night in late 1959. They had both been out for the evening (not together, of course), and, as was usually the case, when Mother went into to the kitchen to mash a pot of tea, a few angry words were exchanged before Mother returned to the front room. Unfortunately, Dad chose to follow her, and, spotting the remains of the Sunday joint on a plate on the end of the table, he snatched at it and said: 'I'll have this if nobody wants it.'

My sister Pat and I looked on in astonishment as Mother promptly put down the tea-pot, plucked the meat from his hands, and, with great deliberation, threw it into the fire. She had just picked up the tea-pot again when Dad suddenly lunged at her, and, in the scuffle that ensued, the pot fell from her grasp and she screamed as the hot tea scalded her arm. They fell into a chair and, with Dad raining blows at Mother, I jumped to her aid, hitting him on the back of the head – first with my fists, then, on the spur of the moment, with a plate which immediately smashed. He got up, grabbed Pat's umbrella from the sideboard, and hurled himself at the three of us brandishing it. After cracking each of us in turn across the shoulder, he suddenly turned and ran through the kitchen and out into the backyard. Mother, having rushed after him, promptly locked the door.

Within moments Dad was hammering on it and shouting to get back in, and, for a few minutes, my parents exchanged verbal abuse through the locked door. Then there was brief silence followed by a shattering crash, with glass flying everywhere – Dad had picked up the dustbin lid and hurled it through the window!

It is easier with hindsight to sympathise with him, and at least start to understand why he acted as he sometimes did; but, at the time, he did not encourage sympathy, and, while it pains me to admit it, my sisters and I felt only pity and shame. He tended to treat any attempt to sit down and discuss the situation on a man-to-man basis as a joke – as if he felt serious debate or any analysis was just so much wasted breath.

He seemed to have simply given up, and, forty years on, I still feel a deep sadness when I remember examples of the way he lived then. When he had money, he drank heavily, and, when he was broke, he would beg and borrow a few shillings, selling anything to raise the price of a pint. He would sell me his cigarette lighter or his prized fountain pen, then buy them back at a higher price a few days later.

One day he was so desperate to get out for a drink that he negotiated an exchange of bedrooms with me and readily removed his belongings into the attic in return for a ten-bob note. This incident was not without its humour at the time, but I remember it now only with sorrow because it not only reveals much about how he was then but no doubt speaks volumes for my own attitude, showing how little respect I had for him.

Dad had long since ceased to work as a clerk, and had a succession of jobs. One to which he settled down better than most was delivering accounts for the Yorkshire Electricity Board – a situation which gave him the bonus of a uniform which, typically, he converted into a Sunday suit by removing the YEB tabs, told the firm it had been damaged in the course of his duties, and duly claimed a replacement!

However, when he gave up this job for a spell to work as a night-watchman on a nearby building site where some high-rise flats were being erected overlooking Pye Bank School, it coincided with a particularly troubled phase at home, and this was a period when I recognised just how badly the situation had affected him.

To assist him in his watchman's duties, Dad bought a mongrel bitch called Tina. The dog was an ugly but placid animal, much too affectionate to scare any intruders off the building site, and, anyway, she was too busy having pups at regular intervals to be a consistent guard dog. All the same, she was Dad's faithful companion – so much so that she even went to bed with him.

Such was his state of mind at the time, he often slept fully clothed – too drunk (even in the middle of the day) to get undressed. The sight of him sleeping, still in his working suit and wearing his cap, with one arm wrapped round a big, scruffy dog, might have been funny if it hadn't been my father. It was like seeing the ghost of 'Billy' Johnstone.

When he wasn't off to the pub, he spent most of his spare time sitting at a kitchen table strewn with newspapers and books devoted to racing form, meticulously noting the names of likely winners. Occasionally removing his cap to scratch his balding head, and with a pair of spectacles he'd bought at Woolworth's poised on the end of his nose, he cut a humorous figure.

When he was in a winning streak, he tended to be full of fun and generous, and even when he'd backed a string of losers, he had a habit of jesting. He often seemed a sad and sorry man, yet, somehow, a sense of humour prevailed which may have been his way of coping with the situation. I sometimes wonder whether it was because he felt he had failed and saw no way back that he so often played the fool in the Rising Street years, but perhaps he felt the whole situation was out of control and he might just as well laugh as cry.

I cannot recall him ever walking upstairs in our house without breaking into song. The moment he put a foot on the first step, he invariably started singing. Amusingly, he seldom sang the proper words and, in fact, preferred to adapt the lyrics in what seemed to us a daft attempt to be funny – and, of course, he was delighted by those instances when we responded and showed the joke was worth sharing.

A typical re-working of a popular Perry Como number would become:

> Buy an evening *Star*
> And put it in your pocket,
> Read it
> On a rainy day.

It was so corny, but it amused him, and, if we pulled a face and called it pathetic, he would repeat the words and go off up to bed unable to stop laughing at himself.

Whatever his faults, he was not without some common sense when it suited him, and there is no doubt he could be serious and had the capacity to have done much better than he did in his life. The sad fact is that he was never able to exploit his strengths, and circumstances somehow conspired to expose his weaknesses. There were moments when it was impossible not to warm to him, and you felt that in another time and place, with some order and discipline in his life, he might have succeeded as a husband and father.

While what happened cannot be changed, my great regret is that, because he died within six years of the final break-up of the family, a time never came when we might really have got to know each other and been able to talk about the past.

I wouldn't want to suggest there were never days when we didn't share laughter and mutual affection as a family. Things might not have been as we would have wished, but my sisters and I adapted to the circumstances pretty well, and, as young people will, individually we got on with our lives even though conditions were dominated by a climate of continuous friction.

However, without wishing to over-dramatise our reaction, the situation left us with a few emotional scars and ultimately sent us in different directions ill-equipped and blindly seeking peace and fulfilment on the other side of the rainbow without a map to help us avoid the pitfalls along the way. Because at the time there didn't seem any hope that things might improve at home, we each sought escape, but the choices we made were seldom the right ones, and we all endured our share of false starts.

I know I felt then that I not only wanted to escape sooner rather than later, but hoped that, when this was achieved, the break would be final. It was a long time before I got my wish.

* * * *

As I've said before, the irony was that whenever I tried to walk away from it all, I invariably ended up coming straight back. For some reason which I can only put down to a flaw in my character or temperament, I found it impossible to settle outside Sheffield. It might have been different if I hadn't been alone, but something in my make up always ensured my heart ruled my head and left me devoid of the courage to reject my roots. Of course, it didn't help that I invariably chose the wrong job, and often acted more on impulse than with any sense of knowing what I was doing.

There was a famous occasion when, after a heated row with my father, I packed a case late one night and went off and caught a train to London. I had £3 in my pocket and vowed I would never see Sheffield again. Paying 32s 3d (£1.71) for a rail ticket and catching the 11.50pm train, I was confident of being able to make a fresh start in new surroundings.

However, when I reached St Pancras the following morning, I was already having doubts, and hadn't a clue what to do next. I was then working for International Twist Drill, and for some reason seemed to think if I turned up at the firm's London Office and explained my plight, the manager might fix me up with lodgings and negotiate a job transfer.

I cannot now remember his name, but, if he had only been a voice at the end of a telephone for months, I knew him to be a friendly chap. In the event, my arrival embarrassed him. To cut a long story short, I ended up catching the 6.40pm train home to Sheffield – and next day was apologising to Intal's sales manager Tony Neill for my absence.

A couple of months later, in the spring of 1959, I resolved to make one more attempt to start again in another town, and came up with the notion of taking a summer job at a seaside hotel as a prelude to finding a clerical position in the same area for the winter. Bournemouth seemed ideal, and, having answered an advertisement in the *Sheffield Star*, I started as a porter at the Devon Towers Hotel.

Crazy as it seems in retrospect, I have to confess that, after travelling down on Monday, 11 May, within three days I spent my last £2 on a return ticket!

My formal duties began at 7.30 on Tuesday morning, when Bernard, the head porter, started me off polishing the front door brasses and scrubbing the front steps before breakfast. Later I was instructed how to feed the boilers with coke, then, before I had time to recover from that task, found myself sweeping out the games room.

It was here that I first fell foul of the owner, Mr Brooksbank. I hadn't realised this small, elderly man was watching me sweeping, but he suddenly appeared and barked: 'You obviously don't know how to use a brush.' Taking the brush, he showed me how he wanted the job doing. Then he marched away, only to return ten minutes later, when he snapped: 'You're taking an awful long time, and, what's more, you're not making a very good job of it.' I wasn't used to this kind of work, of course, and it didn't help that, even at ten in the morning, the sun was out and the humid atmosphere sapped my energy. Anyway, after shovelling coke into the boiler, I was already exhausted.

I survived into the early afternoon, by which time I was overwhelmed by the heat and starting to feel depressed. Bernard kept me busy with all manner of cleaning jobs, and it was when he set me on to sweep out and mop a box room where the windows and a sink also had to be cleaned that I had another confrontation with Mr Brooksbank. I had pushed myself pretty hard with the brush and mop for an hour or so, and felt I had earned a two-minute break for a fag. I had barely lit up when the frosty old owner appeared!

'You seem to be a lazy young man,' he said. 'We must start as we mean to carry on, and I'm afraid you won't make the grade in this job unless you speed up and show a bit more enthusiasm.'

It so happened I was due for a three-hour break before the evening shift, and, foolishly perhaps, my frustration prompted me to use the time to seek an alternative job, preferably as a clerk. Even if I had succeeded, I can't imagine where I thought I might get lodgings with so little money in my pocket.

My break extended into six hours, during which I ended up taking a train to Southampton. It was all wasted effort, and, when I got back to the Devon Towers, tired and hungry, I felt the wisest course was to sneak up to my attic room before anyone could see me. It probably serves to emphasise that I was still very much the dreamer when I note that, dining on a couple of packets of biscuits, instead of planning my next move, I started reading my latest purchase – a book by Dorothea Brande called *Becoming a Writer*!

Curiously, when I reported for duty the next morning, nobody mentioned my absence. I had scrubbed the front entrance steps and was halfway though cleaning out the toilets before an accident occurred which again brought me face to face with the owner.

I knocked over a full bucket, and the water seeped through the ceiling and into the room below. A breathless and angry Mr Brooksbank arrived on the scene, ordered me to the office, and began by asking about my disappearance the previous day. When I said I'd been looking for another job, he said I'd better find one quickly because he was inviting me to pack my bags and leave by Friday.

Had I been able to find more suitable work in Bournemouth, I might not have returned to Sheffield as soon as I did, but the Employment Exchange confirmed a dearth of local clerical vacancies. So, assessing my dwindling financial resources, I decided the wisest course was to invest what was left on a train ticket for home.

So, with my 21st birthday twelve days away, I had no money and no job. I was not only back where I'd started, but worse off. My immediate outlook was bleak, and, moreover, I faced the shame of having to explain my failure to my Dale Carnegie and Authors' Club friends.

You might have thought I would make sure the Bournemouth escapade was my last false start. But, of course, it wasn't.

Knocking on Doors

WHEN, in the hot summer of 1959, I finally managed to get myself back into employment, it was as an £8.10s (£8.50) a week clerk at a firm which dealt in refractories. It was a position that probably had prospects, and I ought to have been grateful for the opportunity, but somehow I never settled. I ended up leaving within less than four months – to become, of all things, a door-to-door salesman!

That spell out of work around the time of my 21st birthday was a chastening experience. There is nothing pleasant about being without money, and few things hurt one's pride more than joining a dole queue and being made to feel like a beggar. Happily, it was the last time I ever applied to the Unemployment Assistant Board for help, but I have never forgotten how humbled and shamed they made me feel as they kept me waiting four weeks (and I faced the third degree from a woman investigator who called at our house) before reluctantly coughing up £5.16s.4d (£5.81).

Ironically, I collected the cash on the way to attend what proved a successful interview for a position at Industrial Products Refractories, a firm based in a large old former domestic residence in leafy surroundings at Northumberland Road. I celebrated by getting a credit check for £13 from my mother's regular collector, and using it to buy a new suit and a new pair of shoes from Banner's store in Attercliffe. Sadly, I spoiled the effect when, trying to be in fashion, I went to a barber's shop on Burngreave Road and got myself a crew-cut which defeated all my attempts to look mature!

They were a friendly lot at IPR, and while at a distance of forty years I cannot remember exactly what I was actually employed to do, I recall my time in that office as a pleasant interlude. I think I was supposed to be lined up as the assistant to sales manager Alan Barthorpe, but for some reason it was one of those jobs in which I drifted along for a few months, never quite settled into a groove or made any serious impact, and left feeling very little wiser than when I had started.

The firm's partners, managing director Paul Wagstaff and company secretary Norman Gill, were a couple of intriguing, likeable characters. They were bachelors and lived together out at Hollow Meadows. Wagstaff was a nervous little man, kindly but somewhat intense and slightly eccentric. Perhaps he was just forgetful. After my initial interview, for instance, it was arranged that I would phone him the following morning to fix a second meeting at which Barthorpe would be present, but, when I called, Wagstaff couldn't remember me. After an embarrassing two minutes during which he was obviously desperately searching his memory, I overheard someone (probably Gill) explain who I was.

Gill was rather suave, immaculately dressed (he always wore a dark shirt and a yellow tie, which seemed to me then the height of sophistication) and self-confident; and, though he tended to be inquisitive, always seeking to quiz you about yourself, I found him good company.

I think Wagstaff and Gill were amused by my ambition to write, which was something they discovered by accident when I happened to leave some auto-biographical notes in a desk drawer. My concern at having my drawer searched after I had gone home was matched by their shock at finding that not only had I spent office time writing up a personal diary on the firm's typewriter, but they as individuals featured in my reflections!

Those notes, some of which still survive, were pretty harmless pen pictures of Wagstaff, Gill, Barthorpe and my other colleagues, accounts clerk Keith Parkin and part-time shorthand-typist Connie Dearkin, all of whom I described as 'characters'. For instance, I mentioned that Keith, who owned a Vespa bike, invariably arrived at the office wearing a huge white crash helmet which made him look like a man from Mars; and I recorded that Connie was totally unaware that her tendency to speculate on the personal lives of the bosses could be overheard by Wagstaff and Gill with a simple press of the switch on the intercom in their office.

I doubt if anyone could have taken offence at my written impressions. However, I did make the mistake of noting that I saw my job at IPR as just a stop-gap until I either got into journalism or wrote my first best-selling novel – which cannot have pleased Norman!

As Northumberland Road, not far from Weston Park, was a fair distance from Rising Street and awkwardly situated in relation to home, I was grateful for the convenience of the No.8 and No.9 Inner Circle bus to get to and from work. You could then catch what we humorously called 'the circular bus' near the bottom of Fox Street, and it used to pass the Crookesmoor end of Northumberland Road after travelling via Rutland Road, the Royal Infirmary and Upperthorpe.

I should mention as an aside that the Inner (8 & 9) and Outer Circle (2 & 3) routes (the latter traversed the outskirts of the city) were not only among the most thoughtfully convenient in Sheffield City Transport's schedule, but they also had the benefit of offering an exercise in local geography to anyone who made the full journey – something I had often done as a small boy at the cost of a halfpenny a time! Incidentally, in those days, too, there were several similar cross-city services specifically designed to meet the needs of workers in local industry until changes in habits condemned them to history

Although I used the bus most days, there was a spell when, perhaps because the weather was so good, I got into the habit of walking home on some evenings via the city centre. The journey on foot took an hour, but, if my notebooks from the period are any guide, I was probably going through a phase when I imagined that consciously absorbing the atmosphere in the central area would provide a useful exercise in observation.

Unfortunately, the only notes that merit a mention here are those which remind me of how I watched crowds of people reading the news bulletins posted in the windows of the *Telegraph & Star* offices in High Street during the newspaper strike of June 1959, and witnessed the demolition of the Norfolk Market Hall in the Haymarket. When the new market opened on an adjoining site, I commented that the second-hand bookstall didn't seem half as large or welcoming as before.

It was typical of me at the time that, when the decision to quit IPR was made, it proved a spur of the moment thing. In this particular case, I can only put it down to the Dale Carnegie influence, for I ought to have known better than to believe I had it in me to succeed as a door-to-door salesman.

As well as being involved in Carnegie Club activities, I was still helping on the courses, and one of the especially interesting characters I met on the latter was a little guy called Frank Toller, who was a regional manager with Betterwear. I would guess he was then about sixty, but he was a bundle of energy, talked with great enthusiasm, and, with his high crowned trilby and a West Country accent which, perhaps because he drove a big imported U.S. car, I mistook for an American twang, he made a big impression on me.

Other people on the courses occasionally hinted at career opportunities, but nothing had developed. Indeed, the only firm offer that had been made came during my spell out of work, when Ronnie Nott, a personnel manager at Sheffield Corporation Transport Department, said if I was really desperate he could get me fixed up as a bus conductor – a situation I politely declined.

Now, old Frank collared me as I was leaving the Grand Hotel one night and asked: 'How would you like to more than double your income by coming to work for me?' When he mentioned the possibility of earning up to £20 a week, the prospect of such riches blinded me to the reality of what would be involved, and, after Frank had spent a few days pushing for a decision, in the end I couldn't wait to leave my £8.10s job at IPR.

Frank sent me out on the first day with a Betterwear rep who operated in the Oughtibridge district, then, on the following morning, we loaded a case of samples into Frank's car and he spent a few hours with me working on the Stannington patch that was to be my own. Frank, a master at his trade, made selling look so easy, but, after he went off back to his Cambridge Street office and left me to my own devices, it soon transpired that I lacked the talent to emulate him.

However, I didn't do too badly in my first week, and earned about £15. It was a long, hard slog, and, of course, it didn't help that having to use public transport made the job just that little bit more taxing; but my initial enthusiasm carried me through. The days were much longer than I had anticipated, and the sheer physical effort over a six-day week was exhausting, but my morale and energy were boosted with every order I clinched.

The idea was to gather orders between Monday and Friday, then make the initial deliveries on Friday evening and finish off on Saturday. On my first delivery day, I found the task of hauling two cases of products rather more demanding than carrying a single case of samples, and my first serious setback came when a succession of clients declined to accept or pay for goods they had readily ordered. It was no consolation to be learning a little more about human nature!

The second week coincided with a sharp decline in my success rate, and by about Wednesday I was starting to doubt my suitability for the role, at least as a long-term occupation. I didn't have the temperament. Every time a housewife slammed a door in my face, I took it as a personal insult; and a succession of failures tended to gnaw at my energy and confidence. There had to be a better way of making a living.

Although it was October, the weather remained reasonably good, but one wet morning during the second week alerted me to the discomfort inherent in doing the job without the benefit of personal transport. Getting wet while succeeding is one thing, but failing in the rain is very different.

Fortunately, I had found somewhere to shelter – my Aunt Charlotte's pre-fab on Stannington Road. Once I had started calling there to have some lunch, then nipping back whenever I was enduring a lean spell, I suppose it marked a turning point. Charlotte was then in the midst of redecorating, and suddenly it became much more appealing to while away an afternoon helping her than to tramp the streets knocking on doors.

Frank, of course, was appalled by my poor sales, and, unaware of my calls on Aunt Charlotte, when he paid me my second week's commission, just under £10, he couldn't understand why I was getting such a low return from long days.

The development which precipitated the inevitable climax to the adventure came when, at the start of the third week, the buses went off the road. That was the last straw. The crews had called a strike which was destined to continue for some weeks, and it meant I had no choice but to walk all the way from Pitsmoor to Stannington. I was worn out before I even started trying to sell my wares.

It is amusing to recall that my notes remind me of how, during this 'marathon' phase, I kept falling asleep over my evening reading – and, ironically, my current book happened to be a novel by Irving Stone entitled *Lust for Life*!

When I reached Monday teatime with only one order in my book, I felt I had had enough. I struggled through the following day, but then gave up all pretence, and, after spending Wednesday and Thursday helping Aunt Charlotte finish her decorating, I plucked up the courage to tell Frank I proposed to quit when I'd made my weekend deliveries.

Yet again I had failed, and, as Frank told me in no uncertain terms, in giving in without a real fight, I had done my reputation and self-esteem no good at all. However, with the benefit of hindsight, I can say it was the right decision, for, in a curious way, it set in motion a pattern of events which, thanks to the influence of a kindly accident of fate, was eventually destined to set me on the right course at last.

All I remember about my last Saturday as a Betterwear man is handing in my case of samples after my final delivery, nipping to the Corporation Street Baths for a good soak, then going back to Rising Street to study the situations vacant columns and write a few letters to prospective employers. The one I wrote to a firm called Newton Chambers at Thorncliffe proved particularly significant – all the more so as I had the sense to walk into town and post it at the GPO.

Thorncliffe Days

WE CAN all look back and identify moments when we made a decision which crucially influenced the course of the rest of our lives, and many of us will admit to having been totally unaware of the significance of the action at the time. Fate is a curious and intriguing thing, and, reflecting on key turning points from our past, it is tempting to wonder what prompted us to instinctively prefer one road when another beckoned, and to ponder whether our choice was pre-ordained or merely a happy accident.

If there is one moment in my life that I look back upon and thank God I was persuaded to act as I did, it was in October 1959 when I responded to a letter from a company called Newton Chambers when it would have been the easiest thing in the world to have ignored it because, just hours earlier, I had accepted a job with another firm.

Newton Chambers was the best firm I worked for in my pre-journalism days, and the four years I spent at Thorncliffe coincided with a dramatic upturn in my circumstances and prospects. The change did not occur overnight, but, within about six months of joining the company, everything began to drop into place, and I suddenly started edging towards the security and stability I had long been seeking. Early in my spell as a Redfyre correspondence clerk, I met the woman who would become my wife and be the major influence in my life over the next sixteen years until her tragically premature death at the age of 37; and I took the first steps which set my career on course for significant progress.

How strange it is to reflect that I so nearly didn't join the firm. That the opportunity arose in the first place was probably fortuitous, and that I answered its knock when it was tempting to turn a deaf ear was surely down to the hand of a kindly fate which had some sympathy with my long-term ambitions. Of course, had I snubbed the chance, I would never have known what I missed, and things might have turned out well anyway, but, frankly, the thought of missing the joy and fulfilment what stemmed from that initial step is too frightening to contemplate.

After rejecting Betterwear and door-to-door selling, I wrote to six or seven companies who advertised clerical vacancies, and, on the Monday and Tuesday of the last week in October 1959, I attended three interviews. At Spear & Jackson's, a tool manufacturing firm in Savile Street, and the *Telegraph & Star* in the city centre, I had no luck. One job was in the export department, the other in advertising, and, while both firms promised they would be in touch, I knew I had failed to make an impression. If I'm honest, neither job would have suited me.

However, when I visited a glass firm called Ellis Pearson, conveniently situated a fifteen-minute walk away at the top of Corporation Street, I got a good reception and was offered a position as an £8-a-week clerk on the spot. As the job was more about costing and estimating than general office work, it wasn't quite what I wanted, but it was something I knew I could master. I agreed to start on the following Monday.

Returning home that afternoon, a letter awaited me from Newton Chambers. The personnel officer, a man called Brotherton, had included an application form, which he urged me to return as soon as possible. I was tempted to dump it in a bin, but then, realising I had nothing to lose, I completed the form and, as was my habit, walked into town and posted it at the GPO in Fitzalan Square.

Frankly, I didn't expect Newton Chambers to process the application before I started at Ellis Pearson's, and, had that happened, I doubt if I would have taken the matter further. However, within less than 24 hours, I was surprised to get a telegram asking me to attend an interview on the Friday afternoon. It was probably the first telegram I had ever received, and I was impressed the firm would take so much trouble.

Of course, I knew Newton Chambers was a big firm, and the more I thought about it the more I fancied the idea of working there. Unfortunately, as they were based well beyond the city boundary in Chapeltown and there was a bus strike on, I did wonder if I really wanted to walk five miles to seek a job I might not get. Happily, I elected to thumb a lift, and, thanks to the generosity of two car drivers who picked me up along the way, I arrived for my interview in good time.

Newton Chambers had existed in the Thorncliffe valley since the last years of the 18th century, and in 1959 it was still a huge, successful and diverse organisation which employed thousands in the chemicals, engineering and excavator industries. Although at the time I was not familiar with exactly what the firm did, I knew enough to be aware that such prominent local industrial figures as Sir Peter Roberts, Sir Harold West and P. J. C. Bovill were associated with the company. Sir Peter, Conservative MP for Heeley, came from a famous Sheffield family, while West, even though he had retired from industry, was widely known as a major figure in the Scouts movement, and, as I learned later, he was something of a folk hero at Newton Chambers, regarded by Thorncliffe veterans as one of the most generous and popular bosses in the firm's long history.

The NC engineering division, which manufactured a remarkable range of industrial plant and products which were sent all over the world, included 'heavy' (HCD) and 'light' (LCD) sections that were each larger than many firms in their fields, plus a Redfyre section which made domestic heating appliances then enjoying immense popularity. The extensive chemicals division included a factory whose Izal products, most notably toilet rolls and disinfectants, had a place in millions of homes throughout the country; while the excavator division was only part of the NC group's activities in this field, with a link-up with an Ipswich-based firm bringing the manufacture of huge walking draglines into the range of products bearing the famous NCK symbol.

The place was like a self-contained village or small town, with a large number of 'supplementary' departments which not only provided back-up services essential to the operation of the separate divisions, but offered extensive social and welfare facilities for employees. Working for the firm was like being a member of a huge family.

There was not one but several restaurants, the firm boasted an extensive sports club with dozens of sections and, as well as a sports ground within walking distance of the works, there was also a golf club and course owned by the company. Other activities included an amateur operatic society, a debating society and chess and motoring clubs. The firm had its own weekly newspaper, too, and a housing department which managed a range of properties which were rented to hundreds of employees from directors to the humblest labourer.

I was certainly impressed by my first sight of Thorncliffe, and there was a feeling about the place which, right at the outset, made me recognise it as something special. I have worked at many different firms, and there are some where you feel comfortable and at home from the moment you walk into the premises. Newton Chambers was one where I immediately sensed I belonged. There was a unique atmosphere, and, somehow, it was unlike any other firm I had known.

This may have been partly down to the fact that it was well beyond the city, and employees hailed not only from surrounding districts like Chapeltown, Ecclesfield, High Green and Thorpe Hesley, but travelled in from Birdwell, Hoyland, Jump, Wombwell, Darfield and other parts of South Yorkshire. The community feeling was part of the firm's tradition, but what I found novel and, indeed, attractive, was my first experience of working with people who, in many cases, were essentially the products of village and small-town life from the mining districts. Moreover, not having worked anywhere before where so many people lived, quite literally, on the firm's doorstep, I became aware of a way of life far removed from what I had known as a city boy.

Now, when I look back, it seems almost unbelievable that such a mighty and diverse company, which meant so much to so many people and enjoyed great success, no longer exists, and I am glad to have been there when it was still thriving and so many great NC characters were still around. In fact, about the time I left, in late 1963, the first signs of an imminent decline were probably evident, but nobody could have predicted that we were so close to the end of a great dynasty.

* * * *

The job for which I had applied turned out to be in the Redfyre department, which was then based in one of the oldest buildings on the site, and it is amusing to think that

I went into the interview not really caring whether I succeeded. Certainly the fact that I had another job to go to made me more relaxed than might have been the case, and it proved to be one of those occasions when I knew I had made a good impression.

After an initial discussion with Brotherton, I was taken across to the Redfyre office, where I met John Marsh, the tall and distinguished-looking sales manager. A manager from another department, a man called Noble, sat in on the interview, and, as the two men fired questions at me, I obviously said all the right things because the discussion soon became very convivial and informal.

They wanted to make a quick decision, but two other applicants were waiting outside. Often in such situations in the past, I had looked at my rivals and instinctively known that I wouldn't get the job. In this instance, noting the other would-be correspondence clerks were younger and more nervous than me, I was sure I had 'cracked' it. I was right.

The firm had overcome the problem of getting their Sheffield employees to and from work during the bus strike by organising a fleet of lorries to collect them at pre-arranged pick-up points, and, after arranging to start on the following Monday, I had my first taste of the novel emergency transport as I went home from the interview on the back of a truck in the company of a dozen other workers.

Unfortunately, come the Monday morning and my first appointment with the Sheffield lorry, the vehicle didn't turn up and I found myself stranded in the Wicker. It transpired that, owing to a lack of demand for transport from the city centre, the first pick-up point had been changed to Page Hall. As on the previous Friday, I thumbed a couple of lifts, but, to my dismay, I marked my first day with Redfyre by arriving thirty-five minutes late.

Happily, the bus strike ended within a few days, and I was able to settle into the routine of catching the 73 High Green bus at just before eight o'clock every morning.

The branch of the business in which I worked was mainly concerned with the sales of fire-grates (continuous burning solid fuel fires that stayed in overnight were a comparatively new thing then) and central heating boilers, and my job was to reply to queries and complaints from customers who had bought their appliances through local builders' merchants. It spoke volumes for the huge sales of Redfyre equipment that we dealt with perhaps three hundred letters every week, mostly from householders, but many from builders and plumbers.

The majority of the queries were trivial, and most of the replies I had to write were simple. It was just a matter of getting the relevant advice from an expert on the firm, then relaying it to the customer. I warmed to the work very quickly, found that most of the correspondence fell into patterns which required variations on a standard letter, and was soon amusing myself by not only seeing how many letters I could rattle off in an hour but experimenting with as many different ways of making the same reply.

Even when dictating a simple acknowledgement, I saw the job as an exercise in writing!

Initially, we dictated our letters into quaint old Ultravox machines which used re-useable magnetic sheets that resembled brown carbon paper, but, within a few months, we were equipped with what then seemed very sophisticated Dictograph machines that recorded on 'once only' red wax rolls which seemed an expensive luxury. Every time we filled a roll with dictation, we delivered it to the typing pool just down the corridor, and, an hour or so later, a typist would drop the finished letters into our 'in' trays.

The typing pool, incidentally, served all the departments in the building, and there were probably about thirty girls in there. It was a room which, as a young man, you entered for the first time feeling rather self-conscious, all the more so as spinster Anne Shardlow, the silvery-haired veteran supervisor, was something of a character and seemed to delight in engaging newcomers in a public conversation with questions designed to provoke answers she knew would amuse her girls.

The dozen or so people with whom I worked proved an interesting and friendly bunch whom I remember with great affection because they were good company and made me feel at home from the start. It was probably the first office I had known where friendships extended beyond the job, and I was encouraged to spend time with colleagues away from work. This, I think, was due to the backgrounds of the people, for, being more 'country' than 'town', they had less of a tendency to keep work and home separate.

Old Louis Gardner, for instance, invited me to spend occasional evenings at his home with his wife and family, and, while he and I had little in common, it was a gesture I appreciated. Then in his fifties, Louis, who was in charge of the office, was somewhat old-fashioned and tended to be regarded as rather unworldly, not quite on the same wavelength as most of the others. In fact, he was more aware and perceptive than many gave him credit for.

He had a reputation for being rather tight with his money, but, in terms of his time and capacity for taking a genuine interest in people, he was never less than generous. A Chapeltown man who spent all his working life with the firm, Louis was typical of the sort of loyal, dependable and unspectacular but knowledgeable and respected veteran employee that every department boasted in those days.

Jack Booth, the chief correspondence clerk and my immediate boss, lived out at Darfield, and, like old Louis, within months of my arrival he invited me to his home. I think Jack had some notion I might join the dramatic society in which he was a leading member, but, if that was never really likely to happen, the experience offered me an insight into an environment far removed from that at Rising Street.

Jack, an ex-naval man, was better at handling people than Louis. He had a natural 'feel' for management at that level, and, while controlling a few correspondence clerks was probably no big deal, his capacity to operate in a relaxed manner gained him respect and made him popular. The pressures of the job were not really great, but, if a major problem arose, he differed from Louis in that he never showed any signs of panic. If there was a rush on to complete a job, Louis tended to fuss, but Jack left you to get on with it.

One of the great characters in the office was a likeable ex-sailor called Jim Cranley. Then in his fifties, Jim, a product of Hampshire, had spent most of his life at sea, serving much of his time as a bandsman. Ill-health had forced him out of the navy, and he was now living in a South Yorkshire village called Jump – the novel name of which still continued to amuse him.

Jim worked alongside a chap called Rowland Wilson, and I think their joint responsibilities covered stock or chasing orders. They were a contrasting pair, with Rowland very serious and Jim so easy-going. Jim would wander around happily whistling and occasionally stopping to share his naval reminiscences with anyone who would listen, while Rowland was fretting over some order that was causing him frustration.

* * * *

Another character in the office was Harry Mellor, regarded as the font of all knowledge about how the firm's range of products worked. For instance, a new oil-fired central heating boiler had just gone into production at a new factory further up the valley beyond the foundry, and it was causing simple souls like myself all kinds of problems. Harry could study the most complex query from a heating engineer and explain in a few simple words why the customer's boiler was on the blink.

Harry was an engineer seconded from the development department, which was based in an impressive modern building at the top of Thorncliffe Lane. The development engineers were a select band, viewed by the clerical staff as a kind of elite because somehow they seemed above the constraints the rest of us had to endure. As our resident technical expert, Harry rather revelled in the added independence his unique role afforded him, but, if he was a man apart in one sense, in another he was essentially one of the lads.

He had an easy-going manner, being one of those people who are invariably chirpy and full of fun, and, when he was in the mood, he would stand at his drawing board and keep the office entertained with his quips and one-liners. A typical Mellor joke was 'Tea and crumpet, fourpence – the tea must be lousy', although, to be honest, much of his humour was essentially of the moment and, being based on situations now long forgotten, it is probably impossible to recapture.

Harry Mellor was a canny, happy and perceptive little man, the sort of colleague you always recall with a smile long after you have moved on and gone in a different direction. I have often regretted that I met up with him again only once in over thirty years following my departure from Thorncliffe. Sadly, when I finally got around to tracking him down and calling on him at his old-people's bungalow at Hoyland Common in 1998, it proved to be only a few weeks before he suffered a tragic death.

The poor man died in a fire in his home, trapped in his kitchen, when an electric kettle failed to switch off – a terrible end for anyone, but especially someone who was such a decent and likeable person. Even at the age of 84, Harry had still been as active and as aware and capable as all those years earlier, and, when I learned what had happened, it seemed an example of how cruel fate can be even to someone whom you could never have imagined falling victim to such circumstances.

In my time at Newton Chambers, Harry lived at Mortomley, just up the road from the works, and, like Louis Gardner and Jack Booth, he made me welcome at his family home. In his case, it happened because he persuaded me to try amateur dramatics with an invitation to join the High Green Players, where he was a leading member and a key backroom figure. The group staged their productions in the local miners' welfare hall, with rehearsals held either in the hall or in an upstairs room at the Crossfield Tavern, and the few months I spent as a member proved enlightening and enjoyable.

It was another insight into community activities of the kind I had not previously embraced, and, but for a trivial dispute which was badly handled and prompted me to concentrate on other things, I might have taken up acting as a serious hobby.

I should mention that, after joining Redfyre, I continued my quest for self-improvement, mainly by seeking to extend my reading, and, if I was still making only limited progress with my writing, I was at least dipping into books and subjects which were gradually extending my knowledge. Few people now will remember that this was a period during which a famous pre-war weekly literary publication called *John O'London's* was revived. I became an avid reader, especially of the leading article. The attraction was the simple way in which the writer discussed the art of writing, and I found it instructive and helpful – though, frankly, when I studied some surviving copies of the magazine thirty years later, I did find it more basic than I had remembered.

However, it was largely due to the influence of the magazine that I discovered the essays of Robert Louis Stevenson and Charles Lamb, and, while there were a lot of other recommended authors whom I found difficult, sometimes a book produced a knock-on effect which was beneficial. For example, Lamb's *Tales From Shakespeare* renewed my interest in the theatre, notably when the local Playhouse put on a production of *Twelfth Night* – a play I attended five nights on the trot. I came away not only having memorised all the main speeches and intoxicated with Shakespeare, but madly in love with the leading lady, an actress called Joanna Craig!

For a spell I became wrapped up in reading plays and books about drama, and I think it may have been as a consequence of talking to Harry Mellor about something I had seen at the Playhouse that he asked me to join the High Green Players. When I went along to a rehearsal of a new play, it was a happy coincidence that the producer happened to be an old Dale Carnegie colleague, Nan Crowther, the optician's wife. It was an even happier coincidence that one of the key figures in the group chose that night to confirm that he was being sent on a course by his firm and would have to drop out of the production. Nan promptly invited me to read for the part of Sebastian Green, a leading supporting role, in *Friends and Neighbours*, which was due to open for a three-night run in three weeks.

Green must be one of the daftest characters in the history of farce, but, though my new colleagues didn't know it, I had the advantage of having seen Danny Ross play the role on television; so it wasn't difficult to appreciate how to get the best out of the part. It was unusual even for the High Green Players to give such a key part to a newcomer, especially a beginner, but, with a crisis on their hands, they were grateful for my readiness to 'give it a bash'.

I revelled in the challenge. Indeed, I lapped it up, especially when, performing before an audience in the welfare hall, I heard people laugh at my funny lines. I even had the confidence to ad-lib on a couple of occasions, prompting gales of laughter.

By the last night, I was milking the laughs and, even at that level, the experience was intoxicating enough to make me understand why some people could never resist the lure of the stage. I knew I was a hit when the weekly *South Yorkshire Times* described me as 'a discovery', and, while I can appreciate now that the achievement was hardly sensational, it was a tremendous boost to my self-esteem.

I was, as they say, rather chuffed with myself, but, while I could well imagine needing little encouragement to get pretty serious about the business, even to the point of cutting back on other interests to ensure I could fully commit myself to the group, there was never any suggestion that my initial success had gone to my head or induced any false illusions. I was just flattered by the kind of attention which was new and novel.

For the next production, Bill Naughton's *My Flesh, My Blood*, I happily accepted a minor part, and, had a situation not unexpectedly arisen which prompted me to quit, I might have been content to continue indefinitely in supporting roles.

The play, a family drama set in a Lancashire town, was in sharp contrast to the previous production, and, having seen it on television, where Wilfred Lawson and Billie Whitelaw had excelled in the main roles as the overbearing father and the put-upon mother, I was looking forward to seeing how amateurs would handle it. I knew my contribution would be small, but was delighted we were doing something which seemed serious and significant. This was more the sort of thing I was interested in, and I suppose I had some notion that a regular link with this kind of play might help my writing aspirations, if only in enabling me to absorb some appreciation of play construction.

The Lawson and Whitelaw roles went to two senior members, Brian Dyer and Betty Marshall, who were typical of the dedicated people who served groups like the High Green Players. Brian was best suited to comic roles in which he had built a big reputation on the local amateur circuit, while Betty was a local lass who took every part in her stride and always turned in a good performance.

Brian and Betty were probably more professional than the majority, but they still did it for fun, and nobody pretended they were Ralph Richardson or Sybil Thorndyke. As in all amateur societies, some set themselves high standards and were 'naturals', while others were on an ego trip and didn't see it as a hobby which demanded more than mastering the words of a part. The majority of those who watched these people perform were uncritical because they knew them as friends and relatives they had come to applaud. People like Brian Dyer, who threw themselves into a role with great enthusiasm and craft borne of experience, were regarded as stars of the local amateur theatre scene.

Unfortunately, a few weeks into rehearsals, Brian suddenly stood down, and, while I cannot now remember why, I think he went off to join another group. Whether it was a consequence of some dispute, or because he had received a better offer, I have forgotten. I seem to recall that the episode took me by surprise in awakening an awareness of the presence of politics and jealousies within the group, but, in my simple way, I accepted the development without criticism.

The next thing that happened was I was invited to replace Brian in the lead role, and, of course, I accepted. The fact that I was a young-looking twenty-two and the part was that of a Victorian-style father in his forties didn't trouble me if it didn't worry Nan, the producer. I was happy to 'give it a bash'. Having read the part a dozen times, and still remembering how Lawson had played it, the kid who had made 'em laugh as Sebastian Green was keen to show he could stir very different emotions as Rafe Crompton!

It was arranged that I would spend a couple of hours each evening in the following week studying my lines and being coached by Nan at her home, and, by the time of the next rehearsal, I was practically word-perfect. Nan allayed my fears about the problem of being too young for the part by suggesting they would disguise my youthful looks with astute make-up.

It was strange to think I had been a member for under two months, yet had stolen the show on my debut, and now landed a major role. Had I been a little more experienced in the ways of the world, I might have been more prepared for the petty jealousies my progress inspired among some more senior colleagues. In the event, I was knocked right off my stride by the open antagonism and criticism of a young couple, a husband and wife, who made it clear they were unhappy that an 'outsider' had grabbed some glory – a felony compounded in their eyes by the fact that I would never have got my chance in the first place had the husband not been prevented by circumstances from taking the Sebastian Green role.

I had been going along to my practice sessions with Nan Crowther unaware that, behind the scenes, prompted by comments from this couple, attempts were being made to recruit an older man for the part vacated by Brian Dyer. Nan must have known what was going on, and, had she explained the situation, I would have accepted the reasoning. I knew I was too young for the part, but whenever I mentioned the subject, she insisted it didn't matter. An hour before I went to the last rehearsal I ever attended, we were still going through my lines together, and she was telling me I was doing fine.

When we walked into the rehearsal room in the pub, I couldn't believe my ears as Nan went into a huddle with the committee and emerged to announce they had found someone else to play Rafe Crompton. When I had had time to digest what had happened, I couldn't dispute the wisdom of the decision, for, according to what was said, the actor in question was very experienced and about fifteen years older than me. However, I was staggered at the way the matter had been handled, and my overwhelming emotion was one of dismay and disbelief. I had worked so hard all week, and I could have been spared the trouble. The only person to express any criticism of the manner in which the deed had been done was Harry Mellor.

Nan invited me to switch back to my original minor part, but, as Harry's son had started studying that, and, anyway, I was hardly in the mood to view the situation philosophically, I declined. The following day I posted a letter of resignation, and have never seriously pursued amateur dramatics since.

My consolation was that the link with the High Green Players had at least made me aware of Bill Naughton, who, of course, later created the play *Alfie*, which was made into a famous film starring Michael Caine. Naughton, who wrote *One Small Boy* and a number of other autobiographical novels and stories, became one of my favourite authors.

It is, perhaps, relevant to note that, a couple of years or so after the High Green Players episode, I had a brief association with the Thorncliffe Musical Society, although I didn't became a member and never aspired to go on stage again. I was asked to act as house manager for their productions of two Gilbert and Sullivan shows, *The Gondoliers* and *The Mikado* at the Newton Hall, and this was a role in which I was able to excel without inspiring jealousy.

* * * *

I remember my years at Thorncliffe as a special time because it was a phase which coincided with a dramatic improvement in my circumstances as I became a married man and took the first serious steps towards a career in journalism. Newton Chambers will always be synonymous with a twin dream coming true.

It was a period when the fates were especially kind to me, but, when I say things suddenly started to drop into place, I have to add that, had I not met Kathleen Hoyland at this point, the other parts of the jigsaw might not have fitted together as they did. Kathleen's influence gave me the stability, sense of purpose and self-discipline which I had lacked until then, and, without her, my career pattern may have been very different and less rewarding.

When we met, she was working in the NC Engineering Division typing pool and occasionally dealt with my letters. Amusingly, Kathleen's first sight of me, on the day I joined Redfyre and Jack Booth took me to meet typing pool supervisor Miss Shardlow, she took one look at the lad with a crew-cut and remarked to her colleague, Pat Oxley: 'He's a bit of a kid!' Little did she know then that we shared the same birthday, I was exactly one year her senior, and she was destined to become my wife. Kathleen, tall, slim and fair, had been with the firm since leaving Ecclesfield school in 1954 and joining the famous NC training college (which was run for many years by the remarkable Miss Mary Berry). There was a sense in which Thorncliffe was in her blood, for her grandfather, Tom Hoyland, had worked in the blacksmith's shop for over fifty years, while her father, Billy, was a former NC engineering apprentice and had only left because, when he finished his 'time' in the mid-1920s, it coincided with a period of mass unemployment.

I suppose Kathleen and I first became aware of each other because we both used the No.73 bus to get to and from work, and we would sometimes make casual conversation as we walked together down Thorncliffe Lane. I wasn't a shy lad, but it took me some time to pluck up the courage to ask her out. Indeed, there was one amusing occasion when, accompanying her part of the way to a city centre college where she was studying to become a shorthand teacher, I spent an hour with her but couldn't quite bring myself to ask the right question. When I finally did so, six months into my Redfyre career, I used the coward's ploy of slipping a note in with some letters I returned to her with some totally unnecessary corrections!

Happily, she accepted, and, as they say, the rest is history. We were inseparable for the next sixteen years, until she died at the age of 37 in 1976, and it all began on our first date, when we went to the Playhouse and sat in 4s 6d (22½p) stalls seats to watch a performance of J.B. Priestley's *An Inspector Calls*. The Playhouse, which was in Townhead Street, has long since disappeared, but it remains vivid in my memory as a theatre synonymous with our courtship. We were regulars over the next two years in a phase when people like Keith Barron, John Pickles, Anne Woodward and Philip Stone were among the Sheffield Repertory Company's favourites in the era of a famous producer called Geoffrey Ost.

In the same month as Kathleen and I started courting, something else happened which ultimately proved a small but significant piece in the jigsaw of my development. You wouldn't think that volunteering to act as scorer for Thorncliffe Rec's Yorkshire Council cricket team could influence my career ambitions, yet, indirectly, it did.

I was by then familiar with the works weekly newspaper, the *Thorncliffe News*, and had noted it carried brief reports of the club's matches. These were supplied by Harry Pickering, the secretary, but I persuaded him to let me provide them. The upshot was a useful regular contact with the NC Press Officer, an ex-*Sheffield Telegraph* journalist called Alf Dow, and his assistant Jack Dodd.

I enjoyed my spell travelling around with the cricket team, for they were a happy group and I liked the atmosphere. Moreover, the experience contributed to my development, not only in getting me out and about and enabling me to mix among people in a way I hadn't done before, but in opening my mind to possibilities of enhancing my journalistic ambitions. For instance, the regular visits to the scorebox of reporters made me aware of the network of local correspondents who served the area's daily and weekly newspapers. It wasn't long before it dawned on me that this might offer me a route into journalism.

It might seem strange, but, at the time, I had no idea how all these things worked. However, once conscious of the possibilities, I learned very quickly. In this context, it was a happy coincidence that Kathleen's family subscribed to the weekly *South Yorkshire Times*, and, once I had started visiting the Hoyland home on St Michael's Road in Ecclesfield, I was able to do some regular market research into the paper.

I have mentioned earlier how going to Newton Chambers took me into an environment which differed considerably from the one I had known. Many of the people with whom I now worked were avid readers of the countless columns of district notes and snippets of news which were the backbone of weekly newspapers like the SYT, and, daft as it might sound, it was a revelation to me to discover that these were produced not by staff writers but by butchers, bakers and candlestick makers – in short, ordinary people who operated as local correspondents. Getting into print was obviously easier than I had imagined!

I think it helped, too, that Kathleen's family was part of my 'new' environment. Her parents, Billy and Edith, were both steeped in Ecclesfield history, and, as dear old Uncle George Shaw, who was then approaching ninety, was living with them at number 68, one way or another I was soon getting regular lessons in local folklore and learning about village characters past and present.

Old George, a retired craftsman who had once been a prominent local sportsman, was a fund of tales about old Ecclesfield, and I have always regretted that, as he died in late 1963, I never got around to recording some of the wonderful stories he used to tell about a cricket team called the Whitley Pondlarks and some of his pals in the local file trade.

* * * *

It didn't take me long to appreciate that there was no sense in aspiring to become the Ecclesfield correspondent for the *South Yorkshire Times*, for an old guy called Percy Brummitt had been firmly established in that role for over forty years, and, indeed, also 'looked after' the area for the Sheffield papers and acted as a 'stringer' for some of the nationals.

Percy, then aged about seventy, was something of a legend in local newspaper offices because he was in his way a larger-than-life character and a man with a remarkable nose for news. Ironically, he had spent most of his working days in the same Redfyre offices where I was now employed, but it was said he earned twice as much from journalistic activities as he ever did from Newton Chambers. He knew everybody in the district who mattered, and, when not gathering news over the telephone in his High Street cottage, he was touring every pub and working men's club in the area seeking information and gossip.

He was the doyen of the old-time penny-a-liners, and, though I didn't know it at the time, he didn't just rely on circulating wedding forms to brides-to-be, or simply spending hours on church steps at weddings and funerals, but organised a network of informants and helpers – most of whom he would reward with a glass of whisky whenever he met up with them in a public house.

To aid his activities, he was a member of countless social and sporting organisations, and even served on the committees of some, which meant he often had access to information before the majority of the other members. In any event, many club officials, keen for publicity, had been trained by Percy to feed him with regular items of news – and most of them thought he was was doing them a favour! There were some old-timers in the village, notably members of the Veterans' Bowls Club, who, as victims of his tendency to use his local fame to steal the limelight, were far from fond of Percy. Yet if they muttered darkly about 'the man who thinks he's the bloody mayor of Ecclesfield', there were plenty of others who were in awe of him.

I must admit that, when I first saw Percy, I was not impressed. He struck me as a bit of a rough diamond, and, more at home propping up a bar than pursuing literary interests, he didn't fit my image of a 'proper' journalist. However, it didn't take me long to discover the high esteem in which he was held in the newspaper world. News and sports editors, on whom he regularly called and insisted on taking for a drink, saw him as a character whom they looked upon with great affection. Indeed, when I tried to submit news items to the Sheffield papers from Percy's 'patch', my efforts were invariably rejected out of loyalty to him. If my stories happened to get into the paper, Percy usually got the payment instead of me!

Later, of course, when I understood better how it all worked, and began to appreciate Percy's status, I accepted him for what he was. When he died, his was one of the biggest funerals witnessed in Ecclesfield for years, and it was widely acknowledged that we would never see his like again.

* * * *

The success of the cricket pieces I was submitting to the *Thorncliffe News* eventually prompted me to make another attempt to get a staff job on a local paper, and, encouraged by Kathleen, in the following winter I applied to the *Rotherham Advertiser*. I ended up being offered a trial as their part-time Wincobank correspondent, which proved an enlightening experience over the following six months.

Now, when I look back, it is amusing to recall the excitement of seeing my own words in print for the first time in a 'real' newspaper, even though the items were only short, trivial paragraphs about a family emigrating to Canada, a social evening at the local church, the election of a new chairman at the district welfare club, and suchlike. I still have a notebook which I bought especially to list my contributions and tot up how many of my lines the paper had used at a penny a time, and it's amusing to think how wonderful those entries once seemed!

Operating in a district where I started out not knowing anyone and being unfamiliar with the local groups, I found the task something of a slog which demanded much more effort than the financial return justified. I never earned more than thirty shillings (£1.50) in a week (that meant about 360 lines), but, for a while, the mere fact that I was associated with a newspaper was enough to keep the adrenalin flowing even on the coldest of evenings. Kathleen often joined me on my news-gathering jaunts, and we looked upon it as a great adventure that we felt sure would lead to bigger things.

My enthusiasm, and especially my desire to gather as many items as possible, sometimes led me into situations for which I was ill-prepared. Once, for instance, I arrived at a house to deliver a wedding form, and was immediately attacked by the bridegroom-to-be, who, despite my protestations that my service was free and all I wanted was details of him and his bride, insisted I was tricking them into buying something they didn't want and couldn't afford. When he threatened to thump me, I quickly escaped into the street!

In this spell, I collected dozens of obituaries, and, not surprisingly, had my first experience of being forced to look at the deceased in his coffin when it was the last thing I wanted. However, the death I reported which I shall never forget was one about a man who promptly turned up the following week to prove he was alive and well and in good health. Nobody had told me until then about the need to check my facts, or warned me not to accept second-hand information from people who failed to explain they were passing on a rumour!

The pattern of my progress in this period was in the context of modest aspirations and obscure circumstances, and the most trivial success was a milestone I treasured as a sign that I was moving in the right direction. For instance, when, in my second summer as Thorncliffe's scorer, the works paper started using my initials on the end of my reports, I greeted it as a giant step forward – and a brush with fame!

It was during the same phase that I made what seemed a really significant breakthrough when I was invited to become the Shiregreen correspondent for the *South Yorkshire Times*. Getting a personal letter from the editor of any paper, especially when he was seeking my services, seemed to spell the kind of recognition I savoured even if it was a long way from Fleet Street!

It all came about because Percy Brummitt, who had included the district in his patch for many years, was suffering some ill-health and wanted to reduce his load. The man who negotiated my appointment was Alan Banks, the *SYT's* Chapeltown-based staffman. I met Alan regularly on his visits to the cricket scorebox, and had long been pestering for some help in my quest for a career in journalism.

As Shiregreen, a district which adjoins Ecclesfield, was not only convenient but an area I was familiar with and in which I knew some people, it didn't take me long to make an impact in terms of the volume of material I produced. I started to unearth some good if not particularly sensational local yarns, and, for the first time, I also enjoyed the novelty of selling some of the items to the Sheffield papers. At last I felt I was in genuine contact with the people who mattered in at least three newspaper offices.

I really felt I was starting to make good when the *SYT* began occasionally asking me to cover specific events, and, when I was invited to 'look after' the Yorkshire Council Championship final at Elsecar, I couldn't have been more pumped up with pride if I had been despatched to Lord's. I know I watched every ball of that game, which, incidentally, was the farewell appearance of a local cricketing legend called 'Ike' Baxter, and, in my best Neville Cardus style, I penned a report which I felt sure was a masterpiece.

The men who mattered at the *SYT* must have been impressed, too, for, when I bought the paper on the following Friday, I had the unexpected pleasure of seeing my name in large print above my match report. No journalist ever forgets the thrill of his first by-line – and to get it as a non-staffman, was considered no small achievement in those days!

Of course, down in the Press Office in the Headquarters building at Newton Chambers, Alf Dow and his assistant Jack Dodd had become very familiar with my aspirations, for I developed a habit of calling in on the most trivial pretext. As Alf and

Jack were 'real' journalists, I suppose I hoped to absorb some of their professional know-how and pick up a few tips, but just to be able to listen to them talking about their newspaper days and old colleagues was a source of pleasure and inspiration – all the more so when Jack happened to mention one day that a former workmate, who was now assistant editor on the Sheffield evening paper, had said how impressed he was with some of the cricket items I'd submitted to the *Green 'Un*.

Jack and his wife, Monica, were then living in a company bungalow just a few doors from Kathleen's home in Ecclesfield, so I was able to supplement our lunchtime chats with occasional social calls, and it was on one of those visits that I learned he had decided to quit Thorncliffe and take a job as Press Officer with a firm in Sunderland. The news dismayed me… until it emerged that I was being considered as his successor.

* * * *

Alf Dow had been Press Officer at Newton Chambers for six years when he plucked me from the Redfyre Sales department and made me his assistant, and I shall always remember him with great affection as the man who launched my journalistic career. In fact, our working partnership lasted little more than a year, but, when circumstances conspired to make me a victim of the first major round of redundancies at Thorncliffe, he took it upon himself to help me get my first staff job on a newspaper. In the meantime, he was also instrumental in ensuring Kathleen and I could rent the company house which enabled us to get married in May 1963.

Few people now remember Alf, but, in his heyday, he was one of Sheffield's most respected newspapermen. He had started out as a junior reporter on the old *Yorkshire Telegraph and Star* in 1921, and spent the next 34 years in roles which included a long spell as chief reporter on the old *Sheffield and Rotherham Independent*. In between periods as news editor of the *Sheffield Telegraph* and then *The Star*, he served as a war correspondent with the 49th (West Riding) Division in the Nijmegen campaign. He later pioneered the Kemsley Group's training scheme, guiding the early careers of many young men who went on to reach the heights.

After turning to industry and moving to Thorncliffe in the mid-1950s, he remained at Newton Chambers for thirteen years until retiring in 1969. Sadly, his retirement was marred by his wife's long and painful illness, and, following her death, he spent the last years of his life living with his son in Sussex.

Alf was very much of the old school of reporters, and, if the pressures of daily production were long behind him when we met, he could still operate at a remarkable speed – which, of course, is the essence of journalism. Most of us can write fairly well given the time to compose a report, but to do so within minutes and with the tension of a deadline looming is not as easy as the professional makes it look.

Just to watch Alf in action was an education for a beginner like myself. He would return from an interview, open up his notebook, and sketch the outlines of his story in shorthand on a piece of paper, then knock it out on his portable typewriter – all in the time it took me to work out what I was going to say in my opening paragraph!

When he was in the mood, Alf enjoyed talking about old colleagues and recalling humorous incidents from his early days as a reporter, and I was always a willing listener. I was fascinated by his stories, which aided my romantic notion of a world I hoped I might one day get the chance to experience.

I think my attitude and naivete amused Alf, for, just occasionally, he would say something which hinted that he had some less pleasant memories of his newspaper days. Certainly he felt that in his last years at Kemsley House he had been pushed to one side and fallen victim to office politics, and he resented the way he was removed from front-line journalism and given the training scheme job.

Alf was, in fact, an ideal mentor and guide to the young. I never heard anyone suggest other than that he was a first-class journalist whose ability, experience and knowledge were widely respected; and he was, too, a man of high principles, kind, generous, and ever ready to advise and help younger colleagues. In his time as a news editor, he had correctly identified many a junior reporter as a future star, spotting and encouraging talent others had failed to recognise.

He was typical of his generation of journalists in that he liked a drink but could carry his ale. Often when he returned from a boozy lunch engagement, he would walk about with a wry smile on his face, and these were the occasions when he was most given to reminiscing and story-telling. He had a sharp but gentle wit. Once, for instance, when old Jack Lingard, manager of the works branch of the Sheffield Savings Bank and a great gossip, reported a rumour that Percy Brummitt had died, Alf rang Percy's home. Taken aback when Percy himself answered the phone, Alf asked: 'Where are you speaking from, Percy?'

If Alf had a fault, it was that he tended to fear that every ache and pain signalled an impending serious illness. While he had the ability to talk to anyone, and had the journalist's knack of being able to find something interesting in every person he met, he was by nature an introvert, and, perhaps because his job left him with too much time to think, he had a habit of dwelling on imaginary health problems and ending up depressed. A heavy smoker, he was always fretting that he might get cancer, but it was many years before he gave up cigarettes. I soon grew familiar with his idiosyncrasies, and the challenge of cheering him up was one I enjoyed.

I was always grateful that Alf saw something in me, and it is fair to suggest he took a gamble in inviting me to join him. A man called Hides, a posh ex-public school type who was the NC personnel officer at the time, was not entirely convinced of my suitability for the job, but Alf insisted I was the man he wanted. With the benefit of hindsight, I can see now that one of the reasons I got the post was because, in losing Jack Dodd, Alf had been told he would have to recruit a trainee rather than another experienced reporter. It was, perhaps, the first sign of impending cutbacks.

Alf promised he would teach me everything he could, and I felt that just getting the opportunity was a tremendous step – with an increase in pay from about £10 a week in Redfyre to £14 in the Press Office a wonderful bonus. Moreover, moving into the HQ building and mixing with the 'top brass' at the firm constituted a dramatic rise in status – and I could even start using the staff restaurant instead of the canteen!

It was not without irony that, ahead of my formal switch to the Press Office, out of the blue I was offered a staff job with the *South Yorkshire Times*. By this time I had made a fair impact as their Shiregreen correspondent, and I had written to Sid Hacking, the editor, to explain the need to give it up to concentrate on my new position at Thorncliffe.

Hacking was familiar with my ambition to get into newspapers. Indeed, I had pestered him on the subject on more than one occasion in the past without prompting a response. Now he sought to tempt me with what he described as a job in 'real' journalism at a wage higher than I would get as Alf's assistant.

It created a dilemma which could so easily have induced the wrong decision. Happily, I felt my choice was already made, and, for the present anyway, believed the wisest and most honourable course was to remain at Thorncliffe. I never regretted rejecting Hacking's offer, and have always been grateful to the kindly fate that persuaded me to do so.

I should, perhaps, mention that, a few months into my period in the Press Office, I did renew my links with the *South Yorkshire Times* when, following Percy Brummitt's sudden death, I became their Ecclesfield correspondent; but it was a temporary step which, in solving a problem for the paper, enabled me to bank a few extra pounds in support of the wedding plans Kathleen and I were making.

I enjoyed working with Alf, and, because I was able to operate in an atmosphere in which I could progress gradually and never felt under any great pressure, I developed more quickly than might have been the case had I gone to Mexborough. Alf was very protective, and, while he dropped me in at the deep end sooner than I expected, initially he allowed me to adapt at a reasonable pace. By the time he went off on holiday and left me to produce two issues of the *Thorncliffe News* on my own for the first time, I had the confidence to tackle the task.

Had I gone to the *South Yorkshire Times* as a staffman, my apprenticeship would have been very different, and, in some ways, it might have presented a test at the sharp end of the business which may have been more beneficial in pure journalistic terms. However, I doubt if I could have been stretched more than was the case in those early months in the Press Office.

The step up from clerk to Alf's assistant was a big challenge, not only in terms of the actual work but in having to deal with most of the leading figures in the firm. Facing these people could be an ordeal in a way that many young people today might find difficult to imagine, and to have to act as if I were an accomplished journalist rather than a beginner was a keen test of character and nerve!

I shall never forget the trauma of having to interview the managing director, P. J. C. Bovill, early in the week when Alf first left me on my own. My shorthand was almost non-existant, and here was the biggest boss of them all dictating a statement at great speed. Knowing there was little chance of being able to transcribe my notes with the necessary accuracy, I feared I had failed at the first hurdle. Happily, Bovill's secretary, Barbara Sorsby, spared my blushes by taking a full note herself as back-up!

Bovill was a kindly man, and I think he was aware of my shortcomings but conscious of my enthusiasm. He was then quite close to the end of his career, and, as one of the last of what might be called the Harold West school of employers, he had a genuine interest in Thorncliffe people.

I was astonished one day to discover that Bovill had been discussing me with Alf Dow, and, as a consequence, it had been suggested that, if having a house was all that was preventing Kathleen and I from getting married, we could rent a company property as soon as it could be arranged. I think Alf had put the idea in Bovill's mind, and, in the light of later events, it was not without irony that he made the point that being tied to a firm's house would commit me to a long stay in the job.

The next day, I was called to the office of Mrs Allen, the housing manager, and immediately offered a terraced house on Thorncliffe Lane at ten shillings (50p) a week. I had to smile because, some months earlier, I had asked Mrs Allen, a rather self-important lady, if I might qualify for a company house, and she had insisted there was no chance of going on the waiting list until I was married. She changed her attitude when she found I had influence in high places!

Of course, the wedding had to be arranged in weeks rather than months, but, as is often the case in such circumstances, the planning and preparation went smoothly, and Kathleen's mother, Edith, on whom the bulk of the responsibility fell, revelled in the challenge of organising her daughter's big day at short notice. All I had to do was assist with redecorating the house, enjoy the novelty of helping spend our savings on new furniture, buy a new suit, and prepare my wedding speech for the reception in the Pensioners' Hut.

My biggest challenge was persuading my father to buy a new suit for the occasion. Unfortunately, I failed in this, but, thankfully, Kathleen managed to coax him into having one of his old suits cleaned. At least he looked the part on the big day, and, indeed, he and my mother presented a united front – only faltering when, early in the evening,

Mother left the celebrations on her own and Father couldn't resist saying: 'Give my regards to Thornhill!'

Kathleen and I were married at St, Mary's Church, and, after our honeymoon (a Sheffield United Tour to Cornwall and the Isle of Wight), we settled down to our new life unaware that my days at Newton Chambers were numbered and our stay at No.5 Thorncliffe Lane destined to be limited to barely twelve months.

Curiously, I can recall incidents which, with more experience, I would have recognised as signs that something serious was afoot at the firm. When Bovill retired, everybody seemed to view Ken Walker, the Engineering Division's top man, as the natural successor and automatic choice, but the job unexpectedly went to Chemicals Division director, Shaun Waide, who was considered by some as tough, ruthless, and the sort of realist the group needed to adjust to rapidly-changing circumstances. History was to prove in the longer term that Waide was not as worldly as he liked to think, but, in the meantime, he inspired a dramatic shift in the climate, and by the autumn there were widespread rumours of redundancies.

It was during this phase that I became friendly with one of the great Thorncliffe characters of the period, a Lancastrian extrovert with a literary bent called Frank Whitehouse. Had Walker not responded to being overlooked as Bovill's successor by resigning, I might never have got to know Whitehouse; but Walker's departure prompted Waide to recruit Frank as his personal engineering consultant. Within days of being switched from a works office to one in the firm's headquarters' building, Frank had started the habit of dropping into the Press Office for a daily chat.

Frank, who was then about sixty, had first arrived at the firm as a young married man and made a big impact as the foundry manager. At some stage, he disappeared off to Scotland for ten or more years, and, when he returned to Thorncliffe to become works and then general manager of the Engineering Division, he surprised some of his former colleagues by bringing with him a new, young Scottish bride who had been his secretary. Nobody ever seemed to know much about how the change in his personal circumstances had occurred, but it was assumed he had been the victim of some tragedy. The mystery added a touch of glamour to the image of a man I once heard described by a female admirer as a guy with the looks of an Alan Ladd and the spirit of a Jimmy Cagney.

He was a robust and practical man who was as much at home in a factory as in an office. Physically, he was a bundle of what seemed limitless energy, and, to see him bounce along the valley on his way from the 'light' to the 'heavy' engineering workshop, was to know that here was a chap who knew what he wanted and had the ability to get it quickly. Even on the coldest morning of the year, he never wore an overcoat.

Frank was one of those people who are always full of good conversation, and I liked him because he was not only less remote than most people in his position, but, to my delight, had a keen interest in writing and literature. In fact, as a young man he had published a few short stories, and, after his retirement, his enthusiasm for putting his thoughts on paper was to prompt him to become a prolific contributor to the letters columns in publications as diverse as the local weekly and *The Times*. He wrote his last reader's letter shortly before his death at the age of 97.

Frank kept saying he could see me progressing to a career in newspapers – predicting that one day I would write for the *Guardian* or the *Daily Telegraph*. I treated it as a joke, and I'm sure he had no idea that, many years later, I might actually end up writing in the *Telegraph*; but, with hindsight, I can see that he was really trying to tell me there was no future for me at Thorncliffe. He knew what redundancies were planned, and, as the Press Office was sure to be affected, was well aware I would be the one to have to go.

I was lucky on two counts. First, Alf Dow knew details of the cuts weeks before they were formally confirmed, and, second, he not only wanted to spare me from the blow by getting me out before the axe fell, but was anxious to give me a foothold on the first step of the journalistic ladder. He wrote to one of his 'old boys', Mike Finley, who was then assistant editor of the *Sheffield Telegraph*, and urged him to recommend me for a reporter's job on the paper.

Finley, of course, already knew of my work as a correspondent, and, happily, was impressed enough to respond positively to Alf's plea and give me a chance. The formalities were delayed slightly because, at the time, David Hopkinson, the editor, was preoccupied with the famous 'Rhino Whip' police case, which had just concluded.

However, my appointment was confirmed in late November, and it was not without irony that I arrived on the editorial staff just in time to participate in celebrations of Hopkinson's 'Journalist of the Year' award, which included a dinner at the same Grand Hotel where I had once attended Dale Carnegie sessions and voiced my dream of getting into newspapers.

If my marriage six months earlier constituted the most significant step in my life up to that stage, there was a sense in which my sudden and unexpected move into daily journalism completed the transformation. The day I walked out of Thorncliffe for the last time (clutching a book on journalism, a collection of H.E. Bates stories, and a set of Gilbert and Sullivan records, all gifts from colleagues) marked a break with the past and signalled the start of a new beginning.

The goal I had been seeking since boyhood was beckoning at last! At twenty-five years old, I still had a long, long way to go, with so much to learn, yet it seemed I was finally getting there. The future, I knew, would not be without its problems and pitfalls, and, indeed, so it proved. But the Sheffield Boy was now a happily married man and a 'real' journalist, too. Who said dreams don't come true!